THE UNIVERSITY OF MICHIGAN
CENTER FOR JAPANESE STUDIES

MICHIGAN PAPERS IN JAPANESE STUDIES
NO. 11

# MICHIGAN PAPERS IN JAPANESE STUDIES

No. 1. *Political Leadership in Contemporary Japan,* edited by Terry Edward MacDougall.

No. 2. *Parties, Candidates and Voters in Japan: Six Quantitative Studies,* edited by John Creighton Campbell.

No. 3. *The Japanese Automobile Industry: Model and Challenge for the Future?,* edited by Robert E. Cole.

No. 4. *Survey of Japanese Collections in the United States, 1979-1980,* by Naomi Fukuda.

No. 5. *Culture and Religion in Japanese-American Relations: Essays on Uchimura Kanzō, 1861-1930,* edited by Ray A. Moore.

No. 6. *Sukeroku's Double Identity: The Dramatic Structure of Edo Kabuki,* by Barbara E. Thornbury.

No. 7. *Industry at the Crossroads,* edited by Robert E. Cole.

No. 8. *Treelike: The Poetry of Kinoshita Yūji,* translated by Robert Epp.

No. 9. *The New Religions of Japan: A Bibliography of Western-Language Materials,* by H. Byron Earhart.

No. 10. *Automobiles and the Future: Competition, Cooperation, and Change,* edited by Robert E. Cole.

No. 11. *Collective Decision Making in Rural Japan,* by Robert C. Marshall.

COLLECTIVE DECISION MAKING IN RURAL JAPAN

by

Robert C. Marshall

Ann Arbor

Center for Japanese Studies
The University of Michigan

1984

ISBN 0-939512-17-3

Copyright © 1984


Center for Japanese Studies
The University of Michigan
108 Lane Hall
Ann Arbor, MI 48109

**Library of Congress Cataloging in Publication Data**

Marshall, Robert C., 1948-
    Collective decision making in rural Japan.

    (Michigan papers in Japanese studies; no. 11)
    Bibliography: p. 171.
    1. Aichi-ken (Japan)—Rural conditions—Case studies.
2. Decision making, Group—Japan—Aichi-ken—Case studies.
3. Local government—Japan—Aichi-ken—Case studies.
4. Villages—Japan—Aichi-ken—Case studies.
I. Title. II. Series.
HN730.A34M37    1984      302.3'0952'16      84-3159
ISBN 0-939512-17-3

Printed in the United States of America

CONTENTS

# FIGURES

# TABLES

PREFACE

The origins of this study of rural Japanese decision making lie in my nearly simultaneous discoveries of Niwa Fumio's fine novel of rural passion and intrigue, *The Buddha Tree*, and the transactional analysis of social relations and organizations, or, as it is sometimes called, social exchange theory, which was made especially prominent in political science by Olson (1956), in sociology by Blau (1964), and in anthropology by Barth (1966). Thus, this is a book written with two rather disparate audiences in mind, readers interested primarily in exchange and decision-making phenomena, on the one hand, and readers interested primarily in the unity of experience represented by the Japanese sensibility, on the other.

It is not for me to judge how deftly or ineptly I have combined these two interests in this one study, but I cannot pretend to believe that either audience will be entirely satisfied with the result. To the latter, the ethnography will be thin where it should be "thick," and the argument will be abstract where it should be concrete. To the former readers, the argument will be incomplete where it should be rigorous, and the ethnography insupportably baroque where it should be Bauhaus.

To readers on both wings I can only respond that the people I watched and questioned made their decisions on the basis of a common sense that was not the same as mine. I have therefore tried throughout this study to portray as closely as possible that common sense in action while seeking to generate its double through analysis of hamlet social relations and organization by means of general principles of exchange. It is the major task of anthropology to make explicit those widely held implicit assumptions of a culture that make day-to-day social living possible and to search out the sources of those assumptions. The methods of the discipline remain crude, even violent, like those of physicists who study subatomic particles: smash together some atoms, or individuals from different cultures, and see what results. The effect in both cases is unavoidably reciprocal and impossible to wholly control; one's instruments are altered during the experiment. A rather left-handed complement that I treasure most from this clash of cultures came to me toward the end of my stay in Japan by way of a third party. A Japanese woman who had lived several years in the United States as a student, who knew me well, and who did not care so very much for Americans made a remark at a party I did not attend. "Sometimes," she said about me, "he seems so Japanese I don't see how he can manage to get by at all in America." On the contrary, at first, I did not see how I was going to get by in Japan, and I never would have if not for the immeasurable assistance of many people from many walks of life.

This study is the result of three continuous years of fieldwork in a hamlet in rural Japan. The data presented and analyzed here consist of records from participant observation, formal and informal interviews, casual conversation and formal questionnaires, and public and private documents. Before all other obligations, I must express my deep gratitude to the people of Nohara hamlet and Kawasemigawa ward, who were my friends and teachers. They not only tolerated my research and answered with thought and good humor questions I would now be far too embarrassed to ever ask again but also encouraged my research and made a place for my wife and myself in their community, homes, and lives. But an expression of gratitude is not a return. I cannot hope to repay even the smallest part of their consistent kindness, patience, cooperation, and hospitality.

The subject of this research is group decision making, and the results of this process are, after all, a matter of public record. I do not think there are any data in this study that are unknown to all interested residents of Nohara hamlet. But what is "public" within the confines of the hamlet is by no means necessarily "public" outside the hamlet. In focusing on the process through which alternative courses of action and policies are publicly selected, I have especially tried to record the "who said what and when" of hamlet meetings and private conversations. A significant part of the overall process of decision making in rural Japan, however, is the forgetting of this same information once a decision is made. To the extent I have preserved in this study statements and sentiments never meant for ears outside the hamlet, the need to disguise their authors increases. Where I must fail in a public expression of gratitude to my friends and informants, I must not also fail in discretion. To prevent the identification of individuals whose speech and behavior I have recorded in this study from becoming publicly known, all personal and local place names have been changed, with the exception of the prefecture in which the fieldwork was undertaken.

In addition to specific debts of gratitude to informants who cannot be publicly acknowledged, there remains the pleasure of recognizing another set of financial, intellectual, and emotional obligations. I wish to thank the University of Pittsburgh Andrew W. Mellon Fund for two one-year predoctoral fellowships and the U.S. Department of Education for a twelve-month Fulbright-Hays Predoctoral Dissertation Research Abroad Fellowship. These three awards met the great bulk of my fieldwork expenses. Thanks are also due the C. Itoh Company for a travel and subsistence grant, and the Japan Iron and Steel Federation Endowment Fund of the University of Pittsburgh for a grant for the preparation of this manuscript. Both grants were received through and administered by the University of Pittsburgh Asian Studies Program, which organization and whose administrators have my thanks.

Of those friends and colleagues in Japan, without whose cooperation and assistance this research could not have been begun, continued, or completed, I am especially obligated to Professor Yoshida Teigo, Department of Anthropology, University of Tokyo, who graciously sponsored my stay in Japan. Professor Aoyagi Kiyotaka, Department of Anthropology, International Christian University, Tokyo, established contact for me with Professor Yamada Ryuji, Department of Anthropology, Nanzan University, Nagoya, who suggested Kawasemigawa ward as a possible field site and formally presented me to the ward council. Both of these scholars have my thanks, along with Professor Sofue Takao, National Museum of Ethnology, Osaka, who gave valuable counsel on rural Japan and made the facilities of the museum available to me.

I am also deeply grateful to the faculty, staff, and students of the Kyoto University Primate Research Institute, under the directorship of Professor Shiro Kondo. The consideration extended to me by everyone attached to this institute was unfailing and unstinting. In particular, the Department of Systematics, chaired by Professor A. Ehara, made our stay enjoyable as well as profitable. I also wish to extend my appreciation to Professor Tanaka Jiro, Department of Ecology, without whose assistance I might not have settled in Nohara hamlet, and Watanabe Kunio, Sociology Department. Special thanks are acknowledged here to my friend Dr. Moriyama Akihiko, who was always willing and able to help whenever I needed him.

My debt to the Department of Anthropology, University of Pittsburgh, and to my doctoral dissertation committee is deep and obvious. I wish especially to thank Gary Allinson, L. Keith Brown, John C. Campbell, Arthur Tuden, and Robert Smith for reading various versions of this study and for their detailed substantive and stylistic comments and criticisms. If I had listened more and argued less, perhaps they could be made to bear some of the burden for the shortcomings that remain in this book. But I did not, and so its flaws, at least, are all mine.

More than any other single person, I thank my wife, Betsy, who was willing to go and willing to stay three years in rural Japan. Without her companionship and constant encouragement both in word and by example, I could not have persevered. *Ishi no ue ni mo san nen.*

# INTRODUCTION

The paramount responsibility of any corporate group is to decide to what ends it will allocate its resources. Group decision making is a process of exchange among decision makers, the exchange of consent to relinquish control over something of value for control over something else of value. In *buraku*, the traditional, face-to-face corporate hamlets of rural Japan, group decision making is routinely undertaken as a search for consensus rather than a confrontation of adversaries. Yet it is not uncommon for this process to result in division rather than unanimity. The present study pursues two primary questions with regard to collective decision making in rural Japan. First, what are the exchange foundations of hamlet society that promote this consensual orientation to collective decision making? Second, why and when does this process of public choice in *buraku* sometimes result in unanimity and, at other times, in a division or vote?

Precise answers to these questions are significant not only because they improve understanding of rural Japanese society but also because they increase our knowledge of social organization and social relations throughout Japanese society. Moreover, they advance our understanding both of the more general problem of the emergence of cooperation and voluntary exchange under "imperfect market" and "nonmarket" conditions and of public choice processes in an important alternative cultural setting. These issues combine into the single problem of group decision making in Japanese society insofar as the unique combination of high productivity, stable social relations, and pervasive social harmony, which among modern industrialized nations is found only in Japan (Vogel 1979), is at least in part the result of a public choice procedure that is both practically effective and democratic (Gaenslen 1980).

The major conclusions of this study are outlined below in their simplest and most straightforward form. A hamlet is fundamentally a nexus for the organization of *productive exchange* among member households, the form of exchange through which two or more parties actively combine their resources to produce something of value not available, or as cheaply available, to any of them separately. Defection from productive exchange agreements by hamlet members is reduced by making access to future valuable transactions and corporate property contingent upon the integrity of each current exchange transaction. This method of combining a common interest in production with contingent access to

1

productive resources is termed *mutual investment* and is the major source of consensus in hamlet decision making. When only corporate resources are at issue, decisions regularly result in unanimity. When a course of action can be implemented only if hamlet members relinquish control over individually held resources, a division will emerge among the membership. Whether or not a formal vote is taken, the distribution of differing opinion will be known through more informal means of communication. In all cases of division, by the time the course of action to be implemented is formally announced, the minority in opposition will be extremely small. The question then must be resolved whether those in the minority will participate in the implementation or resign as hamlet members.

This study offers an alternative view of a number of problems in conflict resolution, of which collective decision making is often seen as one aspect. Gaenslen (1980) concludes his excellent review of the advantages and disadvantages of the two modes of decision making and the two modes of participant orientation with the observation that both effectiveness and democracy appear desirable in decision-making processes. While one cannot argue with this assessment of what is desirable, the results of the present study do not support the contention that "the variables of trust and friendship, desire for unanimity, and advocacy are likely to be important in creating the [decision making] process we want" (Gaenslen 1980: 26).

On the contrary, in a setting in which both democracy and effectiveness were present and even prominent, the desire for unanimity was entirely absent. Advocacy was rarely overt, and when it was, it had only a negative effect on the outcome desired by the advocate. Information about the life circumstances of fellow hamlet members was found vastly more important to decision makers than the negligible effects of the few friendships that were found. Trust was found to be a product of the mechanism operating to reduce, but which could never entirely eliminate, the threat of defection from the rate of exchange in the productive exchange relation among hamlet members.

As for the implications of this research for the overall study of Japanese society and culture, we might simply alter a well-known American watchword to read, "The price of membership in Japanese corporate groups is eternal vigilance." The commitment of resources to the productive exchange relation prevents all but the few wealthiest members, or those most willing to risk defecting, from exploiting opportunities outside their ongoing exchange relation. At the same time, this commitment, itself a product of the operation of mutual investment in productive exchange, demands the utmost attention to the public and private affairs of fellow members to insure that that commitment is not betrayed.

Atsumi (1975: 7) suggests that the belief that social relations in other spheres of exchange and organizations in Japan are modeled on patterns of interaction found in rural society is widespread. The present study suggests that this intuition of similarity among organizations of different scope and purpose is due to the equally widespread operation of mutual investment in productive exchange relations throughout Japan. If further research should prove this to be the case, it does not predict great success for the recent boomlet in introducing Japanese management style and technique, and, in particular, Japanese approaches to collective decision making, into other sociocultural settings without providing for the same high degree of commitment to the collectivity that mutual investment does. This point must be emphasized because commitment is produced through the elimination of external opportunities for exchange, as well as through the intensification of collective identity and internal opportunities.

Other important findings of this study in relation to hamlet decision making and hamlet productive exchange relations are briefly outlined below:

1. The consensual orientation of participants—the tendency to dampen down dispute rather than allow it free expression (Bailey 1965: 7; Gaenslen 1980: 16)—remains unchanged from decision to decision, barring discovery of defection.

2. Issues are not treated as commensurate, and the likelihood that a course of action will be chosen and implemented is not increased by making it dependent on the resolution of other pending issues.

3. The consent of each participant depends on his judgment that he will not be made to absorb costs where he has no potential to benefit or where the payment of costs would leave him without the means of production or subsistance.

4. Individual participation in productive exchange transactions is a function of membership rather than opportunity among structurally similar productive exchange relations.

5. All productive exchange within the corporate group only creates opportunities for members and never directly distributes benefits to members.

6. Productive exchange transactions in the corporate group are always accomplished according to the same bifurcate formula:

   Phase 1: All members with any potential to benefit from a transaction assume a share in the capital costs proportionate to their share in the group's total resource pool.

> Phase 2: All members making capital expenditures realize their demand for the results of production independently, using their independently held resources; corporate resources are only used to defray capital, and never production, expenses.

7.   Overt advocacy is much less likely to occur than overt opposition to specific courses of action.

The theory of collective decision making as an aspect of exchange relations among decision makers is predicated on the idea that risk of loss due to defection from an agreement in an exchange relation, whether simple or productive exchange, can never be entirely eliminated, only reduced or made more or less acceptable.  One way of reducing defection is to embed each transaction in a never-ending series of similar transactions among the same participants and exclude those who defect from agreements from future transactions.  With this method, however, the rate of exchange obtaining in any transaction is not *determined* in the decision-making process at each turn but is fixed across the entire series and applied and interpreted to fit the objective circumstances of the issue under consideration.  The interdependence and continuity of the exchange relation creates a corresponding sensitivity to the underlying exchange relation itself and a sensitivity to the long-term effects of collective decisions on the exchange relation.  This sensitivity includes an awareness of the possibilities of "tyrannies of the majority and the minority" to the extent that courses of action that require some members to unilaterally subsidize the consumption of other members, in the regular course of hamlet decision making, are never found acceptable to the entire membership.

The prevalent view of Japanese society and Japanese decision-making processes explains both the consensual orientation of participants and the apparent high frequency of unanimous results in decision making as a function of ideology, the result of socialization into a tradition that prominently sustains ideals of harmony, solidarity, cooperation, and belongingness.  The present study diverges from this perspective insofar as it locates the primary source of consensus in decision making in rural Japan in the operation of the mechanism of mutual investment and the active pursuit of common interest in an institutional setting in which defection from productive exchange agreements is made as unlikely as possible.  The exchange perspective adopted in this study asserts that both the *mode* in which a decision is taken (unanimity or division) and the *orientation* of participants to the decision-making process (ranging from adversarial to consensual) are independent of one another and emergent properties of the exchange relation obtaining among participants.  The specific character of any exchange relationship, in turn, hinges on how effectively and in what manner the integrity of each transaction within it is maintained as a function of transaction itself, not on the characters of the participants.

The operation of mutual investment in productive exchange relations encourages high degrees of individual competence, achievement, and productivity, as well as high rates of successful transactions in corporate groups of all kinds in Japan. But the employment of this mechanism in exchange relations is the strategic equivalent of "putting all your eggs in one basket." This is not a strategy well suited to exchange relations in opportunity structures that encourage participants to "keep your options open."

This monograph is, thus, an examination of the collective behavior of people who have chosen, as it were, to "put all their eggs in one basket." To stretch this metaphor perhaps unreasonably, although only the basket and a few eggs are held in common, all attempt to claim their right to use all the eggs in the basket, even while trying to reserve their own eggs to use as they see fit. The most common result is that everyone watches the basket, the eggs, and everyone else with a consuming intensity. When successful, the eggs hatch into even more valuable chickens. The results of alternative procedures in this situation are also instructive, as The Clover Affair (Smith 1978) demonstrates. But the perennial question "Which came first?" is a primarily historical one and, as such, is not pursued here.

The findings presented here take the form of hypotheses derived from a general theory of collective decision making in productive exchange relations governed by mutual investment, which is explicitly developed in chapter 2. Arguments for the need for such a theory, taken from consideration of sociocultural and historical circumstances of rural Japan, appear in chapter 1. Chapter 3 argues for the applicability of this theory to the circumstances of social organization, social relations, and financial structure of Nohara hamlet, the field site of this study. Chapter 4 contains detailed analyses of cases of decision making gathered in Nohara hamlet, and chapter 5, a general discussion of group decision making in Nohara hamlet and elsewhere in rural Japan in light of these analyses. The conclusion of this study and some brief speculation on possible applications of this theory of collective decision making and productive exchange to other areas and aspects of Japanese culture and society are presented in chapter 6.

# CHAPTER 1:
## COLLECTIVE DECISIONS AND RURAL SOCIETY

### Harmony, Unanimity, and Collective Decision Making

Descriptions and discussion of group decision making in Japan are now widely available and range across the spectrum of settings from rural society to modern industry and politics, from a variety of historical situations to general statements applied to the whole of Japanese society.[1] These accounts broadly agree, in both description and explanation, that group decision making in Japan promotes unanimity in result through consensus, that the tendency to dampen down overt expressions of conflict (rather than allow it free expression) and unanimity in result are equivalent measures of group solidarity, and that these features are a direct result of members' values for such general ideals as harmony, conformity, group solidarity, consensus, and unanimity itself, as codified in the Japanese cultural tradition.

The following passages are only two of many that might be selected as representative of the prevailing scholarly view of Japanese decision-making practice:

It was the general rule that unanimity was required for these decisions. Just as it was thought preferable to select hamlet officers by recommendation rather than by competitive voting, so for other matters every effort was made to avoid decisions by majority vote, for it was considered that voting would damage the solidarity of the hamlet. (Fukutake 1972: 123)

It is most important that a meeting should reach a unanimous conclusion; it should leave no one frustrated or dissatisfied, for this weakens village or group unity and solidarity. The undercurrent of feeling is: "After all we are in the same boat, and should live peacefully without leaving any one behind as a straggler." In order to reach unanimity, they do not care how long it takes—whatever time and trouble they may have in its procedure, all should reach a final consensus. (Nakane 1970: 45)

This view of decision making, widely held as it is with regard to Japan, is by no means limited to the study of Japanese society. It is frequently encountered in studies of "traditional" or "village" societies generally (e.g., Baily 1965; Bloch 1971; Popkin 1979; Ward 1956). It is a view derived from the sociological tradition that analyzes social institutions in terms of the contribution each makes to the overall "maintenance of society" and through these analyses discovers "society" in social interaction. This practice has led to the confusion of motive with result in social interaction and, in the study of group decision making, a confusion of rule-following behavior with choice behavior. Consequently, those few students of Japanese decision making who demur to the logic of the orthodox view (e.g., Befu 1966, 1971; Ramseyer 1969; Silberman 1967, 1973; Cole 1976) either deemphasize the fundamentally consensual orientation of participants in Japanese corporate groups or insist on the historical reality of other than unanimous results in decision making within the Japanese tradition, or both, without yet providing a more coherent theory of Japanese decision making.

Thomas Smith (1977: 114) has written that "historians and anthropologists have emphasized the solidarity of the traditional Japanese farming villages. . . . But there was an equally important competitive side to village life that has been largely ignored: competition between families rather than individuals, covert rather than open, but fierce and unrelenting nevertheless." Among the several reasons that might be advanced to explain this shortcoming, one must certainly be the failure to correctly understand the features of consensus and unanimity in decision making in hamlet public life.

Whatever the traditional form of decision making in rural Japan, it is evident that decisions were never taken as they were because hamlet members valued "tradition" in and of itself in decision making. Customary practice emerges and remains as tradition because it constrains competition in such a way that no alternative strategy permits better long-term performance to any participant. With regard to the "tradition" of decision making of rural Japan, Befu (1971: 91) carefully observes that

> the hamlet assembly as the governing body is present in just about
> every hamlet, and is composed of one person from each family, no
> matter what the size of the family. Generally speaking, unanimity of
> agreement is desired in reaching decisions, and every effort is made
> to convince and persuade dissenters. (This unanimity requirement,
> however, does not imply that a single dissenting vote constitutes a
> veto.) At the same time less influential members are no doubt more
> or less coerced into going along with the more powerful members.
> There is evidence that by the end of the Tokugawa period already the
> hamlet assembly was resorting to voting as a decision-making proce-
> dure, although there was no legalistic, strict provision as to the

number of votes necessary to decide any issue. But it is evident that nothing like unanimity was required or expected in many hamlet assemblies even in the Tokugawa period.

Explanations of decision-making practice within solidary groups in Japan that are not based on simultaneously competitive and cooperative strategic inter-action among group members but rely on uniformity of participant beliefs and values with regard to the decision-making process itself are open to four specific criticisms: (1) they cannot demonstrate sufficient stability over time to have permitted institutionalization as the "traditional" basis for current practice; (2) they suffer from circularity in their reasoning; (3) they participate in the logical error of affirming the consequent; and (4) they cannot account for the regular variation found in decision results.

(1) The prevailing view of Japanese decision-making tradition cannot yield historical stability. It is axiomatic that decision making only occurs under condi-tions of scarcity. No decisions will be made where it is not necessary to choose among competing claims on limited resources. It is here that the "boat" metaphor fails to float as either an unambiguous description of informant belief or an ex-planation of observed practice. This view implies that decision making is an opportunity to exhibit altruistic behavior as represented by the claim that unanim-ity in result is preferred by all decision makers to the implementation of any specific course of action. This is to suggest, because hamlet members are not individuals but stem families, that the continuation of the hamlet itself is of greater importance to any hamlet member than its own continuation. This impli-cation is false. Altruism cannot emerge as the underlying principle of collective decision making in the hamlet context precisely because it is so easily invaded by any member who defects from it.

Under circumstances of finite and diminishing resources, as represented by the situation found in a lifeboat, the participant at each decision point who is least altruistic will secure more of life's necessities for himself. Over a series of decisions, the participant least opposed to relinquishing his own resources to others will be the first left without further resources. The metaphor of the life-boat is actually a metaphor of musical chairs, an ultimately untenable situation, an absolutely "worst case." In fact, hamlet society is based on cooperation and on the collective intensification of production. Cooperation need not be altruistic, and when cooperation results in increased production, questions of altruism need never arise.

If it is true, however, that stragglers are not *always* left behind, it is still legitimate to inquire into the conditions under which they are allowed to falter and finally fail. An adequate explanation of decision making in hamlets must account for both competition and cooperation among members, for both unanimity and division in decision results. Simple participation does not, as a matter of course, force some members to subsidize the welfare of other members in the name of "the good of the hamlet as a whole." This is a more difficult task than accounting for the persistence of a public morality that endorses the virtue of altruistic behavior. It will always be in everyone's interest that others behave altruistically.

(2) Bailey (1965: 5) has already demonstrated that "to say a council strives for consensus because its members value consensus is evidently a circular argument." For all that, this is an argument frequently encountered because it lies at the core of the "myth of the harmony of the natural village" (ibid.: 4) and the illusion that conflict is not inevitable and a part of human nature, but the product of pernicious institutions.

The logic behind this widespread belief is at the same time even more, or perhaps less, than exactly circular. To prefer unanimity in result is ultimately to prefer unanimity to the implementation of any particular course of action. With such a preference among participants, the preference of form over substance, there can be no logical grounds for the preference of one course of action over another. Decision making as a process of determining member preferences across a set of alternative courses of action vanishes from consideration, and we are left with the absurd situation in which members of the hamlet, "acting as a council" (Kuper 1971), are eager to arrive at a consensus they can unanimously endorse but are unable to support any specific course of action. Here is the hilarity of the classic "Alphonse and Gaston" comedy routine, in which neither man, from excessive deference to the other, is willing to proceed through the open door first.

(3) Explanations of group decision making that require participants to have preferences for unanimity often are expressed in a form that violates another principle of logic, that of affirming the consequent of the argument. This false argument has the form "if A is true, then B is true; and since B is true, then A must also be true." The prevailing view of Japanese decision making takes this form when it finds expression as a variant of the following: "Unanimous decisions, because everyone must agree, seem difficult to obtain. They are so difficult that everyone must really want them to be unanimous, or they would not go to all that trouble. Since group decisions are characteristically taken unanimously in Japan, it must be that participants very much want them to be taken unanimously." The argument is then often reinforced with statements of informant belief that they in fact do place a high premium on unanimity in result.

The preceding section has already shown that the minor premise is false: wanting a unanimous result cannot lead to a unanimous result. The error of affirming the consequent, however, leads to premature closure of causation, a denial that some cause other than A might result in the appearance of B. Methodologically, we are not entitled to assert that unanimity in result must arise from a value for unanimity—even if we can show that participants *do* have a value for unanimity—if (a) this relation cannot be demonstrated as logically causal, and (b) there remain alternative means for arriving at unanimity of result that do not require participants to value unanimity at all.

As Cole (1976: 504) has pointed out, the problem of unanimity and consensus building is not unique to Japan, but "can be logically shown to be a universal problem in group decision making." In some ways, the central problem must be to explain why such techniques as have recently been developed consciously and deliberately for use in group decision making in the U.S. have so long been part of the traditional culture of hamlet Japan, developed without the aid and assistance of modern social psychology (Hall and Watson 1970; Hare 1982). Coleman (1964), for example, has shown how unanimous decisions can be, and often are, reached in U.S. municipalities and simulation studies in which there is no desire for unanimity at all and in which contexts participants are accustomed to vote as a matter of course. El-Hakim (1978) has innovatively applied Coleman's decision model to a village in Sudan where decisions are regularly reached by unanimous consent. His data primarily concern case materials in which village factions regularly strive to acquire the resources of competing factions by forming alliances with higher-level political authorities. One of the major techniques these villagers employ to achieve unanimity is to systematically exclude from a meeting at which a decision will be made anyone likely to object to a favored proposal. The applicability of this model to rural Japan remains unclear, however, as a sustained effort is made there to insure maximal participation in all group decisions.

There is also the technique of "squaring," or "horse trading," discussed by Bailey (1965) in a variety of contexts and examined in detail by the several contributors to Richards and Kuper (1971). In this technique, two (or even more) separate issues are linked by agreement and resolved by mutual agreement. Such agreements have the appearance of unanimity. While this technique is largely irrelevant to decision making in rural Japan, it is clear that a group may arrive at one of the two end-points of the decision process, unanimity or division, by different routes. Even within the homogeneity of Japanese society, we must allow for this possibility.

(4) Those explanations that rely on the desires of participants for a particular mode of decision result do not adequately account for the variety in the available data. Most attempts at explanation reduce this variability by simply discounting its relevancy and locate the decision mode of unanimity itself as a component of Japanese culture. This pattern is then treated as an independent variable in accounting for other interesting sociocultural phenomena. Kerlinger (1951: 38), for example, records a four-to-three vote taken by a school board in the appointment of a school superintendent; the vote was reported as unanimous in the local newspaper. He suggests that the newspaper reported unanimity rather

than division because the culture, in general, and the newspaper's readers, in specific, require all decisions to be taken unanimously, whether they are or not. Whether or not explanations of this sort are sufficient at any level of analysis, they can never account for actual division when it occurs. Silberman (1973) is entirely correct in deploring the extent to which students of Japanese decision making have allowed this view of "unanimity as culture" to displace actual observation.

To suggest that Japanese methods of taking decisions in groups are "traditional" and then reduce this tradition to a simple desire for unanimity through consensus denies the significance of the range of variation in the actual cases of decision making. Where this variation is not denied, however, contradictory analyses have arisen within the work of the same authors. To cite only two of many prominent examples, Nakane first (1967) reports intense levels of competition in hamlet society and later (1970) suggests that stragglers will not be left behind. Lebra (1976: 158) observes that "belongingness . . . . puts one under pressure to comply with the will of the group against one's own will" but agrees with BenDasan that "the Japanese believe that 'no decision binds people by a hundred percent'" (1976: 30).

Ramseyer, too, leaves unreconciled this "cultural tradition" and his own observations in the field. He writes: "Decisions within the community are made on the basis of consensus and unanimity. Once it is arrived at it is considered binding on all residents" (1969: 208). He records specific instances, however, when all residents clearly do not consider such decisions binding: "K-4 feels that the community is against him in this, . . . but that he is entitled to half the old road and will wait forever if necessary to get his rights" (ibid.: 220). When issues involve productive resources such as arable land, "forever" may not be hyperbole. Thomas Smith (1959: 199) discusses a village dispute begun in 1713 that was still unresolved over 150 years later. Such lengthy disputes are possible because the entities at odds are not individuals, but hamlet members, corporate stem families.

When a decision fails to yield a unanimous result, the prevailing view of Japanese decision making can only point to a breakdown in hamlet harmony and solidarity resulting from external social or cultural impact. This view suggests that because unanimity is the result of the pursuit of harmony, results other than unanimity must imply either an initial lack of harmony or its loss along the way. This is also the native view of the decision process itself, and it differs only from the scholarly view in that its program suggests a search for the deviant personalities responsible for the failure to achieve unanimity rather than inadequate institutional arrangements. As an explanation, however, this approach fails from the same shortcomings as the original argument that gave rise to it. It is a conceptual framework unequal to the task assigned to it, presenting a native political tactic, the invocation of "harmony," as an explanation for the results of regular social interaction. There is no reason we should accept such reasoning and conceptual schema in explanations of political phenomena, however, when we have long since rejected them from discussions of religious belief and practice. Yet "harmony" occupies exactly the same epistemological status in Japanese social relations as does *mana* in Melanesia and "witchcraft" among the Zande, two examples familiar to all anthropologists from introductory texts.

Neither can we admit the methodological slight-of-hand of substituting the "apparent" for the "real"; even if a hamlet council only strives for "the appearance of harmony" rather than "true" harmony (Beardsley, Hall, and Ward 1959: 355), the original question of why some decisions are resolved unanimously and others result in a division remains unanswered. Whether a real, or only an apparent, harmony informs native consciousness, neither state of mind is sufficient to produce a result of any kind in a decision. Even if it were possible to distinguish authentic from feigned harmony, the fact remains that the desire for harmony is no more necessary for unanimity than its lack is to results other than unanimity.

There is a way out from this impasse, however, as Ramseyer observes: "When the vital interests of the household are seen to be involved, . . . solidarity is not an absolute value" (1969: 217). He goes on to suggest that a household's "vital interests" are involved when issues are "a threat to the livelihood" of a household, such as land or water rights (1969: 221).

But if harmony and solidarity are not "absolute values" all of the time, they are never absolute values. Since this is the case, Ramseyer's suggestion that the vital interests of the household must be threatened can only be used as a rough rule of thumb in the most obvious cases of conflict. An adequate theory of hamlet decision making must at least produce a generally applicable principle that predicts when a hamlet member will "draw the line" and refuse to "yield to the will of the group." At this point, however, it is sufficient to show that such a "line" is actually drawn in hamlet decision-making situations. This particular act is revealed most clearly through an examination of the ultimate hamlet sanction, ostracism (*murahachibu*). Robert Smith (1961) has collected and analyzed the few recorded cases of this sanction.

In the eight cases of *murahachibu* reported by Smith, three families were ostracised for refusing to meet additional assessments levied by the hamlet council (Cases 1, 5, and 7). In another case (Case 8), the hamlet council adjusted upward the fertility rating of a field, and the agrieved owner refused to participate further in hamlet affairs other than those related directly to irrigation. The council let stand its decision. Another case involved a local rash of petty potato theft by several different hamlet members, each from the other under cover of darkness (Case 6). Ostracism was threatened anyone caught in the act when even the guard hired to halt the practice before it became routine was caught stealing the very potatoes he was ostensibly guarding.

The final three episodes involve revenge against a former high-status hamlet household in reduced circumstances (Case 2), the revelation of election-law violations within the hamlet to a local newspaper by a child who took her civics lessons at face value (Case 4), and the removal of an especially obstreperous member from one hamlet "moiety" to that in which he had kinsmen (Case 3). Only in Case 2 is it clear that accumulated resentment within the hamlet led to ostracism, and in this case the punishment specified that the family would be excluded from hamlet society for only one year. With the aid of a go-between and an acceptable show of contrition, this family was readmitted after only two months without the pale.

That in six of the eight cases presented, one episode, one event, was sufficient to precipitate ostracism shows clearly that a definite "line" is drawn. Only one case (Case 3) provides insufficient evidence to make any judgment at all. Only Case 2 involves the exploitation of an opportunity for revenge, and this case was settled without a protracted period of suspended social relations.

One reason cases of *murahachibu* are so difficult to resolve is that while the sentence is invoked by the hamlet against one of its members, it is not always a judgment actively avoided by the outcast. As Beardsley, Hall, and Ward (1959: 257-58) point out, it is often difficult to distinguish expulsion from withdrawal. This difficulty arises precisely because a major and certain cause of ostracism is the failure of a member to abide by the (obviously not unanimous) decision of the hamlet council. And while ostracism is in fact a rare event, it is difficult to persuade outsiders that it is not done almost as if on a whim. To nonmembers, the content of such disputes often appears trivial in the extreme (see Smith 1961).

The very fact that decisions that result in *murahachibu* often do seem so trivial to nonmembers has been used by students of rural Japan (e.g., Smith 1978: 237; Dore 1959: 343) to support the general thesis that a "last straw" model is useful in understanding the eruption of open conflict in hamlet society. Conceived in this way, any event, although itself unimportant, when added to the total burden of hostility long suppressed for the sake of the appearance of hamlet solidarity and harmony, can create the "critical mass" that releases feelings of animosity so strong that they can no longer be restrained by public sentiment. Like the entire view of decision making that recommends it, this model fails as an adequate explanation for several reasons. Among these are: (1) it does not give sufficient attention to the nature of the event that gave rise to the conflict; (2) it does not distinguish between the source of the conflict and the expression of conflict; and (3) it does not distinguish between conflicts arising among neighbors as neighbors and conflicts arising directly out of participation in hamlet affairs.

This same evidence, however, also supports an alternative view that the very "triviality" of the causes of overt conflict in hamlet society demonstrates how exceedingly sensitive hamlet members are to the dependency and fragility of their status as hamlet members and, from such an "exposed position," how willing they are to "draw the line" on participation in hamlet affairs. This approach suggests that hamlet solidarity must be actively re-created with every decision and that under appropriate circumstances any apparently solidary group can experience the shattering effects of overt conflict without warning. It is a question of whether each hamlet member will abide by or resist a particular decision, however trivial that decision seems. It need not be an issue that itself threatens a member's livelihood, merely one that alters the member's rights and duties as a member of the hamlet.

In order to understand ostracism as an expression of the inherent delicacy of the hamlet alliance, it is necessary to draw attention to the distinction between the member-hamlet relationship and the neighbor-neighbor relationship. The two are not the same. As the sanction of *murahachibu* demonstrates, the member-hamlet bond takes precedence over the neighbor-neighbor bond. In many, if not most, cases, ostracism is almost as hard on members still in good standing since they must break off relations with the outcast. In some cases it may be harder on the outcast's friends, neighbors, and relatives because their suffering is unmerited, at least in terms of the neighbor-neighbor relationship. But a man who despises his neighbor cannot, for that reason, have him ostracised.

Ostracism operates to protect the hamlet as a corporate group from exploitation by its individual members; withdrawal from hamlet society is the only recourse a member has to exploitation by the hamlet as a whole. Ostracism results from irreconcilable differences in interpretation of a member's duties as hamlet member in particular instances. The apparent triviality of the instance itself only serves to further emphasize the possibility of differences in interpretation of what, concretely, can and cannot be required by the hamlet of a member. This is not a quantitative, but a qualitative, matter.

There is, however, no similar means of organizing tensions and differences of opinion within the neighbor-neighbor relationship, and it is not a matter for public concern (as opposed to gossip) within the hamlet that a man and his neighbor are not on good terms. As hamlet members, even neighbors not on speaking terms must still interact as hamlet members. While it is theoretically possible for two feuding households with sufficient influence to organize their sympathizers and allies into conflict groups that have the appearance of factions and to prevent the hamlet from functioning, this is actually quite rare. Most neutral households have too much to lose to allow feuding neighbors to engage in behavior damaging to their interests and too little to gain by siding with one party against the other. Thus, tensions that do not stem from the member-hamlet relationship and are not allowed to disrupt that relation can still accumulate within the neighbor-neighbor relationship. This may be what is meant by the idea that a hamlet should preserve "the appearance of harmony," i.e., that grievances that did not originate in the member-hamlet relationship must not be permitted to disrupt that relationship. This does not mean, however, that grievances can accumulate in the same way in member-hamlet relations that they can in neighbor-neighbor relations. Either hamlet members participate in hamlet decisions and abide by them, or their member-hamlet relationship is dissolved by one side or the other, or both.

There are, thus, two reasons for the intensity of acrimony expressed when conflict does erupt in a hamlet. First, given the priority of the member-hamlet relationship, whatever personal complaints and suspicions one household holds for another can be given overt expression once the member-hamlet relationship is breached. Such complaints can be, and are, used to show that the bond has been severed because of flaws in the personality of the offender and not because of structural weakness inherent in the relationship. This venting of rage, however, should not be mistaken for evidence that the weight of accumulated grievances finally caused the collapse of the relationship. Indeed, such matters can never be the cause of that failure unless they have affected all hamlet members uniformly.

Second, there is frequently an almost total lack of structural alternatives to the member-hamlet relationship since it is virtually impossible for a member excluded from one hamlet to join another. Even the content of neighbor-neighbor relations is altered by conflicts arising in member-hamlet relations. Thus, outrage is expressed in such great measure not only because the failure of a member to participate has prevented a pet project from being realized but also because all future benefits deriving from participation in the member-hamlet relationship are certainly made more expensive, and possibly threatened. The fragility of the member-hamlet relationship is forced into the consciousness of all members.

## Hamlet Society and Productive Exchange Relations

The distinction between the member-hamlet relationship and the neighbor-neighbor relationship is critical for the problem of group decision making not only with regard to the capacity of either to affect the course of conflicts originating in the other but also with regard to the qualitatively different foundations of these relations within the bounds of hamlet society. While the words competition and cooperation spring easily to mind, it is an unacceptable oversimplification to view the former relationship as one of unalloyed competition and the latter as pure cooperation since both relationships combine both forms of interaction. But whatever the varied relations among neighbors in a hamlet, the hamlet alliance itself is of a piece, a relation of *membership* of equivalent social entities in a different social entity of the next higher order of inclusion. The hamlet is a corporate group in which other corporate groups (*ie*, stem families) hold rights of access to corporate and other members' resources.

The hamlet alliance is founded on *productive exchange*, the exchange process through which two or more parties organize and combine their resources to produce some good or service not (as cheaply) available to any separately (Emerson 1976: 357). Through productive exchange, producers are able to take advantage of both division of labor and economies of scale. This is not to say that the member-hamlet relationship is necessarily freer from competition than the neighbor-neighbor relationship. It is evident, however, that the more formal qualities of the member-hamlet relationship and the rewards of increased production that the relationship promotes do afford all hamlet members a clearer view of the risks and rewards of participation in hamlet affairs than can exist from neighborly relations alone.

Since approximately 1700, if not earlier (Nakane 1967: 47-49; Smith 1959: 157), production in rural Japan has been carried out by small domestic units, stem families (*ie*), in local competition for the often extremely scarce resources necessary to survival: fertile land suitable for irrigated rice cultivation, fertilizer, and water. In discussing the historical conditions of production and land tenure in one rice-producing hamlet, Thomas Smith (1977: 107-8) writes,

> Farming at Nakahara was intensely competitive, with land changing hands continually in response to even very small setbacks and successes. Few families worked exactly the same fields for many years running. Fields were lost in bad years, added in good, and good and bad years sometimes came in clutches. In a decade or two, holdings could double in size or melt away to nothing.

Smith continues that competition for land was ultimately competition for family survival, and "when a family could no longer survive as a group, its members dispersed and its identity was forgotten" (1977: 108). Such competition was not necessarily the result of the commercialization of agriculture, which was negligible in Nakahara. Rather, it was the direct result of the variations in the productive capacities of families as they passed through the phases of the family cycle, of the quantity and quality of arable land, and of the weakness of restraints on the alienation of land from the stem family.

Rice fields were the property of individual households, and main families did little to cushion the effects of competition on their branch households: "Altogether, the impression is that mutual aid among kin in Nakahara was limited and that each family's fate was essentially in its own hands" (ibid.: 113). Nakane (1967: 113) also observes that competition for scarce resources was keen even among close kin:

> What is important to notice about these changes [in plot ownership] is the high degree of independence of the household. Even a household

of one's close kin, or a close neighbor, seldom offered help to their own detriment, and envied the rise of another household.

Smith (1977) offers evidence that close kin may have in fact been among the fiercest competitors. Branch households seem to have been founded not to provide for the subsistence of collateral members but to solve the problem of labor surplus in the main household, thereby maximizing the main household's land-labor ratio. Thus, the establishment of a branch family could result in a higher level of per capita consumption for the main household by shifting the problem of labor surplus onto a newly established branch household. We would then expect that branch families would always receive less land than would have been available to them on a per capita basis if they had remained in the main household. Smith (1977: 112) records that in Nakahara

> the division of property was almost always extremely unequal: main family shares in Nakahara averaged 23.1 koku of arable land, and branch family shares only 10.4. Property other than land was divided even more unequally: the house, the farmyard and heirlooms usually went intact to the main family.

Nakane (1967: 80-81) also suggests that the fundamental relationship between families in the hamlets of rural Japan was one of persistent competition:

> Every household, as an independent property-owning and farming unit, theoretically stands equal to any other member of the village. Superiority over others is made possible only by the social and economic advantage historically accumulated by the household, and can be maintained only by constant economic and social superiority over others.

Hamlets themselves are corporate groups that do not depend for their existence on the continued membership of any member household, and they may continue to exist over long periods despite the vicissitudes of fortune to which individual households are subject. Smith (1978: 43) notes that while genealogies in the hamlet of Kurusu only go back four or five generations, the settlement itself is not of recent origin: "There are many gravestones in the Kurusu cemeteries that bear family names no longer found anywhere in the district."

Hamlets serve their members as "a means of maximization of economic, political and social activities" (Nakane 1967: 81). The hamlet only exists for the welfare of its members, and only as long as membership offers a net gain to member households would we expect membership to be continued. Conversely, we would not expect other members to tolerate among them a family that expected the hamlet to subsidize its existence. The hamlet is only maintained because it serves as a nexus for productive exchange relations through which maintenance, capital investment, and operation costs are kept maximally low for all members.

> A *kumi* [hamlet] is not merely a neighborhood group, but has importance as an exclusive economic body in which labor, capital and credit circulate. In other words, it is a common economic pool, upon which the group's economic life depends closely. . . . In this way the households of a *kumi* are linked together by limitless, long-term obligations and duties which bind its members together, both economically and socially, into an exclusive group, so that it is difficult to leave or a stranger to enter. (Nakane 1967: 137)

Much of the exchange among hamlet members is simple reciprocal exchange, such as help with transplanting, house construction, firefighting, and hosting religious festivals, and all of these activities can be organized at the hamlet level. But the fundamental exchange relationship upon which the hamlet is founded is productive exchange. This relationship is most clearly seen in the most basic cooperative activity in which the hamlet engages, the irrigation of wet rice fields.

Large-scale irrigation systems may indeed require the organizational capacities of an "oriental despot" (Wittevogel 1957), but the small-scale systems that have supplied and continue to supply so much of rural Japan with water can be constructed and maintained by those who use them (Befu 1971: 70; Fukutake 1972: 90-91). While hamlets often control other valuable corporate property, particularly woodlands in which organic fertilizers and firewood are collected, it is the irrigation system that provides the foundation for wet rice agriculture in Japan and, consequently, the basis for productive exchange in the hamlets of rural Japan (Fukutake 1972: 82).

The cooperative construction and maintenance of an irrigation system offers several advantages to producers organized as small, competitive domestic units. The fact that competition for land and water is severe does not lessen, but increases, the advantages that can accrue from cooperative behavior. Nakane (1967: 73-79) gives several reasons why such cooperation is advantageous to domestic producers.

(1) The labor contributed by a larger group can make possible the construction of a larger and more effective irrigation system. A larger irrigation system can make water available to a much larger area of fertile land for wet rice cultivation.

(2) Because a wider area can be brought under cultivation, fields of optimal size for a family labor force can be constructed and each family's holdings spread out over the entire area.

(3) Because water must be worked into the dry fields until the field has the consistency of a thick paste, a family must apply maximum labor to each field as it receives water and before the water runs off into the next field.  Thus, it is to each family's advantage to have fields spread over the entire irrigated area, not all adjacent to one another, and to have the water fed into the fields sequentially.  Dispersed holdings are thus desirable, and this seems to be a common pattern throughout the entire country (Fukutake 1972: 83).

(4) The flow of water into all fields depends on the good repair of the irrigation system and the banks of all fields.  Because families' holdings are dispersed over a wide area, all families are assured that the costs of maintenance of the irrigation system will be provided by the owners of each field for each field.  It is to no family's advantage to have any part of the total system in disrepair.

(5) The water supply can be policed with a maximum of security, and the water supply can be distributed evenly throughout the entire area served by the system.  At first glance, this might not seem advantageous to any single family, and thus to no one, because each family can be optimally productive with its fields spread over the entire area.  However, any given family is likely to receive less than the maximum amount of water over its entire holdings if the water supply is not policed.  While a family may get additional water to one of its fields through theft, thefts by other families would prevent it from getting water to the rest of its fields.  As Nakane (1967: 77), among others (e.g., Fukutake 1972: 83), points out, "No one is allowed to have water as freely as he desires, unless abundant water is available.  Everybody wants sufficient water because water virtually decides the annual harvest."

Naturally, quarrels do break out when water is in short supply, and theft of water is sometimes attempted.

> But such malicious conduct can easily be detected:  the person on duty often comes round to see that everything is in order, and also each person will carefully watch the flow of water to his own field, particularly when the water supply is low.  It is said that villagers can tell if someone is stealing water by the slightest change in the sound of the water flow. (Nakane 1967: 79)

Under conditions where the water supply does meet demand, it is

> essential that it should be distributed equally to each field.  Therefore the timing of the water supply to each plot is carefully calculated by the number of plots and according to the size of each plot.  The interval of water supply and the quantity of the water to each field varies according to the available quantity for that year, and the

number of plots to be fed. But whatever the manner of distribution may be, the order of the water-flow among plots is always adhered to. The village rule is very strict on this point. (ibid.: 77)

It follows that changes in the ownership of individual plots neither requires nor allows changes in the order in which plots are watered.

Thus, the system of irrigation makes the village a distinctive social and economic unit and membership both desirable and imperative. "Without being a member of the village, it is difficult to carry on wet rice cultivation" (ibid.: 79).

The fact that individual farming is directly linked with village organization, as appears in the network of water flow, and the way in which households are inevitably bound to each other by water, determines the form of village organization: internally it involves severe economic and political competition among households, and externally it presents the village as a tightly knit organization. (ibid.: 79)

Under these conditions of highly competitive household subsistance farming, which at the same time require extensive cooperation with one's competitors, a family is primarily concerned with its land, its labor supply, and its rights in the corporate group. "In such an economic situation, there is more competition among households over their rights than [over] the accumulation of wealth" (ibid.: 80). The reason for this is that wealth can be quickly consumed or dissipated, but rights in the corporate group are rights to the means of production upon which the survival of the family depends.

These rights in the hamlet, the corporate group, seem once to have been more jealously guarded than they are at present. Even now, however, a new household in a hamlet is often not considered a full member until it has resided in the hamlet a long time and shown itself willing to accept the responsibilities of membership. While a new family may mean additional labor, or, if wealthy, additional capital, it also means "a decrease in the vested rights of the existing households" (Oishi 1956: 18-19, quoted from Nakane 1967: 80). In general, "it costs a great deal and takes quite a long time to acquire *full membership* with all rights" (Nakane 1967: 138). Smith (1978: 76, 210) has recorded an interesting method of securing the acceptance of responsibility by new members in Kurusu hamlet: upon joining the hamlet, new members are promised full shares in the profits to be gotten after the hamlet's commonly owned woodlands mature in about fifty years. Presumably they must, until that time, remain on their best behavior.

Rights in the corporate group can be lost in either of two ways: a member can resign from the group or be expelled. In actuality, it is sometimes difficult to understand which has occurred (Beardsley, Hall, and Ward 1959: 257-58). Nakane (1967: 140) records an interesting case of the loss of rights in the corporate group as recently as 1962. A man who had been a hamlet member left the hamlet for several years but finally returned. Although known by all the members of the hamlet and allowed to reside in the hamlet, he was not given full rights (including access to communally owned land) as a hamlet member. If he had either sent money to meet hamlet assessments in his absence or left a member of his family behind to participate in hamlet undertakings, he could have continued as a full member. But he did neither, and he returned to the hamlet with the same status accorded any new family just entering and gaining membership.

Conditions of extreme competition within the corporate group do not preclude cooperation in the form of productive exchange, as the fundamental paradigm of hamlet economic organization—the corporate control of irrigation— demonstrates. All other productive exchange transactions are founded on the productive exchange paradigm implied by and exemplified in the local irrigation system. But neither does cooperation in the form of productive exchange at the hamlet level imply reduced competition among hamlet families as independent units of production and reproduction. By far the commonest method of acquiring land by families within a hamlet has been to foreclose on other families in default on usually small loans (Smith 1959: 158; 1977: 107-10; Nakane 1967: 48-51; Fukutake 1972: 4).

Internally, competition for scarce strategic resources was keen even among close kin and neighbors, but it was a competition at least in part ameliorated by the obvious advantages of productive exchange at the level of the hamlet as a whole, the inclusion of all families using the local irrigation system. The exigencies of competition among hamlet members were not, however, lessened by conditions in the surrounding society. By law (often, it must be noted, more commonly observed in the breach than in attendance), farmers were

> forbidden to sell their land; their right to subdivide it was limited; they had no freedom to change their place of residence; and even the crops they could grow were restricted in order to pay their taxes. Practically forced into self-sufficient subsistence economy in small villages, and bearing collective responsibility for the annual payment of their rice tax, the individual was submerged in an isolated and exclusive community. (Fukutake 1972: 5)

The dilemma of the household during the period that gave rise to the tradition of decision making found in hamlet society was whether or not the prospect of increased production was worth the risk of increased dependency in the face of diminished external opportunities. The means most likely to insure the success of a family's continued survival was participation in the productive exchange opportunities offered by the hamlet as a corporate group. Households could survive without interaction with their neighbors as neighbors if they could interact as hamlet members. Within the hamlet alliance, security lay in numbers. Yet households could not permit themselves at the same time to become victims of the very relationship from which they benefitted. If membership in the hamlet provided access to corporate and other members' resources, it also required the reciprocal duty of making one's own resources available to other members.

The one certain way a family could go extinct was to yield its control over the means of production, and it was difficult enough to avoid going under at the hands of other individual families without the inclusion of the hamlet as a whole as an additional competitor. Only by reserving the right, in some form, to refuse to participate in hamlet undertakings could a family have any hope of survival. Conversely, the hamlet could not allow a family to benefit from its productive exchange transactions without making it assume an equitable share in the burden: the right to refuse to participate must always be on general grounds. A family that could only lose by participation in hamlet undertakings would always be better off resigning from the hamlet. Relative to each member, the strength of the collective allows all members to share this perspective on the limitations of participation in collective undertakings. This is the attractiveness, and also the risk, of the member-hamlet relationship over the neighbor-neighbor relationship: that everyone in the hamlet agrees that a member's refusal to participate in any particular hamlet undertaking is unjustified. Although competition for local resources is greatly reduced in the hamlets of Japan today relative to even the recent past, hamlet members still have no desire to subsidize the consumption of other hamlet members as a function of hamlet membership. The hamlet remains a nexus for productive exchange among hamlet members, and hamlet members alone.

Through the decision-making process, the hamlet, in its capacity as hamlet assembly, chooses among alternative courses of action, discovering and creating its members' preferences and their willingness to participate in the implementation of an authoritative decision. That this process is maximally inclusive and consensual reveals both the presence of common interests within the hamlet and the fragility of the hamlet relation. We are not entitled to assume that the effort to discover a common interest is prompted by an underlying identity of interest. On the contrary, such care in the decision-making process suggests an acute awareness of the limits of common interest and the lack of an identity of interest. The assumption that hamlet members are willing to exchange their right to withdraw from participation for the appearance of an absolute identity of interest that can never become a reality is not justified.

Beyond its utility in understanding hamlet conflict management and the organization of hamlet-wide collective undertakings, there is a third reason for drawing attention to the distinction between member-hamlet and neighbor-neighbor relations. Methodologically, analytically separating these two orders of social relations among the same households within a hamlet makes possible the development of a theory of hamlet decision making based on a simple model of productive exchange, the basis for hamlet-wide interaction. A hamlet is not merely a collection of neighboring households, but a corporate entity in its own right.

There are several reasons why it is desirable to analyze hamlet relations apart from neighbor relations, not the least of which is that previous analyses of hamlet decision making have attempted to view interaction between member households at the hamlet level as a function of the total system of social relations. The results of these attempts have not been satisfactory. If an alternative approach is desirable, then it must be one that is not as ambitious and that is willing to exchange a complete picture for additional clarity in some selected area. This clarity can be achieved through a return to simplicity, to underlying principles.

It is possible for a model of hamlet relations to be simple insofar as the hamlet relation is at least much simpler than the agglomeration of all neighbor relations within the hamlet. The hamlet alliance is in fact the essence of simplicity since hamlet members are either "in good standing" or they are not, and this status is not affected by the particular state of its relations with other households. A member's standing is entirely a function of its participation in hamlet affairs, particularly its willingness to abide by hamlet decisions. Relations among neighbors can, and do, range widely, but the relationship of member households to the hamlet as a whole is uniform. It is based on participation in productive exchange transactions among all hamlet members in good standing.

A few comments on the nature and use of models are appropriate here. In Schelling's words, "models tend to be useful when they are simultaneously simple enough to fit a variety of behaviors and complex enough to fit behaviors that need the help of an explanatory model" (1978: 89). The virtue of a model is that it allows simplification and at the same time provides an explanation insofar as the system described by the model behaves like the model. A model, again in Schelling's words, is "a precise and economical statement of a set of relationships that are sufficient to produce the phenomenon in question" (ibid.: 87). The "phenomenon in question" in this case is the fact that sometimes decisions are arrived at unanimously and sometimes they are not. I do not believe that a sufficient explanation for this phenomenon is yet so simple and so obvious that no abstraction is required. On the other hand, hamlets and the issues with which they deal are not so diverse that something useful cannot be said about hamlet decision making as a unified phenomenon and a theory of hamlet decision making not developed on the basis of a relatively simple model of hamlet relations. Even where such a theory is inadequate as an explanation, it at least retains the virtue of being explicit and open to examination in both its assumptions and its logic.

An adequate theory of hamlet decision making should, at a minimum, provide a number of related explanations: (1) it should offer a reason to expect division and unanimity; (2) these results should be related to the issue at hand; (3) it should provide a clear statement of when a hamlet member will and will not agree to participate in hamlet undertakings; (4) it should be based on reasonable assumptions about member interaction at the hamlet level; and (5) it should explain the relative frequencies of division and unanimity within the overall consensual framework of member-hamlet relations. To be at least provisionally acceptable, such a theory should do all of the above better than competing theories, but it should not be required to explain any and all questions of interest to students of rural Japanese society.

The basic assumptions of the model on which the theory presented in the next chapter is founded are (1) that the fundamental relation of hamlet members is one of productive exchange and (2) that hamlet members choose rationally among available alternatives on the basis of *expected utility maximization*, but that with regard to hamlet membership itself, members follow a *minimax loss* principle. That is, within the scope of any issue, hamlet members examine and rank alternative courses of action with a view to maximizing expected utility, but all alternatives are also divided into those that are acceptable and those that are not (Heath 1976b: 26-27). However imperceptibly, each issue raised in the hamlet also raises the question of continued membership for every hamlet member. It is from this perspective that we must expect hamlet members to "consider the worst outcome which could follow from each course of action and . . . then select the course which will have the least ill effects if the worst outcome occurs" (ibid.: 27). To draw upon Schelling once again: "There may or may not be a unanimously preferred outcome. And even if one of the outcomes is unanimously chosen, we cannot infer that it is preferred from the fact that it is universally chosen" (Schelling 1978: 98-99). After all, the view of hamlet decision making presented here rests on the view that hamlet members belong to the hamlet because to do so makes their continued survival more likely than other available alternatives, and they cease to belong when survival is less likely. All hamlet decision making must ultimately refer back to this fact. Hamlet decision making is the active element of the productive exchange relation represented by hamlet membership. The following chapter develops a model of productive exchange and derives a theory of hamlet decision making from it. It is not a theory that requires a priviledged vantage point with respect to participant motives, or even supposes that such a possibility exists. Rather, it refers only to participants' revealed preferences for alternative courses of action and asks what the consequences of behavior based on such preferences are.

CHAPTER 2:
PRODUCTIVE EXCHANGE, MUTUAL INVESTMENT, AND
COLLECTIVE DECISIONS: A THEORY OF GROUP DECISION MAKING


Decisions resulting in exchange transactions are necessarily collective decisions. The process of making a collective decision concerning the allocation of resources is a function of the exchange relations obtaining among the decision makers. This chapter develops a model of productive exchange and expands the implications of this model as a theory of group decision making in such exchange relations.

The major contribution of social exchange theory must be found in its treatment of "exactly those topics that economics theory has trouble with: market imperfections" (Emerson 1976: 359). The theory of exchange relations presented below, therefore, begins with a discussion of price and bilateral exchange. The problem of "the paradox of price" is developed as the necessity of avoiding defection from a mutually agreed upon rate of exchange. The principle of "contingent loss" is examined in this connection. The operation of the defection-reducing mechanism of "mutual investment," as a form of contingent-loss exchange regulation, is subsequently discussed. The interaction of price and mutual investment in the formation of a distribution rule operating in this same context is then examined. The chapter concludes with the development of the implications of this model into a theory of collective decision making in productive exchange relations governed by mutual investment.


## The Paradox of Price

Economics theory has generally treated the two separate processes of (1) discovering a mutually agreeable rate of exchange and (2) reciprocally transferring the valued items at issue as a single problem, that of the determination of "price." The paradox of price raises the question of the logical relationship of these two processes. As early as the mid-seventeenth century, Hobbes recognized that the difficulties inherent in consummating an exchange appear as great as the benefits hoped for: "He that performeth first, has no assurance that the other will perform after; because the bonds of words are too weak to bridle men's ambition, avarice, anger and other Passions, without the fear of some coercive Power" ([1651] 1955: 89-90).

The problem of exchange Hobbes identifies is basic, but his incorrect identification of the source of the problem, irrationality, leads to a false conclusion, namely, that exchange could not have taken place prior to the institution of coercive forms of authority. The actual issue Hobbes raises is why persons in agreement on a rate of exchange require guarantees at all. In other words, why is a mutually agreeable rate of exchange not both a necessary and sufficient condition for exchange to occur at that rate of exchange? The answer is not that men are governed by uncontrollable "Passions," but that men remain rational through both processes. The difficulty in consummating exchanges arises directly from the ability to reach a mutually agreeable rate of exchange.

This is the paradox of price, that while a mutually agreeable rate of exchange is a necessary condition for exchange to occur among rational men, it is also a condition sufficient to prevent an exchange from occurring at the marginal utilities underlying that rate of exchange. Men enter into exchanges only because they cannot otherwise obtain the desired results more cheaply. A mutually agreeable rate of exchange, a price, is that point at which no one can obtain a more desirable result. It is here that Hobbes's problem emerges: to reach an equilibrium, possible rates of exchange more desirable to one, and less desirable to the other, must be crossed on both sides. The unilateral release of the valued items at issue must disrupt this equilibrium and thus terminate the transaction at one of the points already passed over. And yet one of the parties must inevitably "go first." "Simultaneous transfer" remains illusory because it too requires an agreement from which defection is possible. On the basis of a mutually agreeable rate of exchange alone, the loss of unilaterally released resources is not a matter of risk but of certainty. The process of reaching a mutually agreeable rate of exchange can never provide a reason to expect reciprocity, only reasons to believe it will not occur. Rational men cannot resolve transactions requiring the reciprocal transfer of valued items solely on the basis of a mutually agreeable rate of exchange.

It appears that economics theory has not treated this necessary relationship between the processes of reaching an agreement and carrying it out as problematic. Instead, it has focused attention on problems of price alone, precisely because of the apparent inevitability of Hobbes's solution, namely, the presence of coercive forms of authority. Those economies in response to which economics theory has developed have themselves evolved in the context of complementary political and legal systems with the power to enforce agreements (Klein and Leffler 1981: 615-16). Recent advances in "transaction-cost" economics (e.g., Williamson 1979; Telser 1980; Klein 1980; Klein and Leffler 1981), however, lead to the inevitable conclusion that supply and demand schedules for the valued items at issue alone are insufficient to account for the total utilities of the resources involved in any exchange transaction. Exchange itself is simply not "free," but a necessarily costly social product. The "Invisible Hand" of the classic marketplace has the form of an outstretched and open palm.

## Defection-reducing Mechanisms

From this point, discussion of exchange turns from the determination of price toward an examination of those mechanisms, with their associated costs, that function to insure the integrity of exchange transactions. A mechanism that provides this function is called a *defection-reducing mechanism*. *Defection* is any attempt to increase one's resource levels through an exchange transaction at a rate of exchange other than that to which the other party willingly, and in full knowledge, consents. Thus, broadly defined, defection includes both open and closed designs, such as robbery and theft, cheating and fraud, as well as any action taken on the basis of unilateral interpretations of the agreement.

While exchange is not possible without the operation of defection-reducing mechanisms, such devices can never entirely overcome the risk of loss that the possibility of defection introduces into exchange transactions. This is because defection-reducing mechanisms are themselves integral to the exchange process and are implied by the process of reaching a mutually agreeable rate of exchange. The costs of utilizing these mechanisms must ultimately be paid for from the marginal utility of the exchange. As with all things consumed, the law of diminishing marginal utility applies. As more units of defection reduction are consumed, the utility of further units and the likelihood of defection declines. When the likelihood of defection has been removed from the exchange transaction, the marginal utility of the transaction itself will also have been reduced to zero.

No exchange transaction can be made entirely free from the possibility of defection. Thus, if there is to be an exchange transaction at all, some uncertainty as to whether defection will occur must be borne by the party who first relinquishes his resources. In common language, estimates of the degree to which a transaction has been made free from the likelihood of defection are often expressed as a matter of "trust" or "trustworthiness."

The cost of defection reduction is exacted for all transactions and is unavoidable. Because this cost is part of every transaction, it is often left undifferentiated, and the operation of the defection-reducing mechanism is frequently left unnoticed or taken for granted. When recognized, they are usually seen either as aspects of the sociocultural setting in which exchanges customarily take place or as attributes of participants' personalities or personal relations. They are rarely taken as components both integral to, and essential for, consumated exchange transactions.

There are two fundamental defection-reducing mechanisms. That suggested by Hobbes and assumed by economics theory is called *contract*, which relies for its efficacy on the coercive powers of a superordinate third party to enforce the terms of agreements. The other mechanism is called *contingent loss*. It reduces defection through the anticipation of loss of access to a source of valuable future transactions.  The only recourse this mechanism provides against defection is refusal to transact in the future.  To be effective, contingent loss requires an indefinitely distant horizon for the terminal transaction in the series of future exchanges.  Axelrod (Axelrod 1981; Axelrod and Hamilton 1981) employs the principle of contingent loss in an iterated Prisoner's Dilemma, a simulation of the general conditions under which stable patterns of defection-free exchange will emerge in the absence of coercive third parties.  He shows that defection can only be reduced by restricting the participants' opportunity structures to the point where the search for new partners is more costly than defection-free exchange with a current partner.  Thus, while payment of the costs of contract are made directly to third parties (or even indirectly, as in the form of taxes, tribute, and license fees), the costs of contingent loss are accounted as opportunities foregone.

The major differences between these two different mechanisms can be brought more sharply into focus.  By means of contract and explicit agreements, attractive single exchange transactions can be consummated with a variety of different partners.  The resources lost in payment for this opening of opportunity, however, become unavailable for inclusion in proposed exchanges.  Contingent loss can never support even the most attractive single exchange transactions, and thus, many desirable exchanges will not be transacted.  However, as none of the resources involved in the transaction are extracted to pay for increased defection reduction, for equivalent exchanges, marginal utilities in exchanges governed by contingent loss will be higher than those governed by contract.  Contract is more advantageous in a social field characterized by diversity and intermittent contacts; contingent loss is more effective regulating exchanges in homogeneous social fields with high frequencies of interaction.  Because both mechanisms are costly, however, each will tend to dominate entire social fields and maintain those characteristics of the social field that foster that defection-reducing mechanism.  Thus, utilization of contract will tend to encourage further intermittent exchanges of diverse resources, and contingent loss will encourage further homogeneity and high-frequency interaction among circumscribed sets of partners.

### Forms of Exchange and Defection Reduction

There are two means of increasing the utility of resources, exchange and production.  Production is not necessarily a social activity, while exchange always is.  When production is organized socially, it is called *productive exchange*:

> Unlike the direct transfer of valued items in simple exchange, here items of value are produced through a value-adding process.  In general, the separate resources of two or more persons, A, B, C, . . . N, are combined through a social process involving division of labor.  The result is a valued product.  (Emerson 1976: 357)

It is obvious, however, that even in multiparty productive exchange relations, defection-reducing mechanisms are still necessary. As Williamson (1979: 242) has observed, even where there is "a long-term interest in effecting adaptations of a joint profit-maximizing kind, . . . governance structures which attenuate opportunism and otherwise infuse confidence are evidently needed."

It is not only a matter of relating productive exchange to a defection-reducing mechanism. The relation of labor to the means and results of production must also be considered. Economics theory is strongest when production is modeled as a process of multiple and simultaneous simple exchanges governed by contract. For production to be modeled as a simple dyadic exchange of "valued resources," labor theoretically must be treated as alienated from the means and results of production, which are themselves the property of the party to the exchange who purchases the labor of the other party. In this view, a man either works "for himself," in which case he produces alone and production is not socially organized; he works "for someone else," the owner of the means of production; or he "organizes production," meaning that he purchases all of the means of production and markets the product profitably.

That production *can be modeled* in this way, however, does not mean that it must necessarily be organized in the same way. One alternative means of organizing production is the partnership, a situation in which two or more people can work "with" each other without any of them acting directly as buyers or sellers of labor or talent. Partnerships can combine many partners of diverse statuses, but it is a fiction to believe that the major difficulty of a partnership is that the partners are reluctant to organize themselves in this way only because partners are personally liable for claims against the partnership. The difficulty lies at a deeper level.

Partners must satisfy themselves that there is an agreeable rate of exchange available to them outside considerations of the "market value" of the contributions each brings to the partnership. Where production is highly individualized, as in law and brokerage firms, and where individual contributions can be measured with high and unerring degrees of accuracy by all partners, this difficulty diminishes. Where production is highly interdependent and complex, however, the problem of aligning returns with contributions becomes virtually insurmountable. Increases in the number of partners makes the dyadic model increasingly inappropriate and unworkable, determination of a mutually agreeable rate of exchange difficult, and defection more likely. Rather than a relationship of production "infused with confidence," interaction among partners easily becomes reduced to the accusatory mode.

A more successful solution to the problem of rate of exchange in productive exchange relations is the corporate enterprise that, as a social entity, owns assets, purchases the means of production, and markets products through its agents.  It is in turn owned by those persons willing to invest in it.  Corporate organization at once makes possible the total integration of labor and capital, as well as their total separation.  That is, within any corporate group organized for production, it is possible to specify that only those who have invested in the corporation can be employed by it, that no one employed by the corporation can be a shareholder, or that no specific and necessary relation between ownership and employment need exist.

The success of this solution as a theory of production has been due to its ability to maintain the view that all exchange is simple exchange and that production results from the purchase and application of labor.  Practically, it has been successful insofar as exchange agreements within corporate enterprises are enforced by superordinate third parties.  A third, more recent solution to the problem of rate of exchange in corporate production has been to reduce the triad "buyer of labor, seller of labor, enforcer of agreements" to the dyad "worker-planner, distributor."  This latter approach has not yet proven altogether satisfactory from a number of points of view, at least as represented by current examples of "state socialism."

Corporate production governed by contract relies on the "market price" to determine the rate of exchange obtaining in productive exchange relations; state socialism attempts to improve on this distribution rule by introducing notions of "social equity."  A fourth solution to the problem of the social organization of production is the combining of corporate production with the defection-reducing mechanism of *mutual investment*, as contingent loss will be termed when applied to relations of productive exchange rather than simple reciprocal transfers of valued resources.

### Productive Exchange, Mutual Investment, and Rate of Exchange

A mutually agreeable rate of exchange is, at the same time, a condition necessary for exchange to occur and a condition sufficient, in the absence of any defection-reducing mechanism, to prevent an exchange from taking place.  Contingent loss, or mutual investment, has been discussed above as one means of reducing the likelihood of defection in productive exchange transactions.  Contract has been discussed as another defection-reducing mechanism.  As well as making exchange possible, however, defection-reducing mechanisms also condition the social fields in which they are employed.  For example, the economist's "market price" depends on the possibility of large numbers of "buyers" and "sellers" coming together and reciprocally matching their individual supply and demand schedules to the commodity at issue.  Such conditions can only be made possible by the presence of superordinate third parties with the ability and willingness to enforce single exchange agreements.  This section takes up the question of the determination of rate of exchange in corporate productive exchange relations governed by mutual investment.

In simple exchange transactions, the reciprocal dyadic exchange of valued items, rate of exchange is a matter of negotiation to the point of mutual agreement. When governed by contract, single simple exchange transactions become feasible, and, as shown above, production can be modeled and organized as a series of simultaneous, simple, multiple, single exchange transactions.

Contingent loss can never accommodate single exchange transactions and tends to confine simple exchange transactions to multiple exchanges over time among a limited number of regular partners. In productive exchange transactions, however, the benefits of mutual investment are clearer insofar as the costs of reducing the likelihood of defection from an agreement are not removed from the ongoing exchange relation to a superordinate third party and remain available to the relation for productive exchange. How these benefits are achieved is not immediately obvious, however, because of the apparently conflicting requirements of the two necessary mechanisms in the productive exchange relation, price and mutual investment.

A mutually agreeable rate of exchange only emerges in negotiation through the successive comparisons of participants' supply and demand schedules for the valued items at issue. Exchange transactions governed by mutual investment, however, are not total and autonomous transactions because future transactions are made to depend on the integrity of each present transaction. Thus, each transaction is merely a partial transaction embedded in a series of similar transactions with an indefinitely distant horizon. This fact is obvious in simple exchange transactions but must be kept in mind constantly when considering productive exchange transactions. Productive exchange transactions governed by mutual investment have the capacity to appear as independent transactions because the amount exchanged with each transaction is not directly a function of a finite amount of resources left to be exchanged over the entire series of exchanges. In simple exchange, the resources to be exchanged are known and finite, but precisely because value is added through productive exchange, the pool of resources to be exchanged in the future of a productive exchange relation is unknown and potentially infinitely large.

The embedding of productive exchange relations in a series of indefinitely numerous similar transactions has the effect of reducing ostensibly autonomous transactions to interrelated partial transactions. This method of reducing defection from an agreement has one particularly important implication for the determination of rate of exchange. In productive exchange relations governed by mutual investment, the rate of exchange obtaining in any one partial transaction will be related to the rates of exchange of all other transactions in that exchange relation. What we see is not the negotiation and emergence of a novel rate of exchange with each transaction but the application of a constant and previously determined rate of exchange to the specific features and requirements of each proposed transaction.

Constant rate of exchange and embeddedness can also occasionally be found in simple exchange transactions governed by contingent loss. They remain little developed where production is not a part of the transaction, however, precisely because of the fixed nature of the total amount of resources to be transferred in the exchange. In such cases, when a mutually agreeable rate of exchange has been reached, the total resources to be exchanged will then be subdivided into a series of exchanges (with an unavoidable terminal transaction). Some fraction of the total amount to be transacted is exchanged, and the sum to be exchanged is arrived at step by step. This practice has been institutionalized in requiring "deposits," "down payments," and "earnest money." Whatever provision is made for exchanges internal to the complete transaction, however, the mechanism of contingent loss is inadequate to insure the total transaction because there must always, when the total amount to be transacted is finite, be a terminal transaction.

When we observe a subtransaction of this sort in simple exchange, we cannot immediately recognize it as a function of an exchange agreement already negotiated and agreed upon. It appears in itself to be a complete transaction. Imagine, as an example, the exchange of ransom for hostages between two sovereign groups and, within this simple exchange transaction, the transfer of some fraction of the ransom for one hostage. If we did not know that this one partial transaction was embedded in a single transaction, we would not be able to account for the very different appearances of the first exchange, a somewhat later exchange, and the final exchange (if it could be consummated at all). While such an imaginary situation could become quite sticky toward the end, if the first exchange was successful, the middle exchanges could, and probably would, go comparatively smoothly. The points to be noted here, however, are that each subexchange, while appearing in itself as autonomous and possibly different from some of the others, is embedded in a single simple exchange agreement. Each subexchange acquires its character from and is a function of this single agreement, and the consumption of such subexchanges has no effect on the overall rate of exchange. (That the consummation of such subexchanges may have a definite effect on the consummation of the total simple exchange transaction is not a matter of rate of exchange but of defection from the agreement. This fact once again draws our attention to the inherent deficiency of contingent loss in governing single simple exchange transactions.)

The relation of rate of exchange to defection reduction and partial exchange transactions embedded in a series of transactions in productive exchange relations is not any different. Exactly as in simple exchange, the rate of exchange must be determined prior to exchange in order for mutual investment to operate effectively, and it cannot be allowed to vary from partial transaction to partial transaction. Such apparent variation does not constitute a renegotiated rate of exchange between partial transactions but defection from the originally determined rate of exchange. What is changed is the expected marginal utility from continuing to engage in partial transactions within the relation. In simple exchange, the expected marginal utility of successive partial transactions diminishes. In productive exchange transactions, it need not diminish and can even increase, depending on how productive the transaction actually was. Because the rate of exchange obtaining in productive exchange relations governed by mutual investment does not change from partial transaction to partial transaction, it must be capable of expression in general terms as a fixed ratio across the entire series of partial transactions. It is not merely an expression of participants' supply and demand schedules for the resources at issue in any specific, partial productive exchange transaction.

The rate of exchange obtaining in productive exchange relations governed by mutual investment is arrived at through the accommodation of the requirements of the price mechanisms, mutual investment, and external conditions. Each of these three components requires the satisfaction of two conditions.

Mutual Investment

1. The number of transactions in the series must be indefinitely large.
2. All members of the relation must make their resources available to productive exchange transactions within the relation before taking advantage of external opportunities.

Rate of Exchange

1. Demand for the results of productive exchange transactions must be allowed to vary among members for each transaction.
2. The willingness to supply the factors of production must be allowed to vary among members for each transaction.

External Conditions

1. The pool of resources available to the relation must be finite.
2. Capital costs, production costs, and consumption must be met from this resource pool.

What we wish to know is the rate of exchange obtaining under these conditions. But if the rate of exchange is a function of demand for, and willingness to supply, factors of production at *each* transaction, mutual investment cannot operate. If mutual investment is to operate, then the participants' supply and demand schedules for the resources at issue cannot specify the apparent rate of exchange obtaining in each partial transaction, and hence any partial transaction.

Reconciliation of rate of exchange and mutual investment in productive exchange relations is made possible by viewing production as the uniting of two separate processes, capital expenditure and operations. Where the entire process of production is undertaken by one group of participants and governed by mutual investment, capital expenditure and operating costs can be separated in each partial transaction and later reunited across the entire series of productive exchange transactions. This separation and reunion insures that the required capital will be provided without a specified rate of return and provides an incentive to meet operating costs. This is most commonly the case when demand for the specific end result of production does not correlate with participant access to sufficient surplus resources to meet capital costs. This separation of capital and operating expenditures through time and across productive exchange transactions within a single relation governed by mutual investment allows the rate of exchange and defection reduction to operate in tandem, rather than in opposition, within the constraint of finite resources across the entire series. This separation and reunion of capital and operating expenditures is accomplished in the following way:

1. Capital requirements are met by any and all members with potential to benefit from the opportunity for the productive exchange at issue. They are allotted such that each member meets that fraction of the capital requirements represented by his own fraction of the total resource pool.

2. Those members of the productive exchange relation who have contributed to the capital expenditure make whatever production expenditures are necessary to meet their individual demands, independent of the expenditures of the other members.

3. Productive capacity becomes the property of the corporate group made up of the members of the productive exchange relation, with rights in use restricted to those who have made capital expenditures. If a member is expelled or resigns, he forfeits all rights in and claims to corporate property. A member can be expelled only for defection from the above rate of exchange.

With this rate of exchange, or distribution rule, capital expenditure and production costs, as well as supply and demand schedules for the resources at issue in each proposal for productive exchange, are reunited across the series of transactions. This reunion occurs because a differential benefit through increased production in a present transaction entails a proportionately larger share in capital expenditures in the next transaction. As complex as this rate of exchange first appears, it optimizes productive exchange for all members of the exchange relation from several different perspectives. (1) It encourages a maximum level of productive exchange transactions, which provides a minimal risk within the relation. (2) It provides each member with the greatest possibility of benefit at the lowest possible rate of capital expenditure, leaving the greatest amount of resources available to meet production costs to those members with the highest demand for the specific results of production. (3) Maximum levels of resources are allocated to those transactions for which there is the greatest aggregate demand. (4) The outward flow of resources in the form of transaction costs is minimized. (5) Across the entire productive exchange relation, production is maximally intensified.

In brief, no cheaper solution, which satisfies the second requirement of the price mechanism, is available to any participant. The first is satisfied by reuniting the supply and demand curves of the participants across the entire series of transactions. The specified relation of production expenditure to capital expenditure across transactions implies the first requirement of the defection-reducing mechanism of mutual investment and makes the second unavoidable. As long as transactions actually consummated remain productive, and investment lead time does not preclude subsistance consumption (a most unlikely event), the requirements of the external conditions will be satisfied. Further, this rate of exchange actively encourages members of the relation to search for opportunities for productive exchange transactions. As each member's stake in the corporate enterprise increases, the demand for resources for further productive exchange transactions will grow at the expense of consumption, and external opportunities will appear less and less attractive. This follows from the relation of capital expenditure to production expenditure. Insofar as capital expenditure must be made where there is the potential for benefit by individual members, resources that might otherwise be consumed or committed to transactions external to the productive exchange relation will be used to meet production costs of the newly created productive capacity within the exchange relation.

### Productive Exchange, Mutual Investment, and Collective Decision Making

Resources are allocated to productive exchange transactions through a collective decision-making process. Even dyadic simple exchanges are the result of a collective decision-making process. To the extent that participants desire to reach a mutually agreeable rate of exchange and consummate that exchange, their orientation to the decision-making process will be cooperative and consensual. But because the process of reaching an agreement requires movement across points of disequilibrium, participants' orientations are at the same time antagonistic. Mechanisms that reduce the likelihood of defection from an agreement do so by reducing the benefits that can be obtained through defection, and thus they dissuade participants from pursuing strategies in exchange transactions based on an antagonistic orientation.

The interaction of mutual investment and the price mechanism results in a rate of exchange that is optimally cheap, productive, and free of defection within the relation. But this interaction leaves untested and unknown whether opportunities outside the group might not provide a greater rate of return. Continued membership in the relation implies doubt that such is the case, and consequently, the process of allocating resources within such relations to specific productive exchange transactions allows a maximally consensual orientation in the collective decision-making process. This is not to say that the potential for an antagonistic orientation is not present at all times, but that such an orientation becomes less useful as the possibility of benefiting from a strategy based on defection becomes remote.

The fundamental difficulty in collective decision making in productive exchange relations governed by mutual investment arises from the interaction of two unavoidable constraints. The first, that the pool of available resources must sustain diverse demands, has already been met. The second is that in cases where the initial distribution of resources is unequal, demands for subsistence consumption become inelastic at the lower end of the scale. It is simply easier for the wealthy to temporarily cut back consumption in favor of capital investment than it is for the poor.

The interaction of these two facts has the primary effect on the range of productive exchange transactions open to the group as a whole. Demands for opportunities for production by those with greater resources are limited by the demands for consumption and production by those with fewer resources. This, in turn, creates a dilemma for those in the middle. They must either help the wealthy create more opportunities and thus force the poor out of the relationship, or sustain the demands of the poor for consumption and risk losing the wealthy and their resources to other productive exchange relations with higher productive potentials. This dilemma cannot be resolved in the abstract but only through consideration of members' external opportunity structures in relation to the proposed exchange transaction at issue. In general, however, to the extent production costs and lead time are low relative to capital costs, initial intervals in resources levels will be maintained across the series of transactions.

Before entering into a specific discussion of the relation of modes of resource control to decision modes, two preliminary points must be raised. First, "voting," as an institution coupled with majority or larger rule, is not necessary to the effective operation of collective decision making in productive exchange relations governed by mutual investment. What is necessary is a recognized and legitimate means of voicing objections to any proposed course of action. Voting is merely one possible, and rather formal, means. The second point is that the distinction between privately held and corporate resources is maintained in terms of control and the ends to which they can be allocated. No member of the productive exchange relation can unilaterally allocate corporate resources to any end. All members have the right to request that both privately and corporately held resources be allocated to meet capital requirements for productive exchange transactions. All members are free to allocate privately held resources to consumption, capital expenditure, or production costs, provided they share in capital expenditure for productive exchange transactions within the relation from which they have the potential to benefit.

This last constraint leads directly to a fundamental problem concerning the application of the rate of exchange outlined above to any proposal for productive exchange. While all members with the potential to benefit must share capital costs at a fixed ratio, it may sometimes be the case that after poorer members of the relation have provided capital costs, they have insufficient resources left for consumption and production costs. The very real question then arises whether these members have any potential to benefit from productive exchange, at least at the proposed levels of capital expenditure. Whether or not such members have, in the abstract, any demand for the results of the proposed transaction, they will be unable to satisfy their demand.

There is a further "political" variant on this problem. Those with high demand for a specific transaction will presume the widest distribution of potential benefits, and those with low demand, the narrowest distribution. But for any proposal involving individually held resources, implementation will require the clear specification of the distribution of potential benefits. Members of both types, those who cannot meet consumption and production expenditures after sharing in capital expenditures and those with very low demand for the results of the transaction, have or believe they have no potential to benefit. They will resist making capital expenditures. If they are not to resign or be expelled, they must have some means of voicing objections. It is also in the long-term interest of those with both a clear potential to benefit and the resources to realize that potential to provide the means through which objections can be raised.

A means to object will be provided not merely because "someday the shoe might be on the other foot," although this effect might be present. Rather, those members with high demand will have calculated the distribution of capital shares in relation to production costs and potential returns as widely as possible.  The ultimate refusal of those with no demand or potential to benefit will affect the results of those calculations, lowering overall demand by raising levels of individual capital expenditure.  In a fixed resource pool, rising capital costs will have the effect of reducing not only the ratio of capital expenditure to potential return but also the level of resources available for production costs.  For any member then, as successive members decline to participate, an increased share of capital costs will exponentially lower demand until all demand for the collective undertaking has disappeared at the level of capital costs required.  It will always be cheaper for everyone to discover the most likely rates of participation before attempting to implement a decision requiring individual participation.

A major consequence of this model for group decision making is that decisions to use only corporate resources in productive exchange transactions result in unanimity, while those requiring privately held resources can, and often do, result in voting and always result in a division of opinion.  When a division results, the question of whether or not it will remain permanent and alter the composition of the exchange relation must be resolved.

This expectation results from an examination of the grounds for objection to participation, and it is in the interest of all members of the exchange relation to make them clear.  Objection to the use of corporate resources to increase the capital assets of the corporate group cannot be raised on the belief that a "cruel choice" is being forced or that a member has no demand for the opportunity being proposed.  Objection on the first ground, that a choice between subsistance and investment is being required, obviously cannot be true because corporate resources are never unilaterally available for consumption.  Objection on the second ground, even if true, is simply a form of "dog-in-the-manger-ism," the ability of those who cannot use resources to prevent those who can use them from doing so.  Such objections cannot be collectively sustained because even if a member has no demand at all for the specific transaction proposed, his consent will provide those with demand an opportunity to benefit and an ability to pay a larger share of capital expenditure in the next productive exchange transaction.  When corporate resources alone are at issue in a decision involving productive exchange transactions, the only objection that can be raised is that some alternative proposal, in relation to the existing distribution of resources, will prove more productive.

When corporate resources are at issue even in cases where contending proposals might immediately benefit various members differentially, the threat to resign is hollow.  Resignation cannot raise the immediate capital costs of those with demand and will not assist a member who resigns in retaining additional resources he could unilaterally allocate to alternative ends.  But resignation does entail both a loss of rights in existing corporate property and access to future productive exchange transactions.  There are, consequently, no reasonable grounds on which to object to the implementation of sound proposals if all capital expenditure can be met from corporate resources. Such is the benefit of division of labor, that those who currently have no better proposals but do not wish to make use of the opportunity proposed would be expected to encourage those with high demand to proceed with their proposal.

Issues that require individually held resources for capital expenditures, however, inevitably lead to division precisely because individually held resources can be unilaterally allocated to alternative ends. Again, some members will have high demand and insist. Others will have low demand and resist. Within the consensual orientation brought to the decision-making process, compromises can often be reached, but it is the specific nature of these compromises that is important. When a compromise is reached, it will be made in terms of liability to shares in capital expenditure, the interpretation of the criteria, and the distribution of "potential benefits," not in terms of "who will pay how much." That is to say once again, the rate of exchange obtaining in the productive exchange relation is already settled and not altered from transaction to transaction. Its application to the concrete features of the proposal must be made precise in terms of who will make any capital expenditures.

Below follows a theory of collective decision making in productive exchange relations governed by mutual investment. The major hypotheses examined in this study are presented systematically here as derivations from the model of productive exchange already developed.

1.  *Decisions allocating corporate resources alone will result in unanimity; those requiring individually held resources will lead to division.*

2.  *When a decision results in a division, or vote, the opposition will be an extremely small minority.*

Proposals for which there is not already widespread support are unlikely to ever be seriously considered for implementation. Widespread demand implies widespread potential for benefit, which in turn implies capital costs approaching the minimum. As capital costs decrease to the point at which those with demand are willing to meet those costs without the marginal contributions of the opposition, the opposition will be required either to meet their share of capital costs or to leave the exchange relation. Those in opposition either will be without resources at the required levels or will object to the collective interpretation of their own potential to benefit. There will always be one member in the opposition most lacking in resources and one member who feels most keenly that he will be exploited by the decision (although both slots may well be held by the same member in any decision).

When there are larger numbers in the minority, a proposal will lack sufficient support to even approach a more formal division. Such a proposal will fade
informally from consideration and be reintroduced only if objective conditions
change significantly. If implementation of a proposal is attempted without support extremely close to unanimity, the group will fission, an extremely rare event.

3. *Barring the discovery of defection, the consensual, cooperative
   orientation of the members remains unchanged across the series
   of decisions, regardless of the particular mode in which any
   decision is made.*

Attempts to apply the prevailing rate of exchange result in unanimity or
division. With unanimity, the process of productive exchange continues without
interruption. When division results, those in opposition meet the required capital
costs, have their vetos sustained, or withdraw. In all three cases, whether the
group retains its original roster or is reduced in number, there are no grounds
present for altering the rate of exchange, and therefore, there is no reason for
members to alter their orientations to the decision-making process.

4. *Issues are not treated as commensurate; the likelihood that a
   proposal will be implemented is not increased by making that
   proposal dependent on the implementation of other proposals of
   interest to members of the group.*

One frequently suggested means of reaching consensus is "squaring," or
"horse trading" (Bailey 1965: 11; El-Hakim 1978). This method of arriving at
unanimity in collective decisions is actually an attempt to discover a mutually
agreeable rate of exchange. To say in such cases that a "consensus" has been
reached is merely to say that a series of bargains has been struck in which the
reciprocal transfer of valued items (most often votes) is delayed. Such agreements may be, and often are, enforced by contingent loss. Indeed, "horse trading"
is only possible in settings where future interactions are highly likely (Axelrod
1981). Even so, this method is not easily extended beyond small numbers of participants. Its effectiveness is severely reduced through "bookkeeping" problems
and the tendency for defection to increase as the amount of time the total exchange requires for consummation also increases.

In productive exchange relations governed by mutual investment, a mutually agreeable rate of exchange is already in place. What is at issue is the distribution of interests in the proposal at hand and the application of the rate of exchange to that proposal. This rate of exchange already provides for unanimity
when corporate resources alone are at issue. When privately held resources are at
issue, grounds for objection to participation are available, and it is in the interest

of all members that valid objections be heard.   But all proposals are already maximally "linked" through the feedback component of the distribution rule.  Any superficial linkage can only move the decision away from the equilibrium point. Over the series of transactions in which participants are embedded, each proposal will be dealt with solely in terms of the distribution of interests with regard to that proposal and the objective conditions it provides for the application of the rate of exchange.

5.   *The consent of each participant depends on the satisfaction of the two legitimate grounds for objection with regard to the proposal at hand; past decisions and their outcomes are irrelevant.*

While the distribution rule presented above appears complex in its full form, in application it is in fact extremely simple.   The crucial questions each participant must be able to answer in the affirmative are: (1) Does this proposal offer me objective potential to benefit? and (2) If so, can I meet the capital and production costs, as well as the necessary lead time, and still maintain subsistance levels?   The "information search" segment of the decision-making process will normally provide all the information needed for comparisons with personal circumstances.   Negative answers will result in vetoes and consideration of the desirability of continued membership.   In the subjective mode, negative answers can only be the result of comparisons with personal opportunity structures external to the group.   To deny group access to one's resources in order to commit those resources to external opportunities is one form of defection.

Past decisions and their outcomes are irrelevant for the same reasons that issues are not commensurate and orientations do not change across issues.

6.   *Participation in productive exchange transactions is a function of membership rather than opportunity among structurally similar productive exchange relations.*

This follows from the prior commitment of resources to productive exchange transactions within the corporate group and the lack of defection-reducing mechanisms outside the productive exchange relation.   The obligation to honor claims on one's resources for productive exchange transactions is also the right to participate in corporate productive exchange transactions and to propose such transactions to the group.   Whether this condition is felt as a right or an obligation is entirely subjective and, again, results from comparisons with personal opportunity structures external to the group.

This is not to say, by any means, that hierarchies of corporate productive exchange relations are not possible among structurally equivalent groups.   They are, and hierarchies become likely to the extent such relations open up new opportunities and transactions become numerous. While problems of coordination may present difficulties, the rate of exchange underlying such relations remains unchanged.

7. *Productive exchange transactions within the corporate group create opportunities for production but do not directly distribute benefits to members.*

This is one implication of the integration of capital and labor. Because benefits derived from the creation of opportunity directly determine successive rates of capital input in future transactions, capital will not reproduce itself without the provision of differential demand for production and a proportionate distribution of capital costs. That is, differentials in willingness to produce rather than differentials in access to capital will ultimately determine the course of proposals for productive exchange transactions.

8. *Corporate productive exchange transactions governed by mutual investment always follow the same bifurcate procedure.*

This proposition follows from the concept of contingent loss applied to productive exchange and the interrelationship of future to present transactions. It deserves particular mention because the replication of the procedure demonstrates consistent application of the rate of exchange. For individual members, this application is the comparison of personal circumstances to the objective conditions of the proposal. Where this procedure is truncated, however, we must expect defection. Unlike simple exchange transactions governed by contract, in which the infrastructure of the governance mechanism, a coercive third party, is paid independently and available whether called upon or not, mutual investment does not account costs of defection reduction until defection has already occurred. Because the only recourse available to the discovery of defection is the termination of the relation, each transaction must be regarded as likely to lead to defection. What is lost to defection are not only the resources immediately at issue but also expected future opportunities, the loss of one's investment. From this perspective, each transaction is equally "crucial" to the continuation of the exchange relation, and its importance is not merely a function of the resources immediately at issue. Consequently, the care given to insure the absence of defection in each transaction will not appear as a function of the utilities of the resources to be exchanged but as a function of the entire relationship, including the dimension of one's own and other members' opportunity structures outside the corporate structure. When productive exchange transactions governed by mutual investment are viewed in isolation, the care given to the decision-making procedure may appear either extremely casual or extremely petty with regard solely to the resources immediately at issue.

9. *Overt advocacy of a particular course of action by individual members is much less likely than overt opposition.*

The more desirable a course of action is to a member, the less he will wish to be identified with advocacy of that course of action. This follows from the fact that the more widespread the demand, the more likely the implementation. To the extent that an individual continues to support and advocate a course of action in the face of low demand, the more likely either (a) that proposal will require other members to subsidize his consumption at a higher level or (b) the return on investment cannot be justified in competition with alternative proposals. If the demand for an opportunity does not rise with the presentation of the objective circumstances of the proposal, continued advocacy will only contribute to the suspicion that the advocate is withholding relevant information. Consequently, the most successful advocate is the one who is least prominently associated with a proposed course of action and who appears impartial, allowing each member the opportunity to assess independently his own potential for benefit.[1]

On the other hand, legitimate grounds for objection are available, and knowledge of legitimate objection is in the interest of all members because it is directly related to present and future capital costs. Given the inherent inclination to participate rather than refrain from participation, only objections that are crucial will be raised. But because information concerning the relation of individual circumstances to the objective conditions underlying the proposal is always imperfect, to the extent it is imperfect, objections will be raised. Advocacy, however, is always a strategic error.

One question this theory raises but does not attempt to answer is how to distinguish between defection and mistakes. Of course, the extension of the "information search" phase of the decision-making process will help prevent some errors in fact and judgment, as will the consensual orientation of members and the lack of advocacy in the procedure. But both mistakes and defection remain possible.

Fjellman (1976), in his critique of the assumptions and findings of experimental decision-making science, catalogs at least a dozen reasons why people are not able to make "good" decisions and why experimenters are unable even to discover what a "good" decision is. Humans are not computers; they must make crucial decisions on a wide variety of issues under severe constraints. While we are able to adjust our beliefs to accommodate our behavior, we still make mistakes, often failing to choose that course of action hindsight shows to have probably been the more desirable alternative. It is even tempting to conclude that human beings, even in groups working toward a common end, can only stumble on the relatively "best" solution available to them and most often are even unable to see what that solution might be.

But it is also true that we pay for our mistakes in judgment one way or another, and the "best" choice is, of course, a singularity amid the variety of less desirable alternatives. The costs of mistakes may be either minor irritation or large numbers of ruined lives. What is critical is often not so much the mistakes in gathering information on the future outcome but the probability of defection from what appeared to be a mutually agreeable rate of exchange.

Another way of viewing the accounting procedure of mutual investment is to regard those resources that might otherwise be expended on mistakes in judgments of "character" as transfers of resources to improve estimates of objective conditions underlying proposals for exchange transactions. While it is the central thesis of this study that Japanese society, certainly rural Japanese society, relies much more heavily on the mechanism of mutual investment than contract, the Japanese have no inherent corner on good decisions. If they are able to devote relatively more resources to gathering information on the objective conditions underlying proposed exchange transactions, however, it is at least in part because of a reciprocally greater reliance on recruitment procedures and the "sincerity" of members of the exchange relation. Consequently, tokens of that sincerity appear correspondingly larger, as in the prominence of public apologies, early retirements, and suicides in the acknowledgment of "responsibility" for corporate losses. In productive exchange relations governed by mutual investment, "honest mistakes" will be discounted and losses absorbed without an adversarial finding of fault. Defection, however, can never be an honest mistake, only a strategic mistake. It is always deliberate. It must result, consequently, in the dissolution of the relation and not merely the failure of a single exchange transaction. Contract does not require the distinction between honest mistakes and defection, but mutual investment depends upon this distinction entirely.

# CHAPTER 3:
## HAMLET SOCIAL ORGANIZATION AND FINANCIAL STRUCTURE

The social organization and financial structure of Nohara hamlet presented in this chapter provides the figured base over which the hamlet decision-making process is performed in endless variation. Although *buraku* have not been recognized as administrative units with "legal personality" since 1947 (Beardsley, Ward, and Hall 1959: 350-51), where they remain intact socially, they still retain at least a touch of distinctive personality and the loyalties of their members, to whom they provide a wide variety of services. As partners in the exchange of access to public resources for political support, they continue to be recognized by politicians and municipal bureaucracies.

Nohara hamlet is one of the six hamlets that make up Kawasemigawa ward (*ku*) of Sagi City (*shi*) in Aichi Prefecture (*ken*). Until the Meiji Restoration, Kawasemigawa ward was an autonomous village (*mura*) in the Owari fief (*han*). The amalgamation process began in this village in 1889 and continued until the village became a ward in Sagi City in 1954. But this former village, more lately ward, retains its geographic isolation from the city and neighboring wards. It is located in a narrow valley that stretches like a slim finger from the palm of the Nobi Hanto into the westernmost foothills of Aichi Prefecture.

The plaque that hangs in Nohara's shrine to its tutelary deity (*ujigami*) asserts that the shrine (and presumably the hamlet as well) was established some twenty years before the battle of Sekigahara in 1600. This claim is repeated on similar plaques in the *ujigami* shrines of four of the other five hamlets (Beniya, Usoda, Kitabora, and Yanagida) of the ward. The smallest of the six hamlets, Nishioka, was established in 1937 with the withdrawal of eleven families from Usoda hamlet; it has no *ujigami* shrine of its own.

The narrow valley, along which Kawasemigawa lies and through which the river of the same name flows, once served as the bed of the main road from Sagi City and its once important castle to Gifu City, Gifu Prefecture, and its once even more important castle. The ancient road has long since been replaced with a paved prefectural highway, and the electric train that stops in the ward, only a local, has run through the ward's rice fields in the valley bottom and stopped in Kawasemigawa since the early 1930s. But one can still only enter or leave the ward from either end of its valley.

47

Each hamlet, again with the exception of tiny Nishioka, is located in its respective and even narrower valley, all of which enter the main valley at right angles. The main tunnel of the irrigation system that provides water for all of the southern region of Nagoya City lies *under* Kawasemigawa. Each hamlet in the ward still irrigates its own fields from the series of ponds located high in the hills surrounding each hamlet's individual valley.

### Hamlet Membership and Recruitment

The most important aspect of "tradition" in *buraku* is the continuity of social relations among members. In this sense, Nohara hamlet is a "traditional face-to-face community." There are about 215 households in Kawasemigawa ward, and all of them belong to one or another of its six hamlets. Thirty-five of these households belong to "Nohara-gumi," as its own members and the other residents of Kawasemigawa refer to Nohara hamlet. Of these thirty-five households, twenty-four have been members for at least two generations, and eighteen for three or more generations. Six member households are first-generation branch households of these older twenty-four households, and only five member households have come to Nohara from outside the hamlet during the lifetimes of their respective current household heads. Two of these "outside founder" households have relatives in other hamlets in the ward. Thus, only three of the hamlet's thirty-five member households have no kinship or historical connection to the immediate area. Only one land-owning household of the hamlet sold its land and left the hamlet within living memory, an episode that occurred in 1926. The ward's other hamlets exhibit an equally high degree of social continuity.

Hamlet membership is still formal, exclusive, and the prerogative of households rather than individuals, as is customary throughout Japan (Beardsley, Hall, and Ward 1959: 351-52). A household wishing to join the hamlet must reside within the general area of the hamlet, or at least near another hamlet member, and petition the hamlet for admission and recognition as a member. It is still the practice that a member household acts as sponsor for this petition. A bottle or two of sake and a cash gift of, currently, ¥10,000 accompanies petitions for admission to membership.

The hamlet membership still decides whether a new household will be admitted, but as the hamlet no longer administers corporate resources of great significance, such as woodlands or productive fields, no request for membership by a sponsored family has been denied in recent times. This is not to say, however, that this decision is perfunctory and not thoroughly discussed within the hamlet. There was open opposition to the readmission of a former member in 1978, although this household was finally allowed to resume its membership.

It appears that in the past the areas of the ward that bear hamlet names were coterminous with the distributions of the hamlets' respective memberships, but this is no longer the case. Many old Kawasemigawa families own land in several different hamlets, and branch families have occasionally been established on such properties. When the site is close to the center of an area bearing a hamlet name, no problem arises: the new household joins the hamlet in which its house is located. But these areas locally known by hamlet names are not so labeled on maps. While their centers are well-known, their boundaries are vague and diffuse. Thus, if a branch family builds in an area away from a center, which most do, it must make a choice of which hamlet to petition for membership. As the hamlets have grown primarily at their edges, there are areas in all these hamlets where one's neighbors are not all members of one's own, or the same, hamlet. This is particularly the case in Nishioka hamlet, in which the nonmembers outnumber the members and which is bordered on one side by Nohara hamlet.

Occasionally, this failure of identity of membership and residence creates administrative and organizational difficulties, but perennial suggestions that hamlet membership and residence be "rationalized" draw little more than hypothetical support from anyone. It is a local source of long-standing amusement that Nohara's meeting hall is not even in "Nohara," but in Nishioka. But then again, neither are five of the hamlet's oldest households and three of its newer ones.

This dislocation of territory and residence, however, makes it clear that hamlet membership is not merely a function of residence and kinship. The hamlet itself is an autonomous corporate group, and membership is a function of mutual recognition of members. While several factors enter into the judgment on admission to membership, the primary question is the accessibility of new member's resources. Residence and kinship provide a basis for potential interaction and access to a member's resources, but neither criteria is a sufficient or necessary condition for membership. What is important is a mutual willingness to engage in productive exchange transactions, and this can only be discovered over a lengthy period of interaction within the hamlet context.

## Hamlet Internal Organization

The thirty-five households of Nohara hamlet find occasion to meet as a body, on the principle of "one household, one representative," about once a month. Within the hamlet, these households are also divided into "lower and upper halves" (han) and into five "five-family groups" (gonin-gumi). Both divisions are functional groupings, and their functions do not overlap.

The functions of the han are limited to the collection of local, municipal, and property taxes and participation in hamlet funerals as, per han, "helpers" (*tetsudai*) and mourners.  It is possible that these *han* at one time had a more functionally important position in the hamlet than they do today, but there is no record now of additional functions.   The *han* do maintain at least a symbolic identity on a regular basis through the circulation of two lanterns of religious significance.   The *han's* respective lanterns, lit by each family in the order of circulation at night and taken the next day to the next family, are identical in appearance.  These *han* elect no officers, have no collective property other than their lanterns, make no decisions as a group, and have no treasuries.  There is no evidence that any sentiment attaches to this division.

The finer and much more functional division of the hamlet is that of the *gonin-gumi.*  At present there are five groups of seven families each.  For several years prior to 1977 there had been four such groups, with the hamlet membership only approximately evenly divided among them.  The *gonin-gumi* have two primary tasks, which they perform by rotation:  to serve and prepare meals taken in the hamlet hall and to clean the hamlet hall and the hamlet's two shrines.  Each group also provides a representative, the "five-family group head" (*gochō*), to the *gochōkai.*

The *gochōkai* serves as the hamlet's representative assembly and is composed of the *gochō*, the hamlet head (*kumichō*), and the hamlet treasurer (*kumi-kaikei*).  The *gochō* serve by annual rotation within their groups and have two primary responsibilities, attending the meetings of the *gochōkai* and informing their group's members of the results of these meetings and any other information the hamlet head passes on to them.

The meetings of the *gochōkai* are generally relaxed and informal.  As a representative body, it has only the power to set dates for hamlet activities and to make recommendations on matters brought before it.  It occasionally serves as a filter for "trial balloons" as well, by refusing to place issues on the agenda for discussion and decision by the hamlet meeting as a body.  The *gochōkai* has virtually no authority to allocate hamlet funds to novel ends.

The rule of the thumb by which the *gochōkai* operates is if there is any difference of opinion among its members on an issue that requires the allocation of hamlet resources, the matter must be referred to the whole hamlet meeting as a council.  The *gochōkai* is empowered, however, to assign one or more of its members to do "research" (*kenkyū*) into an issue facing the hamlet and make recommendations.  Such recommendations are generally taken very seriously by hamlet members.   The most common issue on which the *gochōkai* deliberates and makes recommendations is the nature, location, and date of hamlet labor service (*kinrōhōshi*).

## Hamlet Offices

The office of *kumichō* (hamlet head) is the hamlet executive office, which has only responsibilities and virtually no discretionary powers. Until the early 1950s the office circulated among a limited number of prosperous hamlet families, "the families with *kura* (stronghouses)." From the early 1950s until 1968 the office was elective, and hamlet members voted by secret ballot annually for the coming year's new *kumichō*. In 1968 the office was put on a rotational basis, an order of circulation was established, and all households were expected to serve and discharge the office responsibly.

The *kumichō* serves without remuneration as chairman of all meetings of the whole hamlet and presides over the *gochōkai*. He acts as the hamlet's liason with the ward council (*kukai*) and sits on the *kukai* as the hamlet's representative.

While the responsibilities of the *kumichō* are general in nature, there are several other hamlet offices oriented to very specific tasks (see table 1). The roster of these other offices has also undergone substantial changes in the recent past. Perhaps as much as any other index, the changes in hamlet offices that have taken place since the end of World War II demonstrate the gradual and continuous disengagement of the hamlet from local agricultural production. In 1965 there were still ten hamlet offices directly concerned with agricultural production within the hamlet. By 1979 this number had dwindled to four.

The *dōryoku-kakari* (motive power officer) was renamed the *momisuri-kakari* (rice-hulling officer) when the Agricultural Practices Association purchased a self-contained rice-hulling machine and sold its old traction engine. But the six offices once concerned with sericulture were discontinued as hamlet members discontinued cocoon production entirely. The purchase and sale of commodities in bulk is now handled by the head of the Agricultural Practices Association (*jikkō-kumiaichō*).

By 1967 all of the ward's six hamlets had their own small fire pumps, and in that year a "ward fire brigade," in name only, was begun. This "brigade" does not meet and does not have officers. It is not an organized group in any sense of the term. The young men appointed to the brigade from each hamlet are simply responsible for the maintenance of their respective hamlet's pump and for promptly getting that pump to any fire in the ward.

The most important and recent addition to the list of hamlet officers is the *kumi-kaikei*, the hamlet treasurer. During the 1970s a number of hamlet projects were undertaken that required more than the remaining term of the hamlet head to complete. Responsibility for completing projects begun during the tenure of a hamlet head remained with the out-going head. Many hamlet members expressed dissatisfaction with the effective extension of the term of the hamlet head and

Table 1: Comparison of Hamlet Offices in 1965 and 1979

| 1965 | | | 1979 | | |
|---|---|---|---|---|---|
| Office | Number of Officers | Year Ended | Office | Number of Officers | Year Begun |
| 1. *kumichō* (hamlet head) | 1 | | 1. *kumichō* (hamlet head) | 1 | |
| 2. *jōkō-kumiaichō* (Agricultural Practices Union head) | 1 | | 2. *jōkō-kumiaichō* (Agricultural Practices Union head) | 1 | |
| 3. *jōkō-fukukumiaichō* (APU vice-head) | 1 | | 3. *jōkō-fukukumiaichō* (APU vice-head) | 1 | |
| 4. *yōsan-kumiaichō* (Sericulture Union head) | 1 | 1976 | 4. *omiya-kakari* (shrine officer) | 1 | |
| 5. *yōsan-fukukumiaichō* (SU vice-head) | 1 | 1976 | 5. *momisuri-kakari* (rice-hulling officer) | 1 | 1969 |
| 6. *omiya-kakari* (shrine officer) | 1 | | 6. *ike-kakari* (irrigation pond supervisor) | 1 | 1974 |
| 7. *yama-kakari* (hamlet woodlands officer) | 1 | 1966 | 7. *nozei-kumiaichō* (hamlet tax collections officer) | 2 | |
| 8. *sanshu-kakari* (silkworm egg-card officers) | 2 | 1974* | 8. *gochō* (neighborhood group heads) | 5 | |
| 9. *hanbai-kōbai kakari* (sales and purchasing officers) | 2 | 1974* | 9. *ku shōbō kakari* (ward fire brigade) | 2 | 1967 |
| 10. *dōryoku-kakari* (motive power supervisor) | 1 | 1969 | 10. *kumi-kaikei* (hamlet treasurer) | 1 | 1978 |
| 11. *gochō* (neighborhood group heads) | 4 | | | | |
| 12. *nozei-kakari* (hamlet tax collections officer) | 2 | | | | |

*In 1973 both of these offices were reduced by one officer; they were eliminated the following year.

the overlap in responsibility that resulted. It was decided that a treasurer, who becomes the next year's *kumichō*, would provide continuity between administrations. The treasurer is familiar with the progress and financial details of all hamlet projects and assumes responsibility for the incomplete projects of the previous year. The hamlet head no longer keeps the hamlet account books, a task that is now part of the treasurer's functions.

The office of hamlet treasurer was begun in 1978, and there is still some doubt in the hamlet that this office will succeed (see Case 6 below). The advantages of dividing the responsibilities of one office into two are obvious, but whether or not these offices will function as intended and allow greater satisfaction throughout the hamlet still seems to depend largely on the specific features of hamlet projects. As both the hamlet head and the treasurer attend all *gochōkai* and hamlet council meetings, the redundancy in the system will require about 100 extra man-hours per year from hamlet members. But the treasurer still will not regularly attend ward council meetings. In addition, minutes and hamlet records will be kept separately from hamlet financial records. Whether two sets of hamlet records will add confusion to a system designed to promote continuity remains to be proven.

All hamlet offices are limited to one-year terms, and, with the single exception of the vice-head of the Agricultural Practices Association (*jikkō-fukukumiaichō*), who is selected by secret ballot and serves as the Association's head the following year, all hamlet offices are assigned by rotation from a fixed schedule.

## Subhamlet Groups

The hamlet is a corporate group composed of families, and it embraces the entire family in its activities. Within Nohara hamlet are a number of groups that recruit from hamlet families alone. As with hamlet council meetings, most families send an appropriate person to these groups; the "appropriateness" of the member is generally specified by the nature of the group in terms of age, sex, occupation, or interest. Most member families belong to most of these groups, but by no means do all belong to all of them. In most cases membership is automatic and expected. Some, however, recruit solely by invitation, and there are a few families eligible for membership in groups to which they have chosen not to belong or were not invited to belong. These subhamlet groups are:

1. *Jikkō-kumiai.* The *jikkō-kumiai* (Agricultural Practices Association) is the local branch of the *nōgyōkyōdō-kumiai* (Agricultural Cooperative). Membership is entailed in ownership of Co-op stock. All hamlet households engaging in agriculture belong.

2. *Yōsan-kumiai.* The *yōsan-kumiai* (Sericulture Association) has as its function the cooperative production of raw silk, but as no hamlet member any longer engages in this industry, this group is moribund.

3. *Hakusan-kai.* The Hakusan-kai is an age-grade association open to all hamlet household heads younger than the group's founder, who organized this group on his forty-second birthday in 1976. Its explicit purpose, as provided in its charter, is "to seek the development of the hamlet and foster comity among the group's members."

4. *Hakusan-chīmu.* The Hakusan-chīmu (Hakusan Team) is the men's softball team. It was organized in 1977 and carried twenty-six active members and five inactive members on its 1979 roster.

5. *Fujinkai.* The *fujinkai* (Women's Association) is open to all wives of the heads of hamlet households.

6. Women's Flower Societies. There are at present in the hamlet three women's groups that travel semiannually for pleasure to areas renowned for their scenic and historic interest. These groups lack a local generic name and individually take their names from the iris, the azalea, and the cherry.

7. *Shinjinkai* and *kannon-kō.* These are two hamlet lay religious organizations of some antiquity for men and women, respectively. They are open to all hamlet members. The *shinjinkai* meets semi-annually, and the *kannon-kō*, monthly.

8. *Kinoesama.* Originally a revolving credit association of the hamlet's prewar *churitsu* class of farmers, this group now meets on a bimonthly basis to promote fellowship among its members.

9. *Kodomokai.* The *kodomokai* (Children's Association) is composed of all hamlet children in grades one through six and their mothers. Its purpose is to gainfully occupy what little free time hamlet children have during summer vacation.

10. *Rojin Kurabu.* The *rojin kurabu* (Old People's Club) sponsors cultural activities for the elderly and is open to all residents age sixty and over.

11. The Anglers. This is a collection of hamlet males who took fishing trips as a group in 1978 and 1979. At present it lacks a proper name.

12. *Wakaba.* The Wakaba (Young Leaves) is the women's softball team.

13. Nursery-school Mothers. These are the mothers of hamlet children who attend the nursery-school outside the hamlet. As their children grow older and their number increases, they will become the next group in the "Flower Society."

14. PTA. The Parent-Teacher Association is organized only at the ward level and up. Each hamlet mother with a child in elementary or junior high school is a member.

The hamlet is composed of member households, which in turn are composed of people of all ages and both sexes. It is tempting to say that the hamlet, through its subgroups, provides "something for everyone," but this is not entirely the case. There is no group to which the young women of the hamlet may belong before they marry. But as they will all leave the hamlet, this is to be expected. There is also no group for the young men of the hamlet, no Young Men's Club (*seinendan*). When the two small rice fields owned by the hamlet's shrine were still cultivated, the young men of the hamlet did participate in a religious ceremony in the fall (*kami-mukae*) and the hamlet festival in the spring. But the young men were never, within the living memory of the hamlet, organized into a regular group, and they were never subsequently organized into an age-grade group as household heads.

Groups in the ward and its hamlets are either organized at the ward level or at the hamlet level and, except for the Wakaba, do not violate hamlet boundaries. When the small hamlet of Nishioka finally organized a softball team and there were too few men to field a team, the hamlet women, rather than men from other hamlets, played on the team in the two tournaments the team entered. These groups are, or can be, both expressive and instrumental for their members, and this is a distinction that cannot be made with any great degree of precision. It would be no exaggeration to suggest that, because all of these groups are explicitly instrumental, they are made at the same time as expressively satisfying as possible. As an illustration of this point, I was told by the head of the ward softball league, "Of course the purpose of softball is to have a good time. But the real purpose is to get to know people from other hamlets and wards in the city. When you meet someone at city hall, for example, you already know each other and are not strangers." But in the softball games themselves, there is very little interaction outside the confines of the game between men of different hamlets and wards. Acquaintances may be made and new faces filed for future reference, but the distinction between hamlets is carefully maintained. Even on the women's team, the small knots of conversation usually take place among women from the same hamlet.

## Funding the Hamlet

Until they decided to have a treasurer handle all financial matters in 1978, the hamlet head acted as treasurer. The new treasurer must now keep the hamlet's books, attend all hamlet meetings, and become the following year's hamlet head. All through the period for which records are still available, 1965-1978, both the number of entrees and the size and detail of the hamlet account books grew. Table 2 presents the figures for income and expenditure on an annual basis for these years.

The hamlet does not prepare a projected budget for the next year's expenses, as fixed sources of revenue and fixed expenditures make up only a small fraction of the total financial activity of the hamlet. By far the greater part of the hamlet's financial affairs is of an extraordinary nature, and most expenses are financed either directly from the hamlet treasury (money already held by the hamlet in its account at a local bank) or ad hoc as the need arises. The hamlet relies on direct assessment of hamlet members only when there is no alternative source of funding available. Also, in the case of fixed annual expenditures, the use of alternative sources of funding is preferred to direct assessment of members. As a general rule, the more distant money is from members' pockets, the more easily it is spent.

The hamlet has several distinct sources of income. Some are directly linked to specific projects to be funded, and others offer casual alternative means of securing general revenues.

### External Sources

*Regular.* Revenues in this category are limited solely to the allowance (*teate*) the hamlet receives from the ward for the maintenance of the fire pump and fire-fighting equipment. This allowance first appeared in the hamlet account books in 1968 at ¥2000 per year. It remained at this level until 1977, when it was increased to ¥2500 per year. This money is part of the ward fee (*kuhi*) of ¥3300 each ward family pays to the ward and is actually money assessed from hamlet members. This allowance is entered directly in the hamlet treasury.

*Irregular.* During the period 1965-1978, Nohara received considerable sums in this category. Much of this money comes directly from the city budget in the form of local assistance. This money is always directed toward specific ends such as drain or road repair, the purchase of the hamlet fire pump, and the restoration of the hamlet's "sacred car," or *kagura* as it is known locally. To receive these funds from the city, the hamlet must make the expenditure first and then present the correct receipts for later reimbursement. Such grants often require an equal contribution by the hamlet or local labor commitments.

Table 2:  Hamlet Income and Expenditure (in Yen), 1965–1978

| Year | Income | Expenditure |
|------|--------|-------------|
| 1965 | 34,157[a,b] | 23,778 |
| 1966 | 78,792 | 64,433 |
| 1967 | 71,091 | 55,437 |
| 1968 | 97,755 | 60,870 |
| 1969 | 110,305 | 57,781 |
| 1970 | 142,614 | 66,454 |
| 1971 | 236,743 | 199,940 |
| 1972 | 88,900 | 50,013 |
| 1973 | 231,127 | 160,254 |
| 1974 | 103,430 | 53,565 |
| 1975 | 856,480 | 281,175 |
| 1976 | 816,651 | 683,240 |
| 1977 | 424,197 | 353,721 |
| 1978 | 336,190 | 200,495 |

[a]The income figure for 1965 contains ¥7527 carried over from 1964. The income figures for all years thereafter contain the unspent balance carried over from the previous year. The unspent balance of 1978 is ¥135,695.

[b]The hamlet account books note only the unspent balance of gifts to the hamlet until 1973, from which year the entire gift is entered as hamlet income. The figures for the years 1965–1972 are adjusted to conform to the later pattern and include all gifts received in those years.

Another steady but infrequent external source of hamlet income is the ward's city councilman.  Sums from this source, received quadrennially, are entered into the hamlet accounts as "rental of hamlet hall by candidate's supporters."

The hamlet also receives occasional rebates from various private enterprises with which it does business.  Actual cash is rarer than substantial discounts or *omake*, additional goods or services provided within the total transaction.

Occasionally single sums are received from unexpected sources.  For example, in 1975 the local railroad closed a crossing used by several of the hamlet's members and compensation was paid directly to the hamlet.  None of this ¥500,000 was distributed directly to individuals.

*Internal Sources*

Sources internal to the hamlet are divided into two categories, corporate property and members' resources.

*Corporate property.*  At present the most regular and substantial source of income from corporate property is the interest on hamlet savings accounts held in commercial banks, the Post Office, and the municipal agricultural cooperative.  This source first appeared in the hamlet accounts in 1973.

The hamlet received money from its forested lands in 1965, 1966, and 1969.  While the amounts received in the first two years were negligible, the sale of timber from the cemetery yielded ¥25,000 in 1969.  The extensive wood lot attached to the hamlet's *ujigami* shrine is seen as a potential source of similar income.

Some small fees are also received from the rental of the hamlet hall.  Until 1974 this money accrued to the hamlet *jikkō-kumiai*, but thereafter was entered into the hamlet general account.  Negligible sums are also received as offerings at the hamlet's *ujigami* and Inari shrines.

*Members' resources.*  Direct assessment of hamlet members to meet extraordinary expenses is the method most frequently used to raise money within the hamlet.  The mechanics of assessment is discussed below, and several occasions on which hamlet members assessed themselves directly are discussed in the case materials.  In addition to such extraordinary assessments, the hamlet also accepts gifts of money and durable goods from hamlet members.

(1) Assessments.  Assessments are made to defray all or part of the expense of some specific purchase or event in the hamlet.  There is also a general fee charged all hamlet members (*kumi-hi*).  With the internal reorganization of the

hamlet in 1973, an annual assessment of ¥1000 per family was established to meet hamlet operating expenses (*kumi uneihi*). The collection of this fee was discontinued in 1978 because of the railroad compensation windfall, but the hamlet head of 1979 was already expressing the desire to see this fee collected once again.

(2) Unsolicited contributions. In Nohara hamlet there are two sources of unsolicited contributions, direct ad hoc presentations (*kifu*) and the unspent balances of gifts given by hamlet families to celebrate auspicious occasions in the domestic cycle (Marshall n.d.). While the former source is more likely to yield contributions of members' special skills or resources in kind, the latter source has contributed ¥182,112 to the hamlet general fund from 1965 to 1978.

(3) Entrance fees. Entrance fees are not overtly solicited but given as a matter of custom. In 1968 this sum was ¥2000, but by 1978 it had reached ¥10,000. There are, of course, no fees solicited when a family leaves the hamlet, but the last two families to leave, both in 1978, each gave ¥20,000 upon departure.

(4) Solicited contributions. Solicited contributions are rarely used in Nohara except for shrine and temple maintenance. In such cases, the amount of the contribution and the contributor's name are made public.

(5) Fines. Although it is common in Japan for hamlets to levy fines on members who fail to meet hamlet obligations or to allow members to commute labor assessments to cash, this technique is not used in Nohara. Discussed in the past, it was agreed that social pressure, especially in the matter of labor contributions, was more effective.

With the inclusion of the use of the corporate status of the *jikkō-kumiai* to obtain loans, the above constitute all of the hamlet sources of income. However, even within recent years the methods and techniques of funding the hamlet have not been unchanging.

Fukutake (1972: 125-31) presents a detailed account of the various methods hamlets throughout the country use to raise money. Nohara hamlet has used all the methods Fukutake lists, at one time or another, although these methods do not always correspond to the classes of expenditure Fukutake mentions. The methods and their successive uses do not suggest that "there has been a considerable rationalization of methods of collection since the war" (ibid: 127). Rather, in Nohara the succession of different methods of collection reflect the constant and always lagging tendency toward funding the hamlet on the basis of the actual distribution of local income within the constraint that no member without the potential to benefit from a specific project is liable for assessments to defray the cost of that project.

A method employed in the hamlet until the 1920s divided the total cost of any hamlet project by the "number of roofs in the hamlet" and allotted shares per roof to the owners.  This method was succeeded by one in which shares were apportioned on the basis of an estimate of annual income, which itself was based on the previous year's rice and cocoon sales, as well as occasional cash income from labor.  This method, I was told by the elderly head of one of the hamlet's two former landlord families,

> was not really fair, because income was estimated for purposes of assessment *before* rents (*nengu*) were paid.  In a few cases, these rents reached from one-third to one-half of the total crop.  People did not complain, however, because there was nothing they could do about it.  In those days, five or six families ran the whole show, and many hamlet families could not make the calculations involved, could not even use an abacus properly.  So if anyone complained, we simply increased the amount they were assessed (*yokeihi o kaketa*).

There is no estimate of how frequently this extra assessment might have been levied or how income from work outside the hamlet was taken into account.  Nor is the extent to which hamlet finances were dependent on this extra money clear.  But the same information was given on different occasions by three men all now in their late seventies.  One was a landlord in Nohara, another had three Nohara families for tenants and lived in a neighboring hamlet, and the third man had been a tenant for a third, different, landlord.

It appears that occasions for the direct assessment of shares in undertakings were infrequent, however.  In Nohara hamlet, in which expenses at the time were largely related to ceremonial events, most of the expenses were underwritten by the wealthy families of the hamlet, as would be expected:

> Whenever there was drinking at the shrine before the war, the landlords usually bought most of the sweets and sake.  The technique we used in those days was, in today's money, to get, say, ¥100 from the richest landlord and ¥10 from the poorest tenant, and then everyone else would find his proper place between these two amounts.  But there never was enough money to cover the whole expense, and so the *omiya-kakari* [shrine officer] and the hamlet head would make up the difference out of their own pockets.  And it was usually the poorer men who drank the most at the shrine.

At the ward level, because all of the ward's several former landlords and prosperous independent farmers were involved, more attention was given to precise calculation.  The formula in use divided total projected expenditure into shares of 50 percent from the previous year's income tax (*shūnyū shotokuzei*) and 25 percent from the municipal property tax (*kotei shisanzei*); the remaining 25 percent was divided equally among all ward families.  This formula was adopted briefly within the separate hamlets as well although it does not appear to have been employed extensively.  Two village halls (one of which is now the ward hall) were built using this method for collection of the necessary resources, and the area school was built in the 1950s using the same formula, with shares distributed among the members of the four villages that would use the school.

After the war and until the late 1950s, an attempt was made to levy assessments based entirely on reported income, and the municipal tax records were used for this estimate of income.  This plan ultimately proved unsuccessful because of the growing numbers of wage earners throughout the ward and in each hamlet who were unable to conceal any of their income from taxation.  Farmers and the self-employed customarily concealed from one-third to one-half of their incomes from taxation.  Consequently, the wage earners felt themselves exploited and forced to carry an unfair burden in projects in which assessments were levied.  The wage earners successfully lobbied city hall to have all tax records kept secret, especially from hamlet and ward heads and the financial officers of the hamlet and ward.  Since that time, around 1957-1958, all ward assessments have been on the basis of one equal share per family.

Within the hamlet, however, there still remained some instances of unequal levies.  The Nohara hamlet hall, erected in 1958, was built with shares levied on membership in the hamlet for the labor involved, and on membership in the *jikkō-kumiai* and *yōsan-kumiai*, so that members in both of these latter organizations paid double shares in expenses as well as contributing labor.  In the late 1950s and throughout most of the 1960s, hamlet cooperative raising of silkworms was also conducted in this way.  A family raising three times the number of eggs that another family raised, for instance, would also pay three times as much for supplies and work three times as many hours.  Even as late as 1970 the purchase of dining tables for the hamlet hall and for funerals was undertaken by means of a similar formula, with the *jikkō-kumiai* paying two shares, the *yōsan-kumiai* paying two shares, and the hamlet treasury paying five shares in the total purchase price.

The discontent of wage earners was not limited to these direct assessments for extraordinary expenditures by the ward and hamlet in the postwar period.  Until 1956 the hamlet annual meeting was also the annual meetings of the *jikkō-kumiai* and *yōsan-kumiai*, and the meal taken at this meeting was funded by assessment.  From the end of the war to 1956, there were from four to eight hamlet members that belonged to neither of these organizations, and they were assessed double the amount of the other hamlet families for this meal.  This expense was not kept in the hamlet account books but in the *jikkō-kumiai* account books.  Unfortunately, the actual division of shares by household was kept separate from either account books on separate sheets of paper, and only a few of these sheets remain in the hamlet record boxes.  Because the relevant documents are no longer available, it is not possible to say when this practice first began. It ended, however, when the hamlet hall was constructed in 1958. From that year onward, the meetings of the two groups concerned with local production were held in the hamlet hall, and the hamlet annual meetings were held, as before, in the house of hamlet head. From 1968, the meetings of all three groups were reunited and assessments for the meal made on the basis of equal shares for each family in the hamlet.

Smith (1978: 223-24) provides from a similar hamlet a clear illustration of the general rule that it is easier to spend money if it is held by the hamlet rather than by the members. A hamlet *fujinkai* planned to take a trip to a hot-springs resort and had been setting aside individual shares to cover expenses beyond what they were able to obtain from the hamlet treasury. Some who had contributed were then unable to make the trip when the time came. They later accused those who did go of using both the hamlet money and the money that everyone had been setting aside. It was not the use of hamlet money that drew the complaints, but the use of the money individuals had been setting aside. The bad feeling that resulted seems to have contributed substantially to the immediately subsequent demise of the *fujinkai*. Smith does not mention that any money was returned to those who paid but did not go on the outing; presumably none was.

The focus of such an issue is a result of the claims that members have on one another's privately held resources and of the difficulty of interpreting the actual source of control over money collected in the above manner. It is difficult to judge whether control over such installments passes to the group or remains with the individual member, but it is not difficult to predict which members will offer which interpretation as the correct one.

Nohara's Hakusan-kai experienced a similar predicament, which was finally resolved satisfactorily. This group's major expense is the annual trip to a hot-springs resort. Originally, the dues (*kaihi*) were ¥5000 annually, and the individual members each paid an additional ¥13,000 annually in monthly installments into an account to pay for the trip. In the first year all members attended the meeting, and there was no difficulty. But in the second and third years, some members (two the second year and four the third year) were unable to make the trip and wanted their ¥13,000 each returned to them. The matter was discussed by the group, and ultimately, each man who did not participate in the trips was reimbursed ¥10,000. It was decided at the same time that, in the future, there would be no distinction made between the society dues (*kaihi*) and the money put aside in installments for the expenses of the trip (*ryōhi tsumitate*). The entire ¥18,000 would thereafter be considered dues and would not be refunded. It was further decided that only as much of an absent member's share as was needed to cover commitments made in his name—primarily reservations and deposits—would be spent; the rest would remain in the society's treasury. Two members then resigned.

The founder of the Hakusan-kai interprets this series of events as follows:

This is a purely voluntary (nin'i) association for the good of the entire hamlet. The people who join and then quit are people who think that there will be something in it for them directly. And then, when they realize that there isn't, they resign. The purpose of the group is to facilitate communication in the hamlet so that when something important does come up, we can deal with it smoothly and effectively. In the old days, in prewar Japan, communications were good and deep between hamlet members, but after the war everyone just let personal relations (ningen kankei) go to ruin. But the ability to deal with people is the strong point of the Japanese, and personal relations must be made to work well again.

When planning such trips in Nohara, group members often raise the issue of whether or not money paid in installments will be returned to the members who cannot go before that money is collected. Most trips are funded in this manner, and the issue is commonplace. If not all the money is returned, it is common to settle the matter of how much will be returned and how much will be kept by the group before the trip is taken. As expressed by one man whose business often prevents him from taking trips with hamlet groups, despite his desire to participate:

On the one hand, it is always easier to get people to pay installments of, say, ¥1000 per month than it is to get them to come across with ¥12,000 all at once. There are always advance preparations that must be taken care of for trips, and they require money. So, should the people who do not let you know if they are going or not until the last minute get their money back or not? After all, the plans were made when they were still planning to go. If you start out clear that the money is in the form of dues and, as dues, will not be returned whether they go or not, then it all goes much smoother. So, everyone decides that from the start the money will be dues, and no one objects at the time. And everyone continues to pay the installments on schedule. Then, all of a sudden they can't go and want their money back. Well, when you belong to a group, you have to abide by the decisions of the group or quit (dakkai suru). It's always true that people have differences of opinion, but when people want to do things unilaterally (katte ni), that's when the problems come up.

This is a problem that can arise whenever anything must be paid for out-of-pocket. In late September 1979, the Anglers took a trip to the east coast of the country. Up to that time all who wished to go had been paying ¥1000 per month

for six months.  The following private conversation between the founder of the
Hakusan-kai and the man in charge of planning the Anglers' trip in early September took place after a softball game.  The "planner" had just shown the "founder"
the itinerary and the specific arrangements for the trip that he had made.

Founder:    "So the date's set then.  Good.  What about the people
            who won't go?"

Planner:    "I suppose we'll have to give the money back, but we'll
            keep ¥1000 each for expenses."

Founder:    "Let's keep ¥2000 each and get them a ¥500 souvenir
            (omiyage) too."

Planner:    "We've got ¥6000 now, and it will take about ¥10,000
            altogether to cover initial expenses."

Founder:    "Then ¥2000 will be good."

Planner:    "Then that's what we'll do.  Give these itineraries to
            everyone who is going to go at the dinner tonight."

On the trip it was unanimously and informally decided to do exactly what
had been discussed above.  During the meal, at which time this question was
discussed by all present, the opinion was expressed by several men that those who
did not go should get some, but not all, of their money back.  The two reasons
given were that the amount not returned would serve as insurance against arbitrary nonparticipation and would pay for the trouble caused those involved in the
planning (mendōhi).  The two men who held the conversation recorded above were
silent during this discussion and spoke only when the question of exactly how much
should be kept was raised.  The founder mentioned ¥2000 and suggested that an
appropriate omiyage for each man might be purchased from the money.  The planner, "taking the sense of the meeting," stated that it appeared that ¥2000 would
be a good amount and that a ¥500 omiyage should be picked up for each man who
did not participate, to let them know that they were being thought of although
they were unable to come along on the trip.  This idea was widely seconded and
the discussion then moved on to other matters.

Over the years the formulae employed in levying assessments have changed
from "simple-differential" to "complex-differential" to "simple-equal" for most
hamlet undertakings.  And yet even recently, there have been occasions in which
the "simple-differential" formula has been employed.  It would be a mistake to
regard this apparent drift in formulae as a fundamental change in methods of securing funding for cooperative projects and the use of different methods, even at
present, as mere "rationalization."  On the contrary, there is no evidence or logic
that supports the assertion that the funding of the hamlet is now more "rational"
than it has been in the past or that the use of any method of funding is more or
less "rational" than any other.  And even the "rationality" in question is not

applicable to some knowable "proper method" of funding a hamlet's activities but is the outcome of political processes occurring within the hamlet, ward, and city. It is, thus, no coincidence that the hamlet's wealthiest member is by far its most outspoken proponent of "equality" (byōdōshugi). Nor was it coincidental that the wage earners, not the self-employed, agitated to have tax records kept confidential in the mid-1950s.

The hamlet and ward have not fundamentally altered their assumptions about the proper way of funding their diverse undertakings. Since the productive exchange relation upon which the hamlet and ward are founded requires the total commitment of members' resources, differential assessments are to be expected where there are differential family incomes. However, in order to make differential assessments, a measure of income that is acceptable to all participants is necessary. Obviously, any measure of income based on tax records, from which wage earners could not hide their income to any significant degree while the self-employed could shield up to half of their income, would not be satisfactory to the wage earners. What set the stage for conflict was not the assumption that differential shares must be absorbed but the fact that those who could not shield their income from the tax records had to subsidize those who could. Equal shares emerged as the point at which compromise was possible only because those who were self-employed proved unwilling to reveal their entire incomes to the hamlet and ward officers. It was not because the wage earners were unwilling to pay differential shares. The difference between past differential assessments and current equal assessments does not lie in a changed cultural perspective on how undertakings *should* be funded or in a failure of different perspectives to be shared by different occupational groups. It lies in the limited possibilities available for measuring incomes to everyone's satisfaction.

The point is not a difference in shared assumptions but in the perceived inequity of income measurement. This fact is well illustrated by the following statement of a ward member in his late seventies, who had served as ward treasurer seven times since 1948 and who is the successor to one of the ward's larger former landlord families:

The old system of differential shares could only work as long as this was a completely agricultural area (nōgyō ippon). In the hamlets, it was even possible before the war to simply come to an agreement by discussion about who made how much, at least relative to everyone else in the hamlet, and to divide shares that way. It took some time, but everyone made his living right here in the village, and so everyone knew pretty well what everyone else's income was. But now nobody knows what anyone else makes, at least not accurately enough to get agreement on it, and so the old system doesn't work any more.

In the old days there were some poor people, some who were not so badly off, and a few who were rather well-to-do. Now everyone says, "He's richer than we are. I don't make anything at all," and so we just hand out shares equally to everyone. That's not fair either, and some people always want to pay less than everyone else. Perhaps the old way could still work, but it doesn't seem to. It takes too long and there are too many arguments. The new system of equal shares is at least as fair as anyone has suggested so far. When there was only agriculture here, and everyone made all their income right here in the village, the old system worked. But now nobody gets even as much as one-third of their income from farming, and half the people don't even farm at all. So there is nothing else we can do but divide the shares up equally.

In fact, even before the war there were families in Nohara that did not get all of their income from farming, although all of the hamlet's families except one (a policeman who sold his fields to his *honke*) engaged in agriculture to some extent. Among the twenty-eight prewar families in Nohara was one family each of tilers, carpenters, dyers, a mulberry leaf wholesaler, and a teacher. Most of the hamlet's families did not raise silkworms, and perhaps as many as ten of those families worked as wage laborers outside the ward on a part-time or seasonal basis.

It was only in the late 1950s, when the bottom permanently fell out of the silk market and most of the men in the ward had begun to work for wages outside the ward, that the system of funding based on differential assessments ceased functioning. The wealthier members of the ward, having supported hamlet and village undertakings previously through differential assessments, did not change their ideologies from a Japanese variation of *noblesse oblige* to a Japanese variation of "grass roots democracy." Nor did the improved position of the class of former tenants cause them to demand the right to pay a greater share in ward and hamlet expenses to match their newly gained rights and privileges. The system of funding changed only superficially, in the matter of a satisfactory measure of income: those who could not shield their income from taxation and the tax records finally gained sufficient strength and numbers to shield this information from ward and hamlet officials. Those hamlet members at the bottom of the income scale still had only the argument against assessments that they had earlier, namely, that they could not afford to pay the assessment and that any assessment, even an equal share, placed them in a "cruel bind," forcing a choice between paying the assessment and reducing consumption below the subsistence level or withdrawing from the hamlet.

This point is illustrated by the negotiations in the smallest hamlet in the ward, Nishioka, concerning the construction of their hamlet hall. This hamlet broke from another hamlet in the 1930s and for many years contained only a handful of families—until 1977, not more than twelve. The members of the hamlet wanted to build a hamlet hall but could not afford the expense until four new families "from the outside" built homes in the hamlet and became residents. The hamlet position was explained to these families, and their pledges were obtained to join the hamlet and help with the expense of the construction of the hamlet hall. With the participation of these four families, the hall was completed in the late spring of 1979.

The following statement concerning the negotiations on the funding of this project is from the above-mentioned informant who is in his late seventies. He is a member of Nishioka hamlet and has supported the construction of the hall from the beginning as a legacy from his father, the hamlet's first head:

> From the beginning it was decided that each family would pay an equal share. But then there were two families that said they would not pay, that they just could not afford it. We talked to them, and it seemed like they would go along after all. But then once more they said they wouldn't. And so we talked some more. Finally, adjustments had to be made because of differences in income. These two families had circumstances that had to be taken into consideration. The one old man lives in a rented house by himself. His wife died about five years ago, and his son has built himself a house in Nagoya. It is pretty certain that this son won't return to the hamlet, and it seems like the father will probably go to live with the son when he can no longer get around. He tried to pay, but he just couldn't manage it. Well, he didn't really pay all that much, and he couldn't keep the payments up. His son didn't pay anything at all for the hall and said that he did not consider himself a hamlet member no matter what his father said.
>
> The other case ended up with two families paying one full share. It's another old man who rents a house by himself. His daughter has a husband, and they built a house here and joined the hamlet on their own. They have their problems too, but everyone knows that sooner or later the old man will have to go over to them. So between them they paid only one full share. If he would just retire and go live with his daughter, they would only have had to pay one share anyway, but he's so stubborn.
>
> But these two are special cases. Everyone else paid full shares. The fact is that nobody wants to pay anybody else's share, especially not his neighbor's. Your neighbors are the people closest to you in the world and yet your worst enemies. You have to depend on

them and yet there's always a conflict of interest (*rigai kankei*) with
them; that boundary is always there between the houses.

The share per family in the construction of the Nishioka hamlet hall came
to ¥12,000 per month for fifteen months, plus an initial payment of ¥50,000, for a
total of ¥230,000 for each of the fourteen families. All families entering the
hamlet after 1979 will be asked to pay a share of the cost at a rate decreasing by
¥10,000 per year over the next twenty years. This provision was thought necessary because there remain in the hamlet four sites classified as house sites, and a
road constructed in 1979 provides access for automobiles to these sites. It is
expected that these sites will soon be sold to "rich people from Nagoya or Osaka
who want a retirement home in the country."

To this point we have seen something of the social context in which decisions in Nohara and the other hamlets of Kawasemigawa ward are made. The patterns of social relations in Nohara hamlet are extremely conservative in terms of
both commitment to the nexus of productive exchange transactions and the circumscribed nature of organizational components. Within this hamlet relationship,
however, there is a constant dynamic that is expressed in terms of the desire to
undertake productive exchange. Accordingly, there is little hesitation to abandon
past projects that present little prospect of benefit. Old organizations become
moribund, and their contents are replaced or new organizations formed. But even
under changed conditions of production and access to both local and external resources, the hamlet relationship remains virtually constant.

The primary change in hamlet life over the past thirty years has been the
shift from locally based agricultural production to externally based wage labor.
This shift in economic relations has not resulted in an overall decline in "hamlet
solidarity" in Nohara hamlet or in the other hamlets of Kawasemigawa ward.
There are now fewer occasions for interaction based on agricultural rituals, but
other occasions for interaction and the amount of resources brought to bear on
productive exchange have increased. There are fewer economic ties between
hamlet members now, but new economic opportunities outside the hamlet have allowed all members to participate in hamlet affairs without a coercive threat to
their basis of subsistence. There is less reliance now on local resources for subsistence, but competition for those same resources has greatly diminished, and the
value of those resources for subsistence has also greatly diminished in the eyes of
hamlet members.

There is little gained in arguing the issue of "hamlet solidarity" outside the
context of the distribution of opportunities for exchange and production for hamlet members inside and outside the hamlet relationship. But changes in the content of exchange transactions should not be taken in themselves as indicative of
changes in or a weakening of that relationship. Although the economic miracle of

Japan during the 1960s has led to a weakening in the position of agriculture in the national economy, it should not be concluded that this change necessarily led to a weakening of the ties among hamlet members *as hamlet members*, rather than as independent farmers, or landlords and tenants. On the contrary, the hamlet is at present able to undertake a wider and more costly range of projects based on the productive exchange relation than ever before. This is precisely because new resources brought into the hamlet from outside can be focused on projects within the confines of constant and enduring relations among hamlet members.

Whatever the content of a productive exchange transaction, however, the problem of the distribution of the costs and benefits across the membership of the hamlet remains. That productive exchange transactions are governed by mutual investment in the hamlet, and that this exchange relationship offers an optimal rate of exchange for all hamlet families with regard to access to productive opportunities for exchange, does not mean that all related problems are automatically solved or that there are rules that can be automatically applied to any problem and that will yield a mutually satisfactory result. Rather, the rate of exchange obtaining in productive exchange relations provides an opportunity for participants to interpret and negotiate the implications of alternative courses of action within the pattern of existing social relations and the interests of all participants in each transaction. Competition for control of hamlet resources remains, and productive exchange transactions governed by mutual investment do not obviate politics. Decisions must still be made and implemented.

# CHAPTER 4: DECISIONS

Cases of collective decision making are presented and analyzed in this chapter. Following presentation of the case materials, each decision is discussed and analyzed in relation to the hypotheses presented in chapter 2. For the convenience of the reader these hypotheses are listed once again:

1. Decisions concerning only the allocation of corporate resources will result in unanimity; those that require individually held resources will lead to a division ("Decision Mode").

2. When a decision results in a division, or vote, the opposition will be an extremely small minority ("Small Opposition").

3. The consensual, cooperative orientation of participants remains unchanged, barring the discovery of deception, whether the outcome of a decision is division or unanimity ("Consistent Orientation").

4. Issues are not treated as commensurate, and the likelihood that a course of action will be chosen and implemented is not increased by linking it to other issues being considered by the group ("Incommensurability of Issues").

5. The consent of each participant depends on the satisfaction of a minimal set of criteria with regard to the decision under consideration; past decisions and their outcomes are irrelevant ("Consent Criteria").

6. Individual participation in productive exchange transactions is a function of membership rather than opportunity among structurally similar productive exchange relations ("Exchange Commitment").

7. All productive exchange in the corporate group only creates opportunities for members and never directly distributes benefits to members ("Opportunity").

8. Productive exchange transactions in the corporate group are always arranged in the same bifurcate procedure ("Bifurcate Procedure").

9. Overt advocacy of a particular course of action by individual members is much less likely than overt opposition ("Overt Opposition").

In the analysis and discussion of individual cases of decision making, these hypotheses will not be repeated each time but referred to by the title given after each hypothesis above. The majority of cases presented here were collected from 1977 through 1979 from decisions made by the council or subhamlet groups in Nohara hamlet. A few of these decisions were made before I took up residence in Nohara; other cases had not been concluded by the time I left.

Before entering directly in presentation of the case materials, two methodological points must be settled: the adequacy of the model presented in chapter 2 to contemporary hamlets of rural Japan and the testing of "negative hypotheses," in particular, Incommensurability of Issues.

There are two questions with regard to the applicability of the model to the hamlet that concern the scope of the application and the nature of the hamlet. Chapter 3 argues that the hamlet is fundamentally a corporate group composed of individual property-owning domestic units of production participating in an egalitarian manner in a productive exchange relation governed by the defection-reducing mechanism of mutual investment. Historically, this seems to be an adequate description of the hamlet of Nohara and, no doubt, many other hamlets in Japan. The question of hierarchy is not relevant to this discussion except insofar as some hamlet members have been required by virtue of hamlet membership itself to subsidize the consumption of other hamlet members through productive exchange transactions organized at the hamlet level. If there is evidence of this practice, I am unfamiliar with it. Again, I am not speaking here of relations between or among families in transactions other than at the hamlet level and not referring to the collection of rents by landlords from tenants.

It is clear that hamlets in Japan have not become more egalitarian since the postwar land reform measures have been implemented, but that the incomes of individual households have become less discrepant. This change in income differential has allowed Nohara hamlet to undertake more diverse and more costly projects within the hamlet. But the change in income differential is a direct result of the de-emphasis of local production and competition for local resources. Consequently, many of the decisions now taken in the hamlet are not related to the purchase of capital goods employed in local production but to the recreation of the hamlet members. And while there is undeniably an instrumental aspect to collective recreational activities, it is difficult to avoid the conclusion that what is involved is no longer productive exchange but simple collective consumption. It would appear at first glance that the Opportunity and Bifurcate Procedure hypotheses cannot be sustained under these circumstances.

One of the individually held resources that is available in finite amounts to all hamlet members, however, is "time." In recreational activities, what is created is the opportunity to benefit, and individuals who wish to take advantage of such opportunities must attend and participate in the activity in order to benefit from it. This is why some money is kept from those who do not participate when activities are planned. The sums that are kept are considered the share in the costs of creating an opportunity for those who stand to benefit, and the remainder of the money individuals have set aside as their "production costs." Conceived in this way, the problem of group recreation and planning can be handled by the model without difficulty.

There is, however, one point at which the purchase of capital goods and recreation differ greatly: recreational activity, to the extent that it is expressive of values of participation, requires several participants for anyone to be able to enjoy the activity. That is, a baseball team must have enough men to play the game. Without sufficient participation, the activity will not be possible. The same holds true for an outing to a resort. Under most circumstances, "the more, the merrier" specifies the potential for any participant to benefit from the activity. Thus, while we would not expect public pressure to be exerted on members of the jikkō-kumiai to use any of its collectively owned agricultural machinery, we would expect members of a baseball team to try and keep the participation level high. In the case of recreational activity, the benefit any member can receive is dependent not only on the participation of other members of the group in the creation of opportunity but also on the second phase of the procedure, production. Consequently, while individuals remain free to invest whatever time, energy, and effort they want in recreation within the group, the amount that they can invest depends on what the other members also do. This set of circumstances has its analogy in agricultural production insofar as those hamlet members who do not cultivate their fields or rent them out (a circumstance unthinkable even a few years ago!) are still required to maintain their field's dykes, keeping them free of weeds and in good repair.

While the problem of historical hierarchy in the hamlet and income differentials is not a problem for which the model is inadequate, the problem of the shift from production to consumption is more substantial. Nevertheless, by considering members' "time" as the major production resource involved in recreation, this problem, too, is brought within the scope of the model.

The problem of the Incommensurability of Issues hypothesis is somewhat different. The theory suggests that "squaring," or "log rolling," is not a part of the decision-making process in hamlets in Japan and is explicit about why it is not. Nevertheless, an absence of evidence that issues are treated commensurably does not constitute proof that they cannot be and never are. While I have no evidence that issues *are* treated commensurably and offer evidence supporting the contrary hypothesis, the method of "squaring" is one of considerable expediency in certain circumstances. While it appears extremely unlikely that this method is ever used in collective decisions in hamlets in rural Japan, I do not rule out the possibility that it might be found employed on a limited basis, as, say, an agreement between two hamlet members. Again, I strongly doubt that this is the case, but if such collusion is discovered by hamlet members not party to the arrangement, such an arrangement must surely be interpreted as defection with regard to the productive exchange relationship. In any case, positive evidence for this negative hypothesis cannot be offered, and its relation to the evidence presented must remain conjectural. The other hypotheses are of a positive nature and generally specify the circumstances under which discrete states in the decision-making process will occur. Positive evidence, in the form of case materials, is offered in support of these hypotheses.

### Case 1:  Softball Equipment

*Narrative*

In this case a decision to purchase softball equipment for the Hakusan Team by means of an assessment of members came to a vote and was carried by a wide margin. The assessment, however, was never levied, and the purchase was ultimately made from corporate resources that were collected in the form of dues (*kaihi*).

In early September 1977, the following notice was attached to the hamlet notice board (*kairanban*):

> Because a number of people have expressed opinions about whether or
> not we should try softball, all those who wish to have a team sign up
> below. (signed) Hamlet Men's Association (*seisōnenbu* = Hakusan-kai).

The following week another note was attached to the notice board stating that the response to the previous call for support had been gratifying and that a meeting of all men who wished to play on the team, whether or not they had signed the previous note, would be held a week from Sunday in the hamlet hall for the purpose of organizing a team.

Twenty-three men assembled for the meeting. Koichi, who had circulated the two notices and scheduled the meeting, acted as chair and called the meeting to order. He then circulated another sheet to get the names and phone numbers of those present. All twenty-three men signed this roster.

Officers were then selected. Koichi suggested that two officers would be sufficient and that he would be willing to continue to act as temporary manager until the team got off the ground. His offer was seconded by popular acclaim. He then suggested that Hirahito, who had already agreed to take on the responsibility, be made his assistant and treasurer. There were no dissenting voices raised, and no further discussion of officers.

Koichi then pointed out that the team would need balls and bats and asked if everyone thought that the team should buy these pieces of equipment. A lengthy discussion concerning the various features of the balls and bats, their prices, and the advantages and disadvantages of each type then ensued. After this question had been thoroughly discussed for upwards of twenty minutes, Koichi gave additional direction to the discussion with the suggestion that three bats of different sizes and construction and a half-dozen balls of regulation quality would probably be sufficient to begin.

Koichi then suggested, after finding that the above proposal was agreeable to those present, that the team dues be initially set at ¥1000 per member "because it would be good to have a little extra money left in the treasury after the purchase of the balls and bats." Beyond a few comments indicating approval, there was no discussion of this point beyond what had already taken place.

On the Wednesday following this meeting, Hirahito collected the ¥1000 from each man who had signed up, plus an additional ¥300 each for accident insurance. When I asked, he told me that I had not missed a meeting at which the insurance policy was discussed, but that Koichi had suggested that the money be collected. He also said that the Usoda team had gotten insurance for its members at a very reasonable group rate.

One week later Hirahito again made the rounds of the team members with a copy of the roster so that members who wished to could sign up to purchase uniforms. Again I asked if I had missed a meeting, and again he replied that I had not but that Koichi asked him to undertake the project of collecting names. He said that there was to be a meeting on Saturday night, when Koichi would bring several sample uniforms of different sizes for everyone to try on. He also said that everyone he had approached had signed up for a uniform, and he was certain that the ten men he had not yet asked would also want uniforms. The price of the uniform, including pants, a shirt, a warm-up jacket, and a hat with the team's initial on the front, was ¥9500.

At the Saturday evening meeting for uniform fitting, another collective decision was taken. All twenty-three men who had originally signed up for the team were present, along with a new person whose name was added to the roster. In addition to the uniforms, Koichi brought a flat rubber home plate, three regulation bases, a catcher's mit, a first baseman's glove, and a catcher's mask. All these items were new.

"The balls and bats," Koichi said, "have been purchased, and some money is left over. So why don't we purchase this additional gear. We can get most of it with the money left in the treasury, but about ¥500 apiece more is needed. What do you think?"

It was at this point that I heard the first objection raised to any of these proceedings:

Let's just hold up on this for a minute. This is the first I've heard about buying all this extra stuff. First we get the balls and bats, then the uniforms. But I don't see why we should get these other things since only two people are going to use them anyway.

The man who raised this objection was not even on the team. He was attending because his son, who was a team member, had to work that evening. This objection was immediately followed by comments of general support from two or three other men who were on the team and who also objected to the team buying the equipment Koichi suggested.

Discussion of this matter lasted about twenty minutes. Only seven or eight men said anything at all; the others remained entirely silent. The greatest part of the discussion was carried by Koichi and Hirao, the father. The others who participated only added an occasional comment or two in support of one side or the other. The lack of general participation made it difficult to judge the degree of support either side enjoyed. The use of "politeness language" (*keigo*) was quickly introduced, with each participant in the discussion speaking more and more slowly and deferentially, and with *gozaru* and *irrasharu* forms becoming frequent.[1]

The arguments of those who objected to the team buying the equipment were primarily based on the observation that the positions each team member would play had been settled at the previous meeting and practice. Therefore, the men who would catch and play first base should either buy their own gloves like everyone else or go in together to purchase the gloves and mask. In any case, those who were not going to play either position and would never use the equipment should not have to pay for it. A secondary point was also made by one of the men objecting to the purchase by assessment. He indicated that it was not the money involved, which was little enough, but the principle of the thing. His comment was in response to the remark—in favor of having the team purchase the equipment—that the ¥500 each required to purchase the equipment would barely pay for two cups of coffee. The idiomatic reply was: "Even ¥100 is ¥100 (*hyaku-en de mo hyaku-en da*). If I want to buy coffee, that's what I'll do, and if I want to buy a baseball glove, I'll do that too."

The argument of those in favor of making the purchase rested on the premise that such specialized equipment would contribute to the good of the team as a whole and that the team should buy the equipment itself for the convenience of everyone involved. Individuals could not be expected to buy such equipment when it was only for the good of the team that they would buy it at all. This general position was buttressed with several specific reasons why the team should buy the gloves and mask in question.

Each argument was countered by the other side, and the discussion gradually began to lose steam. Neither side was at all anxious to give in, and none of the arguments were sufficient to convert any of the participants to the other side. After several moments of silence, Koichi called for a show of hands, asking all those who favored having the team purchase the additional equipment to raise their hands and allow themselves to be counted.

Eleven men raised their hands high enough to be counted. This number included Koichi and the others who had supported his position in the discussion. This number was one fewer than half those present, two short of a majority. Hirao then asked to see the hands of those who were opposed to the purchase by the team, and only four hands, including his own, were raised. All four of these men participated in the discussion. Nine members abstained. The man suggested for the position of catcher did not participate in the discussion and abstained.

There was no discussion of parliamentary procedure, and neither Hirao's request to see the "no" votes nor Koichi's declaration that the motion that the team purchase the equipment had passed was questioned.

Koichi then suggested that they use the ¥12,000 collected by individual assessment to purchase the four bases and the mask. Then later, from the next installment of team dues, they could purchase the two gloves. On this question he simply asked if that would be satisfactory, and there were no objections raised. The meeting was then adjourned to try on the uniforms.

At the game on the next Sunday afternoon, all four bases, the catcher's mask, the catcher's and first baseman's gloves, and the recently purchased balls and bats were used. Hirao did not attend, but his son did. The ¥500 assessment was never collected, and how any of this equipment was purchased never came up in public discussion again. When the team's financial report was distributed in mid-March at the end of the fiscal year, income and expenditures balanced exactly. On 15 September ¥1300 was collected from each of the twenty-three members, with ¥6900 going to the payment of insurance premiums. On 30 October ¥12,000 was accounted received as the bimonthly dues for November-December, and ¥29,000 was paid out for the purchase of "one first-base mit, one catcher's mask, one catcher's mit, six balls, and three bats." No mention was made of the bases that had been in use all fall and winter. The final two entries concern the expense of ¥2500 for refreshments for the January tournament and the receipt of ¥23,000 from twenty-three members for January-February and March-April. At a meeting in October, the dues were reduced from ¥500 monthly to ¥500 bimonthly. The membership remained at twenty-three men, two of the original twenty-three men having resigned and two other men having joined.

The financial report is not a record of all of the team's activities but an itemization of income and expenditure. All the equipment discussed the night the uniforms were fitted, however, was present in the hamlet at least two weeks before 30 October and, according to the treasurer's report, could not have been purchased with team funds because the treasury was then too low to sustain such an expenditure. Money to pay for the uniforms was collected the night the uniforms were fitted, and most members paid in full and in cash at that time. Perhaps it was this money that was used for the purchase of the gloves, mask, and bases, or perhaps they were obtained on credit. It is possible that Koichi "loaned" the team the money either before or after the purchase was approved by the team members, knowing the team would eventually purchase the equipment. In any event, the decision to pay for the equipment in question by assessing each member ¥500 was never implemented, and the money was never collected.

The decision to purchase the equipment having been made, Koichi appears to have been unwilling to pursue the matter of the assessment in the face of opposition. Twice I attempted to discuss this whole episode with him in private, and both times he appeared particularly loath to respond to my questions. Hirahito stated that Koichi made all of these purchases himself and that he himself was not in the least troubled about the episode.

Of the two men who quit the team, one voted against the purchase and another abstained. The man who voted against the issue told me that although he did not think that it was right for the team to buy equipment that only a handful of the team's members would ever use, the decision had nothing to do with his resignation. He simply did not care for softball and did not have the time for it since he often had to work on Sunday afternoons. The man who abstained resigned because of ill-health.

*Discussion*

(1) *Decision Mode.* The issue of whether the team would purchase the two gloves, mask, and bases came to a vote. This was the only decision that came to a vote during the period the team was being organized, and the only time an assessment of team members was required.

*(2) Small Opposition.* The vote was eleven in favor, four against, and nine abstentions. The "pro" votes numbered almost three times as many as the "anti" votes, but what is surprising is the large number of abstentions. In the absence of any information at all concerning the positions of these abstainers (other than that they participated in neither the discussion nor the vote), it is fruitless to speculate on possible divisions for and against the proposal within this group.

*(3) Consistent Orientation.* This hypothesis finds little scope for application within this single decision. This was the only vote I witnessed taken by the team over the several collective decisions it took concerning its activities and the allocation of its resources. Hirao never took part in any of the team's decisions again, and the two members of the team who voted with Hirao and remained on the team never found themselves in a similar situation again.

*(4) Incommensurability of Issues.* This hypothesis is not applicable to many voting situations in this context since issues are linked by decision makers to either achieve unanimity or a majority coalition over a series of specific issues. It is clear, however, that in this case very little discussion of the question of the purchase of the equipment through an assessment of members had taken place prior to the proposal at the meeting. This is no doubt why the abstention rate was so high. But beyond this, there were at the time no other issues of any importance even being considered by the team. From the evidence, it must be concluded that the issue was decided entirely upon the merits of the case and the interests of the members: "the good of the team" versus "the assessment of all members to provide benefits for the few." Although it is difficult to draw a "causal arrow" with any certainty, as the team began to coalesce around a nucleus of the better players, it became clear that (with the exception of the regular catcher and myself, who abstained from voting) those who voted "for" the purchase later became the better and more active members of the team, and those who voted "against" the purchase never played well or often.

*(5) Consent Criteria.* That some members were likely to benefit directly from the assessment of all other members was the primary argument Hirao offered. It was also made clear in the course of the discussion that the issue was not that those who opposed the purchase could not afford the ¥500 that was to be assessed. Those in favor of the purchase observed that it was not those individuals who would regularly use the specialized equipment that would benefit, except as everyone on the team benefited. That is, they argued that the team's overall efficiency would be improved, and therefore the team should buy the equipment.

As minor as this issue is, it throws into relief a persistent question of interpretation in any cooperative undertaking, namely, the division of shares of liability and benefit by individuals in the group. If the primary value being expressed in softball is that of participation and competition, the desire to participate must be tempered by the desire to avoid having one's competence tested in competition. The incompetent, in this instance, can either look on the share in the gloves as "their contribution" or as insult added to injury. But since an impasse resulted from different interpretations of the same information, it is not a question that yields to objective argument. And because some individuals felt that they were subsidizing other individuals rather than contributing to their own benefit through the medium of the team as a whole, they could not consent to the purchase by assessment.

As it turned out, the assessment was never made. The purchase, then, could only be thought to have been made with collective resources. Thus, whatever the ultimate source of these resources, whether Koichi's pocket, team dues, or credit from the store that supplied the equipment, no objection was later raised.

(6) *Exchange Commitment.* This hypothesis concerns relations between groups, primarily, and is not relevant to this case.

(7) *Opportunity.* The question at issue was precisely whether an opportunity for all members to benefit was being created by the purchase of specialized equipment or whether those few members of the team who would regularly use the equipment would be the direct beneficiaries of the purchase. As both views are possible and were expressed, the issue could only be settled by division.

(8) *Bifurcate Procedure.* Interestingly, and precisely because of the values for participation brought to the creation of a softball team, those members who would not use the gloves or mask, or even play, could be considered to benefit without additional expenses related to "production" simply by the victories of the team. But those who the opposition supposed would benefit directly through the use of the equipment would have to consistently expend time and energy using the equipment. The confusion generated in this situation is precisely because, win or lose, it is supposed to be "fun" to participate. But, unless we assume a direct correlation between competence and the desire to play—and the impressionistic data that I gathered in the two seasons I played on the team suggests that this is not at all a sound assumption—those members who are most competent will be the most pressured into playing. This was demonstrably the case with two of the team's best, but busiest, members. These two men always played in the "big games" because they were competent, but they rarely came to practices or other games. One of these two men, when he played, often played catcher.

(9) *Overt Opposition.* It is difficult to separate the advocacy of "Koichi the individual" from the advocacy of "Koichi the manager and team captain." He invested considerable time, energy, and perhaps even money getting the team started and organized. The fact that he ran into opposition may have been due, in part, to his desire to do too much too soon, but it is also due to the inherent possibility of divergent interpretations of "the good of the team." In any event,

his advocacy can be explained entirely as a function of his position as manager: as manager, or chairman, he is expected to articulate the course of action most likely to succeed in gaining the support of the membership.

But the opposition to his proposal came from members who did not have positions of preference within the structure of the team. Rather, it came from men most likely to object on the grounds that they would have to absorb costs in the creation of an opportunity from which they could not benefit. This is where we expect opposition to arise. But to the extent Koichi advocated a course of action that was acceptable to him as an individual, rather than as the temporary occupant of a position in the structure of the group that required him to articulate courses of action, his attempt was a failure. It is necessary to constantly distinguish between the position in the group for the articulation of courses of action and the advocacy of courses of action. In this case, this distinction is difficult to maintain because an advocate was occupying the position of spokesman.

## Case 2: *seimaiki* (Rice Polisher)

*Narrative*

In the spring of 1979 the Nohara *jikkō-kumiai* purchased and installed a new rice polisher (*seimaiki*). The old rice polisher was almost thirty years old and no longer adequate.

After rice is harvested, dried, thrashed, and hulled, it can be either eaten as brown rice (*genmai*) or polished. There is a strong preference for white rice, and no one in the hamlet eats the more nutritious brown rice when white rice is available. Brown rice is polished mechanically by removing the thin outer cover of the rice through abrasion. A rice-polishing machine performs this function.

A rice-polishing machine is one of the few agricultural machines well-suited to cooperative ownership and use because demand is not seasonal. Rice is not polished until just before eating because the flavor deteriorates rapidly after polishing. A machine large enough to provide excess capacity for a hamlet of thirty-five families is not much more expensive than a machine of much lower capacity. Rice is generally polished in 30 to 60 kilogram (2 to 4 *to*) quantities. A typical extended family of six requires about 50 to 60 *to* of rice annually (750 to 900 kilograms). Because rice must be polished in smaller batches in summer than in winter, due to infestations of a moth larva, a family might require the use of a rice-polishing machine roughly twenty times per year.

A new, commercial quality rice polisher takes about ten to fifteen minutes to polish two *to* of rice. Amounts larger than two *to* are not polished at one time because the temperature rises with the length of time taken to polish the rice, and higher temperatures reduce the rice's flavor.  The larger the amount of rice polished at one time, the lower the quality of the finished product per minute spent in the machine.

The old rice polisher had been purchased in 1951 for ¥17,000, including motor and installation.  The purchase was made from the treasury of the *jikkō-kumiai*.  Most of the money required through the years for repairs and maintenance also came from the group's treasury, although some money for extraordinary repairs was occasionally donated by individual users.

In the early 1960s it was decided that the old machine was no longer powerful enough and 220-volt lines were installed.  Shortly thereafter the engine burned out because it had been wired to run on 100 volts only.  It was then repaired and rewired to accomodate 220 volts, but the old machine was not mechanically able to perform well at higher speeds.  From 1963 through 1978 approximately ¥80,000 was spent on repairs.

The old machine was large and unwieldly, requiring an elevatorlike aparatus to lift the grain after it had been through the abrasion screw to separate the grain from the detritus.  This was a rather slow process, and even with the rebuilt 220-volt motor, two *to* of rice required about forty to forty-five minutes for adequate polishing.  The 100-volt motor was even slower, requiring over an hour to polish two *to* of rice.  The slowest method is that employing a water wheel.  This method is said to also produce the best tasting rice.  With this method, four *to*, or one standard size bale (*ippyō*) of rice, takes about five hours.

Because the job of polishing rice was so time-consuming, it was assigned to the grandmothers of the hamlet.  They would come to the hamlet hall where the machine was housed and wait until their rice was polished.  The machine was connected to the motor by a series of rollers and long belts, which often slipped off the rollers at higher speeds.  Since the grandmothers were unable to replace the belts, they had to wait until someone climbed up under the roof and set things in order again.  The old machine was clearly not built to be operated at higher speeds.

A fee for the use of the maching was charged to all users—until 1976, ¥100 for four *to* for members and ¥120 for the same quantity for nonmembers.  From 1976 the rate for the same quantity of rice was increased to ¥280 for members and ¥320 for nonmembers.  The same rates were being charged in other hamlets in the ward at the time.  Although, of course, Nohara families are not members in the *jikkō-kumiai* of other hamlets, many hamlet members began to use the machine of the neighboring hamlet even at the higher rates.  This hamlet had a new machine and employed one of the retired men in the hamlet to run it.  That made it possible for anyone to drop off their rice in the morning and pick it up later in the day.  He did not do a very good job, many grandmothers told me, but at least it was more convenient.

The machine in the neighboring hamlet, purchased in 1975, was at least as efficient as those of commercial establishments. But commercial establishments charged about ¥600 for four *to* of rice, and the nearest facility was in town, four miles from the ward.

The primary effect of the improvement of alternative sources for this important service and the decline of the efficiency of the hamlet machine was that many hamlet families began to take their rice to other facilities or bought private machines. No families in the hamlet bought their new machines on a collective basis, however.

Table 3 shows that while twenty-five families used the old machine to polish some 900 *to* of rice in 1970-71, by 1978 only thirteen families used it to polish 478 *to*. Both the number of uses and the amount of rice declined by half during this eight-year period. This is not to say that the machine's poor performance accounts for the entire decline during this period: four families, although none of them among the machine's heaviest users, discontinued rice production altogether. Nevertheless, the result was such that while the demand for a new machine remained high among some families, demand for a new machine dropped dramatically for several other hamlet families.

The increase in tariff in 1976 was not opposed by the families that no longer used the old machine. The rates were raised to match those charged in the hamlet with the new machine mentioned above, and with the expectation that the money collected would be used to purchase a new rice polisher for the families of Nohara hamlet.

Despite the decrease in overall use of the old machine, the increase in the tariff allowed the *jikkō-kumiai* to accumulate enough money in its treasury to consider purchasing a new machine two years later. Although accounts for two years are missing from the record, the increases in revenue after the increase in tariff was significant.

According to the figures given in the *jikkō-kumiai*'s account book, the group had a balance of only ¥11,502 in 1976. This balance increased to ¥43,217 in 1977 and ¥72,445 by end of March 1979. These increases were due entirely to the extra amounts being brought in by the rice polisher.

On the evening of 20 March 1979, drum practice for the hamlet's spring festival was held in the hamlet hall. Jiro (Family 22) brought a brochure advertising *seimaiki* to that practice and circulated it around the room. On 5 June 1979, a little more than two months later, the *jikkō-kumiai* installed a new *seimaiki* where the old one had stood. The old machine's metal parts were sold for scrap, and the wooden parts were burned as they were brought out of the building.

The decision to buy the new machine was taken very informally over the entire two-month period, and there seems to have been no very strong opposition

Table 3:  Rice Polished in the Nohara *jikkō-kumiai seimaiki*
April 1970 to March 1979 (by family and in *to* of rice)

| Family | 4/70-<br>3/71 | 4/71[a]<br>3/74 | 4/74[b]<br>3/75 | 4/75-<br>3/76 | 4/76-<br>3/77 | 4/77-<br>3/78 | 4/78-<br>3/79 |
|---|---|---|---|---|---|---|---|
| 29 | 2 | — | — | — | — | — | — |
| 30 | 54 | — | 42 | 49 | 59 | 55 | 59 |
| 28 | 51 | — | 18 | 41 | 32 | 52 | 22 |
| 25 | 41 | — | 29 | 44 | 15 | — | — |
| 22 | 61 | — | 58 | 55 | 55 | 66 | 65 |
| 21 | 34 | — | — | — | — | — | — |
| 20 | 42 | — | 53 | 42 | 34 | 22 | 32 |
| 18 | 44 | — | 20 | 46 | 52 | 41 | 46 |
| 19 | 47 | — | 46 | — | 61 | 58 | 20 |
| 17 | 52 | — | 41 | 58 | 66 | 68 | 41 |
| 14 | 61 | — | 44 | 69 | 49 | 48 | 26 |
| 8 | 51 | — | 6 | 37 | 35 | 36 | 26 |
| 13 | 51 | — | 42 | 68 | 68 | 49 | 13 |
| 11 | 22 | — | 11 | — | 11 | 6 | 7 |
| 10 | 27 | — | — | — | — | — | — |
| 3 | 35 | — | — | — | — | — | — |
| 7 | 68 | — | 36 | 50 | 63 | 59 | 58 |
| 6 | 16 | — | 7 | — | — | — | — |
| 5 | 49 | — | 43 | 63 | 52 | 34 | 63 |
| 15 | — | — | — | — | — | — | — |
| 2 | 9 | — | 1 | 1 | 2 | — | — |
| Total (*kumiai* members) | 817 | — | 487 | 623 | 654 | 594 | 452 |
| Niwa, S. | 24 | — | — | — | — | — | — |
| Meada, H. | 23 | — | — | — | — | — | — |
| 31 | 9 | — | 7[c] | 17 | 11 | 24 | — |
| 12 | 2 | — | — | — | — | — | — |
| Maeda, S. | 10 | — | — | — | — | — | — |
| Total (non-*kumiai* members) | 68 | — | 7 | 17 | 11 | 24 | — |

[a]The records are missing for this period.
[b]The machine was broken all of April, May, and June of 1974.
[c]For reasons unknown, this family was charged the rate for *kumiai* members, and its name included in the list of members *in this record only*, from 1974 onward. The reason it continued to be carried with the *kumiai* members is that each year the new record is simply copied from the previous year's list of names. This family does not own rice fields but does work some of its "main family's" (*honke*) fields.

to the purchase; it had been recognized for several years that a new machine was necessary. The question, I was told in straightforward terms the night Jiro brought the brochure to the drum practice, was simply "money." That is, how much was needed, where would it come from, and who would contribute? The question of the machine itself—a supplier, capacity, quality, type of abrasion mechanism—did not merit much discussion since everyone who used such machines had knowledge of them. A rough consensus on these technical requirements was already present in the group.

Jiro, one of the hamlet's most regular users of the old machine, had recently purchased a new trencher for his tea-production enterprise, and at the time of the sale he discussed a *seimaiki* with the owner of the store. As far as I was able to tell, there was no disagreement with regard to either the *seimaiki* that Jiro had circled on the brochure or the price the store owner had indicated. It was this machine that was finally purchased, and at the quoted price minus a 10 percent discount. But the issue had never been the quality or price of the machine.

The *jikkō-kumiai* has twenty-three members. Two neither grow rice nor own rice fields, and none of the living members of either family has ever grown rice as an adult. Both of these families are members in the hamlet *jikkō-kumiai* because they own stock in the city Agricultural Cooperative (*nōgyō-kyōdō-kumiai*), as do all other *jikkō-kumiai* members. Although these two families do not grow rice, they do use some of the other services of the co-op through the *jikkō-kumiai*. In particular, they order seeds, seedlings, fertilizer, and pesticides for their vegetable gardens, at reduced prices, and they occasionally make use of the co-op's credit facilities, which are only available to members.

All of the remaining twenty-one members of the *jikkō-kumiai* own rice fields, but in 1978 only sixteen grew rice and were carried on the books as families planning to plant a rice crop in 1979. Two of the remaining five families grew their last rice in the late 1960s, and the other three families ceased rice production in the early to mid 1970s. Only thirteen of the hamlet's sixteen rice growers used the *jikkō-kumiai's* rice polisher in 1978–79. One family (Family 31), which was not a member of the group, also used the rice polisher that year.

Individually owned private *seimaiki* are not common in Nohara. There are only three machines in the hamlet, two of which are regularly used and a third that is not used at all because its owner ceased rice production in the late 1960s. None of these three families used the hamlet machine after purchasing their machines. These privately owned machines are not considered alternative sources to the hamlet machine by other hamlet families. One owner told me he would gladly let any hamlet member who asked use his machine, but no one had ever asked him. He also admitted that he has never offered the use of his machine to anyone. Even this family's *bunke* continues to use the *jikkō-kumiai* machine. (Figure 1 shows the disposition of *kumiai* membership, rice-field ownership, rice production, and rice-polishing facilities by family in Nohara hamlet.)

The *jikkō-kumiai's seimaiki* was broken for about two months in both 1977 and 1978, and consequently, many, if not all, of the membership had to resort to other facilities in one or both of these years. By averaging the amounts of rice polished from 1974 through 1978 for all families using the *kumiai* machine in either 1977 or 1978, and combining it with the information provided in figure 1, a rough estimate of constant demand in the hamlet by family class for a new *seimaiki* can be constructed (figure 2).

This demand schedule is compiled in terms of family class rather than in terms of individual families for two reasons. First, the question of willingness to supply resources for the purchase of such equipment never arises. Second, the values involved are discontinuous, and there is no opportunity for a family to pay shares in the purchase at other than discrete levels, levels determined by total price divided among participating families grouped on common dimensions.

The first reason becomes clear when we consider the following. Each participant could calculate the amounts beyond which he would prefer to continue to use the old machine, buy a private machine, or have his rice polished outside the hamlet. If the sum of these amounts was less than the purchase price, the new machine would not be bought. If the sum was greater than the purchase price, a different mechanism of redistribution for the surplus contribution would be needed. At least two hamlet families with whom I talked made such a calculation with regard to their farming enterprises and mechanization when their respective labor supply changed by only one person. One of the families thought it was "worth it" to purchase a plow-tiller combination. The other family gave up rice cultivation altogether.

A small family-sized *seimaiki* retails for ¥40,000 to ¥60,000, depending on the quality and capacity of the machine. The polishing apparatus alone, without a motor, costs about ¥20,000. The machine the *jikkō-kumiai* finally purchased cost exactly ¥90,000. This price was for the polishing apparatus alone since the old rewired motor was judged fit for continued use with the new machine.

The above information is the framework within which a family must decide what it will do and what the costs and benefits of alternative courses of action will be. But this is not a calculation that is brought out in the collective decision-making process. The substance of that process is the attempt to accommodate the reservations of members with low demand for sharing in capital costs to the willingness of members with a high demand for supplying those resources. And it is a process that must develop within the framework of discrete levels of shares regardless of how the total price is divided among those who will finally meet that price. As the matter was put by one of the hamlet's larger rice producers active in the *jikkō-kumiai*:

Figure 1

Disposition of *kumiai* Membership, Rice-field Ownership,
Rice Production, and Rice-Polishing Facilities in
Nohara Hamlet

| | |
|---|---|
| I. Nonmembers using hamlet *seimaiki* | 1[a] |
| II. Members owning no rice fields | 2 |
| III. Members owning rice fields | |
|     A. And growing no rice | 5[b,c] |
|     B. And growing rice | |
|         1. Using hamlet *seimaiki* | 13 |
|         2. Using | |
|             a. Own *seimaiki* | 2 |
|             b. Commercial facility | 1 |

[a]Family 31.  This family began regularly using a commercial facility in 1978.

[b]One of the families grows no rice but owns rice fields and its own *seimaiki*, which is in storage and not used.

[c]Until 1977 one of these families occasionally used the hamlet *seimaiki* to polish the rice it received as rent.  From 1977 onward it began receiving polished rice.

Figure 2

Estimate of Demand for New Hamlet *seimaiki* by Family Class

Number of Families

---

1. Families using old machine regularly

   a. Heavy users (over 50 *to* annual average)              5
   b. Medium users (20 to 49 *to* annual average)            6
   c. Light users (1 to 19 *to* annual average)              3[a]

2. Families using commercial facilities                      1[b]

3. Families using own *seimaiki*                             2[c]

4. Families with rice fields not growing rice

   a. Without own *seimaiki*                                  4
   b. With own *seimaiki*                                     1

5. Families belonging to *jikkō-kumiai* not owning rice fields   2

---

[a]Includes Family 31, a rice-growing nonmember regularly using the *kumiai* machine.

[b]A medium user.

[c]Both heavy users.

If only one or two members won't pay a share of ¥1000–1500, then maybe the others can make up the difference. But if three or four people refuse to go along, then we won't be able to get the machine without finding some more money from somewhere else.

That is, if two members will not share in the cost of the machine, then the remaining twenty-one members might be able to agree to divide the ¥3000 among themselves, at a rate of about ¥150 more per member. But if three or four members do not participate, the remaining members would probably not be able to agree to pay the additional ¥250–300 each. I cannot specify more precisely the exact number of members whose refusal to participate would have made the purchase of a new *seimaiki* dubious. In idiomatic speech, this number is the difference, in the context of the hamlet *jikkō-kumiai*, between "one or two people" (*hitori, futari*) and "a few of the members" (*ichibu no kumiai-in*).

The second reason that the demand schedule is computed on the basis of class of member families is because the alternatives available for the division of shares are not functions of individual demand but are the few possible levels into which equal shares by different classes of members can fall. It is likely that none of these levels will correspond exactly to the maximum any family would be willing to pay.

Four or five years of desultory and inconclusive informal discussion only made it clear that there was not sufficient support among the entire membership of the *jikkō-kumiai* to purchase a ¥90,000 machine if the cost was divided among any group smaller than the whole membership. Equal shares in a ¥90,000 purchase would have come to about ¥4000 per member over the entire membership and about ¥7000 each over the thirteen regular users of the machine. Thus, while there were at least three members of the *kumiai* who had been willing to pay from ¥20,000 to ¥60,000 for private machines, and at least a few members who were willing to pay at least ¥7000 for a cooperatively owned machine within the context of the *jikkō-kumiai*, there must have also been more than three members who were not willing to pay even as much as ¥4000 each for a cooperatively owned machine. This follows from the fact that while there had been discussion among members concerning the possibility of buying a machine for the *jikkō-kumiai* by having those who regularly used the old machine purchase a new one, no machine was bought until 1979.

Discussions were taken up again in earnest when it was reported at the end of 1978 that there was a substantial sum, ¥70,000, in the *kumiai* treasury. Even at this point, however, the issue of funding the remaining purchase price was not discussed in terms of individual levels of supply and demand. Rather, the entire *kumiai* treasury was allocated toward the purchase, with the remaining ¥20,000 to be made up through equal assessments of the membership. Thus, the levels of shares that were available during the entire discussion of the purchase of the machine were only (1) ¥90,000 divided by twenty-three members; (2) ¥90,000 divided by thirteen regular users; (3) ¥20,000 divided by twenty-three members; (4) ¥20,000 divided by twenty-one members; and (5) ¥20,000 divided by fewer (perhaps thirteen) members.  Because only these levels were available (with the exception of the purchase by individuals of machines for their own use), it is inconsequential exactly what amounts an individual might have cared to spend for such a machine.

Within the group of regular users, there were differences in demand related to the availability of household labor and access to alternative facilities, but even these differences could only remain as potentials for agreement or disagreement. They could not be expressed in the levels of shares, only in willingness to continue discussions.

For both of the above reasons, the discussion of the purchase of the *seimaiki* was conducted in terms of *kumiai* membership, and the final solution as well was expressed in the idiom of membership.  I will, therefore, continue to present this case largely in terms of differences among classes of *kumiai* members in their willingness to supply the funds for the purchase of a new rice polisher and their demand for its purchase.

From 20 March 1979 to 5 June 1979 I spoke with all of the members of the *jikkō-kumiai* concerning this matter at least once, and with many of them several times.  There were few meetings at which this issue was discussed, and only one meeting called expressly for the purpose of considering this issue.  Negotiations and discussions were almost entirely informal.

The night Jiro brought the brochure on *seimaiki* to the festival drum practice, Akihide, one of the regular medium users, explained to me his understanding of the issue and negotiations up to that time: he was very much in favor of purchasing a new machine through the *jikkō-kumiai*.  The old machine was no longer efficient and often broke down.  There had been talk of buying a new machine over the past several years, but nothing had come of it.  He indicated that although the *kumiai* itself owned the old machine, the entire *kumiai* membership was not going to buy the new one, just the people who used it (*kankeisha*).  Although there were about twenty or so members in the *kumiai*, only about fifteen were *kankeisha* who would buy a new machine when they could finally agree on "money."  It was only money that was holding things up, he continued.  A new machine would cost from ¥100,000 to ¥120,000; the amount per share, divided equally, would be about ¥10,000 for the fifteen *kankeisha*.  Of these members, about ten people wanted to buy a machine at that price, and three of four did not.  It was not, he said, that these people did not want to buy a new machine but that they considered ¥10,000 too much to pay.  This was the first account I received concerning this issue.

Another of the medium users, who is an electrician as well as part-time farmer, attempted (in vain) to introduce me to the intricacies of motors and wiring, currents, phases, and volts because it was his conviction that these were the sources of difficulty in the negotiations. He was convinced that no one in the hamlet really understood the essential nature of the problem but himself, and he was also convinced that they would not be able to buy a new machine until the old one was no longer capable of repair. That time, he said, was not far off because the women who used the machine did not understand anything about machinery and were abusing the old machine fearfully. In short, he added, they would have to buy the new machine for ¥10,000 per family sooner or later. He did not, however, seem at all enthusiastic about the prospect.

One of the two men who owned and used his own *seimaiki* was extremely tentative concerning his own participation in the purchase of a new machine by the *jikkō-kumiai*. When I spoke with him first, he had not yet seen the brochure circulated by Jiro. He had heard talk of buying a new machine for several years and had no doubt that the brochure was merely more "research" (*kenkyū*). He was convinced that members were not yet at the stage of actually making a purchase. Although he was unsure of whether he would participate in such a purchase, he thought that he would, if the price was not "unreasonable"—he would not, however, quote a "reasonable price"—for two reasons.

First, the only reason he belonged to the *kumiai* was because he had rights (*kenri*) in the group and to its property. He was not going to try and change his membership and transfer to another hamlet's *kumiai* just to avoid paying for a rice-polishing machine. "If everyone finally decides to get one, I guess I'll go along," he said. The second reason he gave for his likely participation was that a new machine owned by the *kumiai* would provide him with a convenient alternative facility in the event that something should happen to his own machine.

The owner of the second private *seimaiki* was much less tentative in his response, insofar that he was certain that if the decision was made to purchase a new machine, he would participate. He also thought that another machine would be useful to him as "insurance" in the event his own machine failed. He did not, however, think that a new machine would be purchased in the near future. Although this individual is considered one of the leaders of the older group of household heads still active in agriculture, he was not among those promoting the purchase of the new machine.

The owner of the hamlet's third private *seimaiki* had not resumed rice cultivation after his debilitating accident in the late 1960s and did not participate in *jikkō-kumiai* affairs. He had, he said, heard talk about buying a new machine over the years, but he was not at all certain that he would participate in the purchase. While he readily admitted that he was still a member of the *kumiai*, he would not grant that the talk this time was any different than in the past. He did say, however, that he would pay a share in the purchase if it was necessary and if he was asked. It was his duty (*gimu*) as a *kumiai* member, provided "everyone else pays a share too."

During the period in which I was interviewing members of the *kumiai* concerning this issue, a meeting was held on 30 April 1979, and in the days immediately following I spoke with several other *kumiai* members, some of whom had attended this meeting and others who had not. All had varying notions of exactly what had transpired at the meeting.

This particular meeting seems to have been of some consequence for the final decision, but at a subsequent meeting held only a few days later, a meeting attended by different men in an ostensibly different context, the results of the first meeting were considerably modified. The first meeting was only attended by the *kankeisha* (and *jikkō-kumiai* officers, both of whom were also *kankeisha*), but the second meeting was that of the *shinjinkai* and, therefore, was attended primarily by the older men of the hamlet, especially retired household heads.

Until the first meeting, the assumption was widespread that only the *kankeisha* would participate in the purchase of the new machine, but there was no clear agreement about exactly who would pay shares and how much they would be. This approach had gradually emerged over the years because it was clear that several *kumiai* members were reluctant to pay full shares in the purchase price of a new machine that they would only rarely, if ever, use. At the *kankeisha* meeting of 30 April, three fundamental objections to this solution were made explicit by some of the *kankeisha*. (1) The cost per share, between ¥7000 and ¥10,000, was too high for some of the *kankeisha*. A few of these families would prefer to buy their own private machines rather than participate in the purchase of a collectively owned machine. (2) The solution of having only the *kankeisha* pay shares in the new machine would result in too many members without rights in the new machine continuing to think that they could use the machine at member rather than nonmember rates. (3) If every time the *kumiai* made a collective purchase only those people who wanted to participate did so, then there was no point in anyone belonging to the *kumiai* at all. Nothing would get done, and everyone would lose in the end.

At this meeting the head of the *kumiai* also announced that he had "discovered" (*hakken shita*) about ¥70,000 in the *kumiai* account and that there seemed to be no reason why this money could not be used to purchase a *seimaiki* for the *jikkō-kumiai*. Although he continued to use the word "discovered" even in subsequent conversation, what had in fact occurred was that the books were balanced when the new officers were installed a few weeks earlier. At that time, the account showed a balance of a little over ¥70,000. The man who made the "discovery" was the previous year's *kumiai* vice-head, in which capacity he acted as the group's treasurer. There was no objection to having this money used to purchase the new machine, and subsequent discussion focused on how the remaining ¥20,000 could be raised.

During this meeting there was no call for a show of hands on any question, but neither was the fundamental assumption that the *kankeisha* would bear the cost of the purchase entirely abandoned. Nor was there an immediate drive to directly assess the total membership for the remaining ¥20,000. Rather, the meeting seems to have ended inconclusively but on an up-beat note, since ¥70,000 was now available.

On 2 May 1979 I spoke with one of the regular light users of the old machine, a carpenter by trade, but a part-time farmer as well. It was his opinion that the ¥70,000 could and should be used for the purchase of a new *seimaiki* and that all *kumiai* members should and would pay equal shares in the remaining ¥20,000 sooner or later. He was reluctant to speculate on how long it would take to make the purchase, however, because he did not know how long it would take to get agreement on the exact scope of participation and the levels of individual shares in an assessment. We then had the following conversation:

"Why couldn't the original ¥3500 to ¥4000 be gotten from all the members in the first place?"

Masanori: "Well, we may as well go ahead and use the money we have for the machine since its really money for repairs of the old machine and the like."

"But ¥3500 isn't really very much money, after all. Everyone on the softball team paid ¥10,000 for uniforms, and they aren't necessities like a *seimaiki* is."

Masanori: "It's a lot easier to get ¥1000 from somebody than ¥3500."

"Are there a lot of people in the *kumiai* opposed to paying ¥3500 for the new machine?"

Masanori: "Yes, maybe five or six."

"Is there anyone opposed to paying ¥1000?"

Masanori: "Probably about as many, the same people."

"Are these the people who are members but don't use the *seimaiki* at all?"

Masanori: "It doesn't matter if people don't use the machine or if they do. The point is that they're members of the *kumiai*, and so they still have responsibilities as members."

"Do you think that all of the members will pay their ¥1000 if it comes to that?"

Masanori: "Yes."

"What would happen if these people, the ones who don't use the machine at all, or even anybody, just refused to pay a share?"

Masanori: "I'm sure everyone will pay. It's their duty (*gimu*) if everyone decides to buy the machine."

"Who attended the meeting the night the ¥70,000 was discovered?"

Masanori: "Oh, the regular people, about twelve or thirteen members of the *kumiai*."

(He then listed seven names, excluding himself, and all were regular users of the old machine, with the exception of Yoichi, a man who owns and uses his own machine but is considerd one of the leaders of the agriculturalists in the hamlet.)

"Doesn't it seem like its taking a long time to get a mere ¥1000 from people to buy a machine that everyone claims to want?"

Masanori: "No, not at all. The discussion only started last month, not even one month ago."

"Do you mean when Jiro brought the brochure to the drum practice?"

Masanori: "Yes, from about then. That's when people started talking about it seriously again."

"I wonder why it is so hard to get ¥3500 from people, or even ¥1000, for a machine that will last thirty years and that they will use several times a month, and yet they will pay ¥10,000 for a trip or for uniforms with no trouble at all."

Masanori: "Yes, that's an interesting question."

Masanori's wife (who had been listening to the conversation but had not, until this point, taken part), laughingly: "That much is no mystery. When people take a trip or something, they spend their own money on themselves and no one else, and they have a good time right then and there. Even if machines do last thirty years and you have to have them, they are no fun. People like to go out and spend their money on themselves."

Masanori: "Yes, that's probably right."

"If it was still a matter of every member of the *kumiai* having to pay ¥3500, do you think the *kumiai* could ever get a new machine?"

Masanori: "Well, I just don't know" (*Saa, dō deshō*).

The following night I spoke with another man who had also attended the meeting of 30 April. This man, Hiroki, has only a small family (his aged father and invalid mother) and so uses the rice polisher very little at present. He grows the hamlet's second largest rice crop, however. When we spoke, he presented to me what seemed an exceptionally elegant solution to the entire problem of where the remaining ¥20,000 would come from. His plan was that some of the *yōsan-kumiai*'s remaining ¥40,000 (which was being held in a bank account drawing interest) be used to make up whatever amount remained after using the *jikkō-kumiai*'s treasury. Thus, all the money necessary was already on hand. The machine could be purchased immediately. The problems involved in participation, rights in use, and division of shares in the cost were moot.

The way in which he presented the solution to me left the impression that the issue was settled except for the installation of the new *seimaiki*. But the fact of the matter was that the use of the *yōsan-kumiai* money had not even been brought up at the 30 April meeting, and just moments before I called on Hiroki, the *jikkō-kumiai* head had called him on the phone to ask his opinion of the plan. Hiroki himself was in favor of the plan and said so to the *kumiai* head over the phone, who in turn said that everyone he had talked to so far was also in favor of the plan. I then left Hiroki to call on the head of the *yōsan-kumiai*, the man who held the group's passbook.

This man was a regular heavy user of the old machine, and he had told me earlier that he was willing to go in with the other regular users and buy a new machine for ¥7000 each. He had, however, recognized that this solution would create some problems with other members, especially those using other facilities. Since these people were likely to want to return to the hamlet's machine, they too should be assessed a share in the cost.

When I called on him that night, he told me that it was not his idea to use the *yōsan-kumiai* money, but he agreed to let the *jikkō-kumiai* head see what support there was for the idea. The *jikkō-kumiai* head had come to his house the previous night to discuss the matter. The head of the *yōsan-kumiai* understood that the money would not be given to the *jikkō-kumiai*, but only loaned. The money would be paid back over the next few years from the fees charged for the use of the machine.

When I asked him why it had not been possible to buy a machine earlier by means of assessments on members, he replied that those who did not use the machine did not think that they should pay, or at least not a full share. I then said that I thought that sounded fair enough and that they could not really be expected to be very enthusiastic about buying a machine they would never use. He responded by pointing out that it was not a question of fair or not fair but a matter of duty (*gimu*) as *kumiai* members. He also added that he could understand their point of view and agreed that none of the solutions proposed so far were adequate or fair to everyone.

Most of the members of the hamlet were home on 3 May, a national holiday. The *jikkō-kumiai* head spent the entire day discussing the matter of using the *yōsan-kumiai*'s money to buy the *seimaiki*, and his call to Hiroki was one of his last. It appeared that, whether or not the idea was his originally (and I was never able to find out whose idea it was), support for it among *kumiai* members was overwhelmingly positive.

The *shinjinkai* met in the hamlet hall the evening of 5 May, which was also a national holiday. Very few of those men who had been active participants in the discussions concerning the purchase of the new *seimaiki* attended that meeting. It was at this meeting that the old men of the hamlet rejected the plan to use the *yōsan-kumiai*'s money. They would not allow the money to be loaned or even taken out of the account. In all subsequent conversations, the failure of this plan was laid at the feet of these "old men," who, as everyone knew, were a hard lot and had never been very cooperative even when they themselves were active household heads. Even at this late stage in their lives, they appeared to be acting true to form.

I discussed this matter two days later with the *jikkō-kumiai* head, who gave the following interpretation to the decision of the "old men":

> I tried to discuss the plan for two days with everyone in the *kumiai*. I thought that there was a definite agreement that we would use the money and then pay it back later. But this was just the idea of the "younger men," and I guess that means me as much as anyone.
>
> But the old folks didn't care for it one bit and wouldn't even hear of having the money taken out of the bank. The thing the young men didn't understand was that there were only a few people who really were active in the *yōsan-kumiai* for the past few years, and that now that the account books can't be found, it is going to be hard to sort out to whom the money really belongs. That's mainly why its still in the bank.
>
> But anyway, there are five or six families in the *jikkō-kumiai* who never belonged to the *yōsan-kumiai* at all, and several of those families who did belong stopped raising silkworms so many years ago

that they have no claim on the money now in the account. The young people just figured that it didn't matter whose money it was, since no one grows silkworms at all any more, and it's just sitting there in the bank. But the old folks just wouldn't hear of it, one way or the other.

Once again, the only alternative to waiting longer still seemed to be an assessment on some or all of the *kumiai* membership. We continued our conversation:

"How will it be possible to get everyone to pay shares? I've heard that some people think it wouldn't be fair to those people who don't use the machine to pay equal shares."

Hideo: "Everyone will have to pay equal shares because there is no way shares can be divided up unequally. Some years some people use the machine a lot, and other years other people do. It's not so simple that you can just divide up the cost among those who use it and those who don't."

"Do you think that everyone in the *kumiai* will pay a share, then, even the people who don't grow rice?"

Hideo: "It may be a little difficult to get their cooperation, but the point is not who grows rice and who doesn't, but who belongs to the *kumiai*. Sensei [Taiichi] will certainly pay his share, and Takeshi too. I don't know about Masashi [who owns a *seimaiki* but grows no rice], but he will be told the conditions and asked to pay his share. He owns fields and could start growing rice again if he wanted to, or his son-in-law could. This machine will last for a good twenty years. Who knows what will happen in the next twenty years?"

"Did you ever hear of anyone who quit growing rice and then started up again a few years later?"

Hideo: "No, but that doesn't mean that it couldn't happen. This is a *kumiai* project, and so every member should pay a share in it."

"So you will have to go to each member and ask them to pay, and you think that they will?"

Hideo: "As things stand now, that's the way it looks. After all, it's just ¥1000."

"What would happen if someone, or a few people, just refused to pay at all?"

Hideo: "I don't think that anyone will refuse to pay their share after we explain the matter to them. Everyone will pay in the end."

"Well, suppose that one or two people decided that they wouldn't pay. Could you still get the new machine?"

Hideo: "No, there is no other way now. That's why everyone will finally pay their share."

"It doesn't sound like asking people for the money will be much fun. Do you think many of the people who don't want to pay will complain?"

Hideo (laughing along with his wife): "No matter what you do, some people are never satisfied; some people always complain about everything you do."

He also mentioned that the fee for the use of the machine would not change and that all *kumiai* members would have the same rights to the new machine that they had to the old.

As is common practice with large purchases, the machine was received and installed early in the month and paid for at the end of the month. No formal decision was ever taken, but equal shares in the cost of the machine were collected from all but two of the *kumiai's* members. The money was not collected until after the machine was installed. After the money was collected, I asked each member if he had been called on to pay a share and if he had paid it.

Neither of the members who did not own rice fields were asked to pay a share, and neither paid. When I asked why they were not asked to contribute, both men indicated that they did not grow rice and so did not use the machine. Both also thought that they probably did not have rights, at least as regular *kumiai* members, in the use of the machine, but they seemed unconcerned about that. They both assured me that they would never use the machine anyway.

All other twenty-one members of the *jikkō-kumiai* contributed ¥1000 each. The family that owns its own *seimaiki* but no longer grows rice was asked to contribute and did so. The head of that family explained to me, "We didn't think it was right for us to have to pay since we don't even grow rice now. But since everyone decided to buy the new machine—and after all, it was only ¥1000—when the *kumiai* head came and asked us, we paid."

Two other families who own rice fields but no longer grow rice also paid but made the *kumai* head listen to their complaints when he called on them to ask for their shares. I had the following conversation with Taiichi after he paid his ¥1000:

"Did you pay the ¥1000 when he asked for it?"

Taiichi: "Oh, I paid, but I let him know I didn't much care for it. They [the *kumiai* head's family] are our *bunke*, after all, so he had to listen to me. I've been trying to quit the *kumiai* for years now, but they won't let me."

"What do you mean, they won't let you?"

Taiichi: "We own stock in the co-op, so we are automatically members. But you can't get rid of the stock, and so there's no way out."

"What do you mean, you can't get rid of the stock?"

Taiichi: "You can't just go out and sell it on the stock exchange because no one wants to buy it. And the co-op won't buy it back either."

"Do you mean you couldn't sell it if you really had to?"

Taiichi: "Well, if it came to that, you could sell it. But you wouldn't get anything at all for it, not nearly what it's supposed to be worth."

Another family that no longer grew rice in its fields had made the decision to discontinue rice cultivation after the retired head of the family died. They had made elaborate calculations in order to determine whether they could profit by continued cultivation if they made the investment in agricultural machinery necessary to continue, and they concluded that the best they could do was equal to a two-month supply of rice and that they would rather not continue at that margin. When asked to contribute to the cost of the new *seimaiki*, they did, but the wife of the head of the household told me, "When he came around for the money, we paid all right. But the old man [her husband] really had his say!" She then had a good laugh, remembering the scene.

The fourth family that had not recently been cultivating rice in its fields paid because they intended to use the machine regularly from then on. That spring, the elderly widow of the household had retired from her job in the city. The family decided that with her labor they could afford to invest in a cultivator-tractor that would make rice cultivation profitable for them again. They did not inform the *jikkō-kumiai* of their decision, however, until the *kumiai* head came to ask for their ¥1000.

The fifth family that belonged to the *jikkō-kumiai* and grew no rice in its fields paid when asked, and without complaints. This family is the hamlet's wealthiest, and the household head is the founder of the Hakusan-kai. He explained to me that while he had not participated in the discussion, it was his duty to contribute once the decision was finally made. That was the only way, he said, that an organization could operate effectively. People must be willing to participate once a decision is made. And he joked that perhaps once again he and his family would take up the hoe and sickle.

Other accounts were settled the day the new machine was installed. The notebook in which each family recorded how much rice it polished on what date was examined. The family that had regularly been using the machine at member's rates was noticed: "Oh Tanaka-san, I didn't know you were a member of the *kumiai*. Why is your name here under the section for *kumiai* members?" He replied, "Is that right? I don't know how it got there." No doubt he had no idea, never having himself polished any rice with the old machine. But when the new notebook was hung up on the nail next to the new machine, his name was once again in the section for users who were not members of the *kumiai*, and the family was charged the higher fee once again. But this family, which had been using the old machine at member's rates for several years, was not asked to pay the ¥1000 share. In all, twenty-one of twenty-three member families each paid ¥1000.

*Discussion*

(1) *Decision Mode.* In the absence even of a meeting at which a final decision was taken, it is difficult to state unambiguously that the decision to purchase the new *seimaiki* was taken either unanimously or by vote. Obviously, the difference between a vote and unanimity does not lie in the final participation rates of participants but in the affirmation or rejection of courses of action by the participants.

What is clear in this case is the fact of multiple "divisions." It is precisely because the lines of division were so clear to all participants, and because these lines of division paralleled each family's interest in rice cultivation and rates of use of rice-polishing facilities, that a more formal procedure was unnecessary (and probably undesirable from the perspective of the supporters of the proposal).

As expected, the division among *kumiai* members was not over the allocation of the *kumiai*'s treasury toward the purchase of the machine but over the imposition of assessments. This division varied at each level of likely assessment.

(2) *Small Opposition.* It is likewise difficult to unambiguously demonstrate alignments in favor and in opposition to a proposal when there is no setting in which support and opposition are or can be simultaneously expressed. In this case, the number of supporters of the proposal to have the *jikkō-kumiai* purchase the new *seimaiki* varied at each level of likely assessment. Until the ¥70,000 was discovered in the *kumiai* treasury, the supporters were never numerous enough to secure the actual participation of those unwilling to assume a share in the costs larger than the final figure of ¥1000.

While the status of the two *kumiai* members not owning rice fields remains unclear, three of the four families not growing rice did express opposition to having to pay shares in the cost of the machine even after shares were reduced to ¥1000. That they ultimately all did pay a share does not mean that they were not opposed to the proposal but merely that they were not willing to suffer the inevitable consequences of a refusal.

*(3) Consistent Orientation.* Throughout the entire process of searching for a satisfactory method of funding the purchase, the members of the *jikkō-kumiai* remained consensually oriented to the decision-making process. This process was obviously not limited to the brief period from the end of April 1979 to the beginning of June 1979 but had been in progress for several years prior to this period. During this period, and across the several divisions on this issue among the membership, the group continued to function and no attempt was made to similarly align members on other issues. Efforts were consistently directed toward finding a solution that would be amenable to all members.

That the *jikkō-kumiai* did not hesitate to attempt the exploitation of the *yōsan-kumiai* treasury, and that this attempt was absolutely rejected, does not imply that the orientation of the group was altered. On the contrary, the fact that the "old men" were blamed, if such is the correct word, for the collapse of the plan to use the *yōsan-kumiai* money indicates the strength of the consensual orientation of the *jikkō-kumiai* membership *within the context of the jikkō-kumiai*. Certainly, it is not clear who the "old men" were who objected so strongly, at least not as clear as who was opposed to purchasing the new *seimaiki* by means of assessments on members. And all the men who met that evening were not actually old. Although most of these "old men" are, in general, retired household heads with mature successors in their families, several of the men who attend the *shinjinkai* meetings are still active household heads and were participants in the decision to purchase the *seimaiki*.

Rather than accept at face value the statement that the old men rejected the proposal in either of its forms (as gift or loan) and that their mature sons could not go against their fathers' wishes, another understanding is possible. There was no meeting at which the proposal to use the *yōsan-kumiai* money was discussed. The entire matter was handled by the head of the *jikkō-kumiai* in just two or three days, and primarily by phone. The proposal was presented as a *fait accompli* to which real opposition was not clearly organized. "Railroading," running a proposal through before opposition has time to arise and form, is a common technique in Japan and elsewhere. In this instance, the *shinjinkai* gathering was the first meeting held in the hamlet at which the issue could have been discussed, and it was at this meeting that opposition, which could not be, or was not, expressed earlier, found reinforcement and surfaced.

The old men of the hamlet have the reputation of being hard-bitten, un-cooperative, and concerned more for their own selfish interests than for the "good of the hamlet." As a result, these old men are easily associated with such a seemingly arbitrary refusal. Furthermore, these old men are not answerable for their actions individually since they are not publicly identified except as a class. Neither are they capable of assuming responsibility for the refusal since they are supposed to be retired from public life and no longer active in or liable to hamlet offices.

The explanation that the old men rejected the proposal to give or loan money is not a complete explanation. The intervening variable in this case is that the old men, having discussed the proposal and found it wanting, then said as much to their publicly active sons, who in turn realized that they could not go against their father's (private) wishes in public. But all of this is by way of the shared remnants of Confucian culture, and there was no need to spell this out in public. The sons, who had earlier given an appearance of agreement, could still contend that they stood by their agreement while filially bowing to the wishes of their fathers.

Thus, while the appearance of solidarity and agreement was maintained within the group of *jikkō-kumiai* members participating in the decision to purchase the *seimaiki*, it remains unclear that there ever was an actual difference in values between generations. Any opposition, from whatever quarter and for whatever reason, to the use of the *yōsan-kumiai* money by the *jikkō-kumiai* for the purchase of the *seimaiki* could easily have found a home under the banner of the "old men."

Ultimately, the implicit argument that those hamlet members who con-tinued to raise silkworms until the early 1970s should pay a larger share in the purchase of the new *seimaiki* could not endure. I did not hear any argument raised to the effect that the group about to buy the *seimaiki* had any legitimate claim on the *yōsan-kumiai* money. The entire proposal was one of expedience and conve-nience designed to obviate the difficulty of assessments within the *jikkō-kumiai*. After only a moment's reflection and collective consideration, it was recognized for what it was. As a solution to one problem, and satisfying a few people in the short run, it was quickly seen to prove unworkable as a precedent for the long run. The primary objection raised to the proposal was that which is always ex-pected, that the last members of the *yōsan-kumiai* would ultimately end up subsi-dizing the consumption of hamlet members who had never even belonged to the *yōsan-kumiai*.

*(4) Incommensurability of Issues.* There is no evidence that there were issues facing the *jikkō-kumiai* during this period that might have been "traded off." The issue was treated on its own merits, and there is no evidence to indicate that those in opposition to different levels of assessments were ever approached to see what they might require in return for support of the proposal to purchase the *seimaiki* at any of the available levels of possible assessment.

*(5) Consent Criteria.* Before the ¥70,000 was discovered in the *kumiai* treasury, the question was, At what level of assessment could a new rice polisher be purchased? It was clear that there was no level that was satisfactory to all but a few members. That is, at any level of assessment, and in any grouping of members within the *kumiai*, several were simply unwilling to spend the money.

After the money was discovered in the treasury and the *yōsan-kumiai's* money was not made available, the issue became who had potential to benefit by the purchase. The argument of those who supported the proposal was not phrased in this manner, but it is clear that this was the issue. Although the defining criteria was constantly identified as membership in the *jikkō-kumiai*, which in turn is defined in terms of stock ownership, two members of the *kumiai* were never even asked to pay shares.

Within this broad framework of membership, the actual pair of conflicting interpretations was "people who do not polish rice should not have to pay" and "everyone who owns rice fields must pay." Only a few years earlier this distinction would have been both unthinkable and impossible because all hamlet members who owned rice fields either grew rice or rented them out and collected rice as rent.

There is a great difference between owning land and farming it, but only recently has this difference become apparent. As the family that once again began rice cultivation demonstrates, if a family has land and experience, it can always return to rice cultivation. Consequently, even if the prospects are remote that any of the other families that own rice fields will again grow rice, there is an extreme gap between those families who own rice fields, even if they do not cultivate them, and those families who do not, at least in terms of the interpretation of the potential of these two classes of families to ever benefit from the presence of a rice-polishing machine in the hamlet.

Thus, while virtually no families reenter wet-rice agriculture, that one might do so does not run counter to anyone's expectations. Indeed, the economic miracle of the past twenty years is still regarded as something less than a new and permanent reality (Dore 1978: 87), and the ability to grow a crop of rice is certainly held in higher esteem than the necessity of having to do so. The belief that "a farmer will never starve" still has currency in Nohara hamlet.

In this case, the interpretation of "who has the potential to benefit" is based on the fact that the hamlet will endure, along with the relationship among member families, and that the new *seimaiki* will last at least twenty years. At ¥1000 per share, it would be cheaper to pay a share if a family polishes more than twenty-five *hyō* (1500 kilograms) of rice within the twenty years the machine is expected to be in operation. An average family of six would consume this much rice in about two years. If a family takes its rice to a commercial facility, it would have its share back in only one year. Thus, it is clearly in the interest of every family that intends to polish this much or more rice over the life of the machine to pay a share in it and to see that any family with the same potential does likewise. Conversely, it would be in the interest of any family not now growing rice but that could conceive of polishing twenty-five *hyō* of rice over the next twenty years to hope that their failure to pay a share would be forgotten before the next machine is purchased, if one ever is.

Thus, any hamlet family that might polish more than twenty-five *hyō* of rice over the next twenty years must be expected to contribute a share in the purchase cost. And no family that owns rice fields can say that it will not polish at least that much over that period. It is clear to all *kumiai* members that farm families do not willingly divest themselves of their rice fields except at development prices, and therefore, they retain the immediate capability of resuming rice cultivation at any time. If these nonproducing families keep their rice fields as a hedge against an uncertain future, then those members of the *kumiai* who are currently producing rice must expect these other members to pay a share in the new machine as a hedge against their own future, however small that share might be.

*(6) Exchange Commitment.* This hypothesis predicts the level of organization at which exchange will take place and is relevant to this case in two ways. First, the purchase, made on the widest possible level of participation, was not possible before that level could be achieved. Second, the most expedient solution offered required cooperation from another structurally equivalent group, and exchange was not forthcoming.

Discussion was carried on at the level of the *jikkō-kumiai* as a whole and, with the exception of the two members who did not own rice fields, was implemented at this level. Smaller groups were proposed, but none were feasible. And despite the fact that these two members neither were included in the discussion nor paid shares, no comment was made by either those in favor of the purchase or those opposed to it on the nonparticipation of these members. The reason these two members were irrelevant has been discussed in the preceding section.

However, the superficially most satisfactory solution to the problem of assessments of shares was rejected outright. I do not know whether anyone who never belonged to the *yōsan-kumiai* was against using that group's money for the purchase of the *seimaiki*, but the last five families to stop raising silkworms in the hamlet, and who thus had the most obvious claim to the group's money, all were regular users of the old rice polisher. All five of these families also had retired household heads who regularly attended the *shinjinkai*. Consequently, while the families of both the head of the *jikkō-kumiai* and the head of the *yōsan-kumiai* were among these five families, it is clear that some of these families must have felt that they would rather pay the ¥1000 than risk loaning their part of the *yōsan-kumiai's* ¥20,000 to the *jikkō-kumiai*. And they would not permit the loan despite the fact that all of the families that had ever been members of the *yōsan-kumiai* were still members of the *jikkō-kumiai*.  Although one group was a complete subset of the other in terms of their memberships, they remained totally independent organizations within the hamlet.

(7) *Opportunity*.  Because the use rates would still be collected as before, the purchase of the new *seimaiki* would not provide any member with benefit directly.

(8) *Bifurcate Procedure*.  The issue of who did and did not have potential to benefit was finally settled when the opposition became extremely small.  As expected, all who had potential to benefit were expected to, and finally did, pay a share in the purchase.  After the installation of the new machine, all who wanted to polish their rice in the new machine did so at the rate appropriate to their status as members who had paid a share in the purchase price or as nonmembers.  The status of the two members without rice fields remains ambiguous, but neither of these two families ever used the old machine and were obviously not expected to use the new one either.

(9) *Overt Opposition*.  Overt opposition is seen in the refusal of the *yōsan-kumiai* to allow its treasury to be raided and in the statements of the three of four members who own rice fields but grow no rice.  Overt advocacy is much less apparent, especially with regard to the plan to raid the *yōsan-kumiai*'s treasury.  The *jikkō-kumiai* head would not admit to having originated the plan, and I found no one else who would either.

## Case 3:  Fire Pump

*Narrative*

Nohara hamlet took delivery of its new fire pump about six weeks after I took up residence in the hamlet.  I was not present at the meetings where the issue was discussed and decided.  The data presented in this case come from the minutes of these meetings kept by the hamlet head and from later discussion with hamlet members.

Nohara was the last of the ward's five large hamlets to purchase a modern fire pump.  In the early 1960s the ward bought a new fire pump and loaned its old hand-powered pump to Nohara hamlet.  A concrete-block building was then constructed in the hamlet to house it.

The hamlet had been discussing the possible purchase of a new pump for several years before the decision to purchase one was made; it had been a perennial topic that could not generate either sufficient support to be implemented or sufficient opposition to be abandoned. In early 1977 it was learned that the city had provided funds to another hamlet of similar size on the other side of town to assist in buying a pump. On further investigation, it was verified that the city did have money available to qualified hamlets.

The major qualification was distance from the nearest city fire station, and on this count Nohara clearly qualified: it had been a long-standing complaint in the hamlet that it took too long for city fire-fighting equipment to arrive. Two years earlier the hall of a neighboring hamlet caught fire and burned to the ground before help from outside the ward could arrive. The major purpose of such small pumps as Nohara wanted to buy, and the city was willing to help provide, is to keep a fire under control until the city fire department can arrive. When a wood-frame building of the type so common in rural and even urban Japan catches fire, these small pumps owned and operated by wards and hamlets cannot extinguish the blaze, but they can keep it from spreading.

The first entry in the notebook of the hamlet head concerning the fire pump is from a *gochōkai* meeting of 6 April 1977, to which the officer in charge of fire prevention was invited. A general meeting of the whole hamlet was called for 12 April.

The question of the purchase of the fire pump was the major issue of the 12 April meeting and was taken up last. A vote was taken on whether or not the hamlet should buy the fire pump, but it is not clear exactly how the question was phrased. The number of votes for and against the question was recorded in the personal memorandum of the hamlet head but not in the notebook given to the next year's head. This is a most uncommon procedure.

The memorandum records twenty-five votes for the purchase, one vote against the purchase, and two abstentions. One hamlet member who could not attend the meeting gave his approval to the hamlet head prior to the meeting, and the (at the time) five remaining hamlet members who did not attend the meeting and did not notify the hamlet head of their positions on the issue were recorded by name. The costs of hoses of various lengths, the amount of household assessment, and the entry "city assistance—¥120,000?" are also all recorded in the personal memorandum. Beneath these entries, the hamlet head added that the members should pay their shares to their respective *gochō* between the twenty-fifth and the end of the month and that the application for assistance from the city would be made through the office of the ward head (*kuchō*).

The reason a pump was not purchased sooner was the expense. The proposal to purchase the pump did not make progress in gaining support until it became known that the city would assist in the funding. There is no doubt that the issue always had considerable support within the hamlet, but that support was not growing over time. This is clear from the position taken on the installation of fire hydrants in the hamlet when city water was brought into the ward the previous year. When the plans for fire hydrants were made, none were located in Nohara. The installation of fire hydrants was an expense that the hamlet had to bear. Thus, we see that even two or three years earlier, when plans for the installation of water lines were being drawn up, it was considered unlikely that the hamlet would purchase a new pump in the foreseeable future.

On the other hand, the decision to purchase the pump was taken before it was definitely known that the city would provide financial assistance. As the hamlet head's memorandum indicates, the decision was taken only on the possibility of the city's assistance. But beyond this, the city would at best only provide about one-fourth of the total cost, ¥120,000 of the total purchase price of ¥540,000. This indicates that even before it was known that the city would provide assistance, the question was not whether a pump was desirable but how much the hamlet's members were willing to spend for a new pump. Taken together, this information shows strong, but not total, support for the purchase.

The final opposition was quite small, as expected, but a review of the totals in the vote does not fully accord with the number of households claiming membership in the hamlet at the time. The original ballot records twenty-five "for" votes, one "against" vote, two abstentions, and one prior approval. Of the five families not present, two were later found to be in support, two in opposition, and one abstaining. The thirty-fourth family was not living in the hamlet at that time but continuing to maintain its membership. This family was later informed of the decision by mail and asked to pay a share, which it did, but its opinion was not sought. This gives a total of thirty-five families at a time when there were only thirty-four members in the hamlet.

The discrepancy is the result of one woman, a widow who lives alone, having cast an abstention for herself and another for her daughter, who lives with her husband and two children next door to the widow. The final results of the vote on the purchase of the fire pump are, corrected, twenty-eight "for," three "against," two abstentions, and one family not consulted. Thirty-four shares were collected, one from each family.

At the meeting of 12 April the method of payment was settled by common accord. Each household would pay ¥5000 between the twenty-fifth and the end of the month for three months to their respective gochō (head of a five-family group). Through this method ¥510,000 (thirty-four households at ¥15,000 each) was raised. The remaining ¥30,000 was paid from the hamlet treasury.

The method of assessing each member one equal share was not applied without difficulty because there were entries and exits of families at the time. One family left the hamlet three months after the purchase was made, six months after the decision to buy the pump was taken. This family's share was refunded in

full from the hamlet treasury. About eighteen months after the pump was purchased, another family left the hamlet, and at the same time one family joined.
The family that left did not receive a refund, and the family that entered was not
asked to contribute. It was suggested in a hamlet meeting at that time that the
entering family be asked to pay a half-share in the cost of the pump, but this idea
was rejected on the grounds that if some money was collected from the entering
family, then some money should also be paid to the departing family. The matter
was then dropped.

The pump purchased was chosen on the recommendation and advice of the
city fire department, and this choice was ratified by the *gochō* at a meeting on 10
June 1977. The hamlet head signed the contract with the manufacturer on 8 July
1977, and the entire hamlet turned out to receive its new pump and instruction on
its operation and maintenance from the manufacturer's representative early in the
morning on 10 July 1977. It had already been agreed that each *goningumi* would
practice operating the pump in rotation on Sunday mornings for the six months
following the arrival of the pump, or until everyone in the hamlet, especially the
women and elderly, were competent in its operation. The hamlet head followed up
the paper work on the assistance from the city even after his term had expired,
and ¥120,000 was finally received from the city on 27 April 1978. This money was
not redistributed to the hamlet members but deposited in the hamlet's general
account.

I do not know the identities of those hamlet members who were opposed to
the purchase of the pump and voted against it (either those at the meeting of 12
April 1977 or those who later expressed opposition when the hamlet head called on
them). This question of identity is made more difficult because, just as in Case 2,
everyone with whom I spoke stated that no one was *really* opposed to buying a new
pump, that it was just a matter of money and that, after all, everyone did finally
pay a share in the purchase. Both of the families that later left the hamlet were
not present at the meeting of 12 April when the vote was taken, and both of them
were either for or against the purchase because one abstention belonged to the
family of the daughter of the woman who voted twice. It may have been these
two families that voted no because the two families that were not present at that
meeting but remained in the hamlet both told me that they had been for the purchase of the pump for many years. One family that voted against the purchase
remained in the hamlet, but the hamlet head told me that he was not at liberty to
give me the names of those who were opposed to the purchase: "If they want to
tell you, then they will, but since they paid like everyone else, I think that they
would rather have the matter forgotten now." By the time I was in possession of
the hamlet head's personal memoranda, the issue had already been settled for over
a year, and I did not pursue the matter of the identities of those in opposition to
the purchase further.

*Discussion*

(1) *Decision Mode.* An assessment of ¥15,000 was made on each member for the purchase of the fire pump, and the decision was taken by a formal vote with secret ballot.

(2) *Small Opposition.* The result of the secret ballot was twenty-five "for," one "against," and two abstentions. When discrepancies in the voting procedure are corrected for, and the opinions of those not present for the decision are taken into account, the final result was twenty-eight "for," three "against," two abstentions, and one opinion not sought. It is likely that two of the three hamlet members in opposition were planning to leave the hamlet. I do not know the identity of the third "no" vote and, therefore, do not know that member's reason for voting against the purchase.

(3) *Consistent Orientation.* While the major decision to purchase the pump by assessment was made by a division, all other subsidiary decisions (e.g., which pump to buy, where to house it, whether to return the money to the families leaving the hamlet and collect from the new family, and how to organize "pump practice") were taken informally without overt opposition to the courses of action finally implemented. Throughout the discussion over the years, the question never seems to have been whether or not the hamlet should buy a pump but rather how it should be funded and at what expense. And this matter was handled, albeit without the emergence of a widely supported plan, as a problem to be solved to the satisfaction of all (or almost all) hamlet members. The final solution, of course, made use of funds from the city, and this solution was acceptable to all but three of the hamlet's members.

(4) *Incommensurability of Issues.* I do not know what effect the discussion of the fire pump had on the decision not to purchase fire hydrants when the city water lines were planned and installed, but obviously the two were not "traded off" as commensurable items. And it is clear that hydrants were not installed as a way of lowering the costs of those who did not want to pay for a fire pump because it was not known at that time that the city had any resources to support the purchase. It was that information that made the decision to purchase the pump possible. All information that I was able to get from informants after the pump was purchased suggests that the discussion centered entirely on the relative merits of the presence of a pump in the hamlet against the expense of the purchase.

(5) *Consent Criteria.* All hamlet members' homes and buildings are liable to destruction by fire, and consequently, if a new fire pump is of benefit to any hamlet member, it is of benefit to all hamlet members. If the two hamlet members who were planning to leave the hamlet did in fact object to being assessed ¥15,000 to pay for a fire pump they would likely never use, then their objection

can be easily understood. But for all other hamlet members, there is no question of providing subsidies directly or indirectly to any other hamlet member. The assistance provided by the city seems to have been sufficient to persuade all hamlet members but one that they could afford their share of the purchase price.

(6) *Exchange Commitment.* The fire pump was purchased on the basis of hamlet membership, and each member paid one share in the expense. None of the ward's hamlets ever purchased fire pumps together. After Nohara hamlet bought its own pump, the old pump (which had been purchased by the village in the early 1920s) was returned to the ward and auctioned off to a member of the ward. Each hamlet operates its own fire pump, and the village fire pump is operated by young men appointed for that purpose from each hamlet.

(7) *Opportunity.* Discussion of this hypothesis in relation to this case is somewhat distorted insofar as a fire pump obviously does not provide benefit, but, like insurance policies, only lessens costs entailed in misfortunes. Thus, it is inconceivable that a fire pump could be of positive benefit to anyone. But a fire is a threat to everyone, and a fire pump is, thus, an asset to the entire hamlet and ward.

Precisely because fires are not accounted on the "positive side of the ledger" but only entail costs, use of the pump is not seen as an opportunity for benefit. When a fire breaks out anywhere in the ward, all hamlets bring their pumps as quickly as possible to keep the fire from spreading and even send a small sum of money "in sympathy" (*omimai*) to the family that suffered the loss. The fear of fire in Japan, especially after an earthquake, is a significant concern and a major incentive for cooperation in hamlets and wards.

(8) *Bifurcate Procedure.* Every family with the potential to benefit (or, strictly speaking, have its costs lowered) was expected to share in the purchase of the fire pump and did. Likewise, all families are expected to send all able members to help fight any fire that might break out in the ward. There is, of course, no question of benefit, other than the expectation that any fire in the ward will be fought with the same intensity as any other. Even ostracism does not preclude assistance with fires, and this is no doubt primarily because any fire not immediately extinguished can spread rapidly and reduce an entire neighborhood.

(9) *Overt Opposition.* Like so many other issues settled in this hamlet, its origins are prior to my arrival, and informants do not provide information or seem at all interested in who, exactly, originated any proposal. This is especially true in this case since it concerns an issue of importance to all hamlet members. One might suspect those with the most valuable homes and the largest incomes to be the most interested in securing a pump for the hamlet, but such speculation cannot be verified after the fact.

It is only because there was opposition to an assessment that the pump was not purchased before the assistance made available by the city became known. What is difficult to comprehend, however, is that the city's contribution would have been enough to sway anyone. The city would not, in any event, provide more than ¥120,000. Divided by the thirty-four member households, this amount would reduce each family's share by ¥3500. In 1977 there were no families in Nohara to which this sum would have been a significant amount in contexts other than cooperative purchases in the hamlet from which they themselves could not benefit.

We must also consider that the share of the three families in the hamlet that were opposed to the purchase at the end of discussions amounted to ¥45,000, or about ¥1450 per family if distributed over the remaining thirty-one families. In other words, without the city's contribution, which was never redistributed to the member families anyway, the share per family would have risen only from ¥15,000 to ¥18,500, or by only 13 per cent.

The principle operating in the distribution of shares is that all who have the potential to benefit must absorb a share in initial costs. We can then see that the contribution of the city to the total purchase price, while significant in itself, was primarily a catalyst for renewed effort on the part of those families that wanted to purchase the pump even without the city's support. In effect, the city's contribution made it impossible for those on the fence to remain neutral any longer. As a result, thirty-one member families could indicate to the remaining three families that they were prepared to remove them from the hamlet for a mere ¥1450 each and ask if those three families were willing to leave the hamlet rather than pay a share in the new pump's purchase price. Conversely, opposition that continued after the city's support became known could only be interpreted as the refusal of a few families to allow the other hamlet families to take advantage of (corporately controlled) resources from outside the hamlet resource pool. In effect, those families that already supported the purchase of the pump even without the city's support saw that support as a way to lower expenses, rather than raise them, even though the purchase of the new pump would actually be costly.

Even in "traditional times," any family, even one under penalty of ostracism, could expect fire protection. Thus, there is no way that fire protection can be denied a family, even if it does not pay a share in that protection. Since this is true, it is all the more necessary that all families provide a share in those costs. Hence, any family that is unwilling to assume its share of fire protection costs, the most sensitive area of cooperative activity outside maintenance of the irrigation system, must only be acting in bad faith and, therefore, cannot be allowed to remain a part of the hamlet.

## Case 4: City Water

*Narrative*

Kawasemigawa ward celebrated the completion of the project to extend city water to the ward in the fall of 1976. Until that time, the ward had been entirely dependent on wells. This project involved five of the six hamlets of the ward and was undertaken entirely on local initiative and at local expense, with some minor financial assistance from local, prefectural, and national government agencies. The project required about ten years from start to finish.

Early informal discussion in the ward found sufficient support to justify a slightly more formal and comprehensive survey of opinion within the ward. A committee of residents was formed to examine the possibilities more closely in March 1972. Initial estimates for the project ran as high as ¥360,000 per household. This figure was lowered to ¥260,000 the following year, and to ¥210,000 after two years. This last figure was found widely acceptable and eventually became the final price per household.

A financing plan, worked out during the winter of 1975-76, achieved a high measure of approval within the ward. In the spring of 1976, the Water Lines Association (*jōsuidō-kumiai*, hereafter WLA) was formed in the ward, with each of the five participating hamlets as local chapters. The subscription rate was ¥50,000 per household, and in Nohara hamlet all member families joined at this rate.

Hamlet records for this period indicate that before the spring of 1976 only one hamlet meeting was called expressly to discuss this project. At this meeting the financial plan worked out by the committee formed in 1972, the Water Lines Committee (*jōsuidō-rinkai*, hereafter WLC), was presented. Prior to this meeting, the issue of the installation of city water was handled as general hamlet business. Between March 1976 and September 1976, however, the hamlet met as a body five times to discuss this issue, and there were several other meetings of the WLC, the ward council, and the hamlet *gochōkai* as well.

The general circumstances in which this issue is embedded must be clarified before a presentation of the contents of the minutes themselves can proceed.

(1) As a ward in the city, Kawasemigawa ward qualified for a low-interest loan from the national government. The initial ¥50,000 collected from each household, serving as each family's bond, was deposited in a commercial savings account. The interest on this account was used to pay the interest on the loan. A second loan, to cover additional construction expenses, was then taken out at the city Agricultural Cooperative by chartering hamlet WLAs as auxiliary branches of hamlet *jikkō-kumiai*. Through this manipulation of differential interest rates, an

overall savings of approximately ¥10,000 per family was secured. None of these financial resources were available to individual families, however, and this savings was only possible if the water lines were laid simultaneously by officially recognized organizations. The figure of ¥210,000 was all that each family paid, and there were no additional financial charges paid separately.

(2) Four different categories of water lines were installed. The city's plan for the entire area included the installation of a water main (honkan) to run under the entire eastern region of the city and service the three easternmost wards. The city itself financed the installation of this main.

Intermediate lines (chūkan) branch from the main at intervals throughout the ward. Three such lines service Nohara hamlet. From these intermediate lines, branch lines (shisen) run exactly three meters toward each house and end in a meter. Private lines (kojinsen) connect the branch lines to the plumbing of each house.

The intermediate lines, branch lines, and meters were paid for collectively through the WLA. The lines from the meter to the house were paid for individually by the homeowners. The figure of ¥210,000 covers only the cost of the intermediate and branch lines and the meters; it does not include the cost of having lines laid into the house.

(3) A high degree of participation by ward residents was assured from the beginning by extracting a promise from the city water department that no one could later install water lines from the intermediate lines without first paying the ¥210,000 fee. This agreement applies to houses already built and those that might be built in the ward. I was told that this promise has no expiration date and that anyone wishing to build in the ward in the foreseeable future will have to pay the fee. I do not know, however, to whom, the city or the ward, it must be paid. While I was in the ward, no new houses were approved for construction.

(4) This project was organized at the ward level because the ward is the officially recognized administrative unit within the city. But the most important aspect of the project, the financing of the installation of the intermediate and branch lines, was organized and administered by the individual hamlets. Only by handling the financing as a function of hamlet membership could the project be assured of success. But as a result, there are several members of each hamlet whose homes get water from lines for which they did not directly pay and who paid for lines from which they draw no water.

This anomalous situation arose from the local incongruities of hamlet membership and residence. The only hamlet in the ward in which residence and membership are consistent did not participate in the project. In all other hamlets, there are families that "live in the other hamlet," as this inconsistency is expressed locally. Hamlet members took on shares in their own hamlet's debt and not, when residence and membership failed to coincide, in the hamlet "in which they live."

Early in the preliminary discussion, it was suggested that the entire ward be reorganized to amend these discrepancies of membership and residence, but this proposal was rejected out of hand. Periodically, difficulties in organization and administration arise from this source in Kawasemigawa, and the suggestion that hamlet membership be "rationalized" is a perennial one. Few residents of the ward take this suggestion seriously, pointing in defense of the status quo to the ties of "association" (tsukiai) inherent in hamlet membership and to rights in hamlet membership that cannot be effectively transferred. Since World War II there have only been two changes in hamlet membership involving Nohara hamlet, and both of these families settled in the hamlet from "outside" in the postwar years. I was unable to locate in the entire ward even one case of an "old" family changing hamlet membership within the ward.

While the content of preliminary discussions remains obscure, by 10 March 1976 all thirty-six hamlet members seem to have indicated a willingness to participate in the project. At the annual hamlet business meeting, held 14 March 1976, several decisions were made:

1. Money would be borrowed from the agricultural co-op and from the "Lifestyle Improvement and Modernization Fund" (kindaika-seikatsu-kaizen-shikin).

2. All thirty-five hamlet families would subscribe to the WLA for ¥50,000 initially and at the end of each month pay ¥10,000 until the entire ¥210,000 was accumulated for each family.

3. The one hamlet family then renting would not be responsible for the installation of water lines to their rented house, and a family owning a house in the hamlet and claiming membership, but not at the time residing in the hamlet, would be required to join the WLA.

4. Those members of the hamlet not belonging to the jikkō-kumiai must sign a contract with the hamlet and jikkō-kumiai in order to participate in the loan from the Agricultural Cooperative ("nōkyō no kumiaiin igai no kata wa Nohara-gumi e kaiyakusho o ireru koto").

After a meal, taken in the hamlet hall when the ujigami shrine was cleaned on 4 April 1976, a number of points concerning the project were considered, and all were deferred to the gochōkai meeting held that same evening. At that meeting the gochō adopted the following resolutions:

1. All money would be collected by the tenth of every month and placed in an account in a commercial bank. This account would be handled by the hamlet.

2. A hamlet seal (*inkan*) would be made.

3. The hamlet head would make out the deposit slip and hold the passbook.

The hamlet head duly secured a hamlet seal a few days later.

At a *gochōkai* meeting held about a month later (5 May 1976), however, much of what seemed already resolved had to be reconsidered. Among other things, it was decided that the "modernization loan" would not be used and that everyone would pay as much of the debt out-of-pocket as he could. Further, it was decided that the hamlet would loan money to any member absolutely unable to pay his share. These three points served as recommendations from the *gochō* to the hamlet council, which met in special session three days later. I was unable to discover who was opposed to borrowing money from the "modernization fund."

It was decided at this special meeting of the hamlet council that since they were not going to borrow from the modernization fund or the Agricultural Cooperative, they would not have to form a special group expressly for the purpose of securing a loan within the *jikkō-kumiai*. It was also decided that two hamlet members would take on the assignment of searching out alternative sources of credit. Also, the conditions under which hamlet members would be loaned money from the hamlet treasury were spelled out in greater detail: the hamlet would advance money only to those members "absolutely without means (*dō ni mo komaru hito*) unless a sufficient number of members felt strongly opposed to doing so (*kono hyō wa hantai no kyōryoku na hito ga sūjin de dame ni natta*)." All members should, however, pay as much as possible out of their own pockets.[3]

These decisions, the product of initiatives from within the hamlet, soon came to nought. Investigation into other sources of credit was prompt. Within two days it was reported to the *gochōkai* that the hamlet itself could not get a loan and could not become a legally recognized entity (*hōjin*). Furthermore, no individual member of the hamlet was able to stand surety for such a large loan from a commercial facility. The Agricultural Cooperative was able constitutionally only to transact business with either its local branches or individual members. This *gochōkai* meeting lasted from 8:00 P.M. to 12:30 A.M. and ultimately concluded with a return to the original plan of forming an association within the Agricultural Cooperative and borrowing money from the modernization fund.

The ward council and WLC met on the following night, 20 May 1976, to discuss the construction company's request for one-third of the final cost for expenses related to work already completed.  To this end it was agreed that all of the hamlets would draw up the necessary charters and attempt to get an advance loan from the Agricultural Cooperative as quickly as possible.  A delegation was to be sent to the loan officer at the cooperative, and the city councilman from the ward was to take the matter up with city council.  The tenth of June was set as the date each household would pay ¥40,000, one-third of the ¥121,000.

One week later a charter, in accord with Agricultural Cooperative regulations, was produced.  At the meeting of the ward council and WLC on 29 May 1976, at which time this charter was presented, it was also decided that the city councilman and the ward head would try to negotiate with the construction company for a lesser amount (¥20,000 to ¥30,000 per household) or a slightly longer period of payment.  These negotiations were to be carried out through the city water department on 31 May.

The negotiations were at least partially successful.  On 3 June 1976 a special meeting of the hamlet council was called to discuss the problem of installation of water lines into individual homes and to make applications for the transfer of funds from one account to another for payment to the construction company.  The ¥40,000 could not be reduced, but the payment was deferred for three months.  The ¥40,000 was to be raised as follows:

1.  Each family would withdraw ¥20,000 from the account into which they had all been paying ¥10,000 per month.

2.  The June payment of ¥10,000 would be added to this ¥20,000.

3.  The hamlet treasury would advance ¥10,000 to thirty-four of the thirty-six hamlet households.  This loan was to be only for the month of July and returned to the treasury with the August installment.

One of the families that did not receive this loan from the hamlet treasury was the family living away from the hamlet.  This family was informed by mail that a ¥20,000 payment, rather than the usual ¥10,000 payment, was needed to cover the expenses of the construction company.  The other family that did not receive a loan from the hamlet was not then a member of the hamlet but was in the process of building a house in the hamlet.  This family was, however, a member of the Nohara WLA and had been regularly making payments from the beginning.

The application for an advance on the loan from the Agricultural Cooperative was also successful, and by the time the ward council next met, this money (¥40,000 per household) had been received.  This sum was one-third of the total loan received from the cooperative, but it was in the form of an additional short-term (three-month) loan and was to be repaid in September.  By 24 June 1976, the arrangements with the hamlet *jikkō-kumiai* were finalized, and the loans from the Agricultural Cooperative and the modernization fund were taken out. The hamlet head and two members of the hamlet WLC served as cosigners.  (These three men also had signed the original documents establishing the WLA in the hamlet.)

On 19 July the ward council and the WLC met to discuss provisions for the installation of lines (*kojinsen*) into private homes.  It was reported that the loan would be ready by 1 August, and construction of the branch lines up to the meters was almost completed.  The six provisions relevant to the installation of private lines, taken from the minutes of this meeting, are as follows:

1. In so far as private lines are concerned, in principle each hamlet will see to its own affairs.  Acceptable water line installation companies will be limited to those designated by the city, however, because each person is free and there is the possibility of acquaintances and relatives being involved.

2. Everyone will get detailed estimates from these companies and do comparative research on each enterprise.

3. Everyone will properly enter into his own contractual relations.

4. Continued use of internal plumbing connected to wells is absolutely forbidden.

5. When tying into existing plumbing, pressure should be checked and certified as acceptable (free).  However, if there is a leak, the expense of the repairs lies with the individual.  It should pass inspection after the repairs.  (City recommended faucets:  ¥3000 and up; regular faucets:  ¥700–1500.)

6. Absolutely no exposed pipe outside or under homes.

After discussion of these provisions, the problem of two families in the ward that were unable to keep up with the payments was considered.  The problem of these (and other) families was left to their respective hamlet.  It was also decided that the ward treasury would pay for installing lines into the ward hall. The last item in the minutes recommends that the individual hamlets meet as soon as possible after contacting suitable installation companies to discuss and settle the matter of individual lines.

In Nohara, the meeting to discuss this matter was held on 24 July 1976. Two further issues of monthly financing arrangements were also taken up. The first was the question of the hamlet member who could not keep up with the payments, although he had subscribed to the original association at the ¥50,000 rate along with everyone else. The head of this family had been involved in an industrial accident at his foundry, which he operated in the hamlet. A few weeks prior to this meeting he had moved across town with his wife to convalesce and .later entered the hospital for an extended stay. He notified the hamlet head that he could not continue to make payments because of his hospital expenses. He was self-employed, without sufficient medical and hospitalization coverage, and unable to work during the entire period of his recuperation, about eight weeks. His wife, too, was an invalid. They were childless and in middle age.

This family's hamlet membership had always been somewhat precarious. He did not own land in the hamlet, did not have any relatives in the ward, and was not engaged in agriculture. In 1969 when he applied for membership in the hamlet (with the sponsorship of the hamlet member from whom he rented land), there was some protest against admitting him: it was suspected that he was joining merely because of the advantages it would provide his business. He was finally admitted as a hamlet member, but this point emerged again when discussion of his possible default was taken up.

This case was one of the two taken up at the ward council meeting of 19 July that were referred back to the hamlets. The conclusion of the hamlet discussion was to have the hamlet head visit this man and find out precisely how much money he needed to continue his payments and what his intentions were. The case seemed to fall under the provision of making loans available to members absolutely without means to continue their payments. The minutes do not record this man's response, but at the *gochōkai* meeting of 7 August, it was decided to loan him the money he needed from the hamlet treasury. By the time I became aware of this case, he had returned from the hospital, rebuilt his foundry, and fully repaid the hamlet's loan.

This is not to say that the decision to loan this man the money was not without controversy, but merely that the minutes do not record anything but the conclusions of deliberations. The position adopted earlier by the hamlet was that loans were not unconditional and could be denied if there were sufficient objections to any individual application. The hamlet, as the WLA, would then be liable for the unpaid balance if a subscriber defaulted. Consequently, what the hamlet had to decide was the intention of a member, whether he was truly unable to continue payments or simply cutting his losses. By 7 August the hamlet would have been liable for ¥120,000 for any member who ceased payments. And what the hamlet had to judge, then, was the chances of any member (so badly off that it needed a loan) repaying a loan from the hamlet.

Another case involving monthly payments was also taken up at this meeting. The man in this case owned a house in the hamlet but did not farm. He came to the hamlet directly after the war and had worked, until he retired in the late 1960s, for a company in the city. In 1970 his son moved to a nearby town and built a house there. In 1977 this elderly man joined his son in his new house. The house in the hamlet owned by this man sat vacant from the time he left the hamlet until at least the fall of 1979, when I left the hamlet.

At the time the capital for this project was being raised, there was some question as to whether or not the old man would leave and join his son, or whether his daughter and her family would return to the hamlet and live with him in his house.  As it turned out, the old man and his wife did not leave the hamlet until two years after the lines had been installed. The question taken up at the meeting was whether this person should be expected to maintain his installments, and it was resolved that he should since he owned the house. There is no further mention of this matter in the hamlet minutes, and the records indicate that he continued to pay his installments regularly.

A further issue resolved at this meeting was that the hamlet hall would get its water from the house next to the hamlet hall.  This household was not a member of Nohara hamlet, and it was agreed that the hamlet would pay for the installation of the lines from the meter to the house and one-half of the basic monthly water bill, about ¥2400 annually.  A provision was included that if there was a later rate increase, the matter would be renegotiated.

### Discussion

(1) *Decision Mode.*  The materials of this case were gathered from two to three years after the fact, and the data on this point is inclusive.  Because assessments were required, the model predicts a division.  But the hamlet head's notebooks and minutes, which become part of the records of the hamlet and pass from hamlet head to hamlet head, do not record votes, or divisions, only the results of decisions.  Discussion with informants on this point does not clarify matters:  on the one hand, a very common response is to suggest that no one was "really opposed" to the final course of action; on the other hand, it is widely recognized that "a few people always disagree with everything."

(2) *Small Opposition.*  There is no conclusive data available on this point.

(3) *Consistent Orientation.*  Without data indicating whether a decision is made by division or unanimously, no discussion of this hypothesis is possible.

(4) *Incommensurability of Issues.*  While it is clear that there was a decision made and implemented in this case, there is no data indicating involvement of this issue with any other.

(5) *Consent Criteria.*   Discussion of data relevant to this hypothesis is taken up in the discussion of Hypothesis 8, Bifurcate Procedure.

(6) *Exchange Commitment.*   Although the municipal and national governments, as well as the Agricultural Cooperative, could not deal directly with the ward's hamlets, to the greatest extent possible this project was organized by hamlet members around hamlet membership.  This is clear from three facts:

1.  Although the project was ostensibly a function of the ward and the local *jikkō-kumiai,* one whole hamlet did not participate.

2.  Suggestions to organize by residence rather than hamlet membership were completely rejected.

3.  In Nohara, in order to avoid including hamlet members not belonging to the *jikkō-kumiai,* an attempt was made to discover sources of financing for hamlet members as hamlet members rather than as special *jikkō-kumiai* members.  When it became apparent that the hamlet itself could not secure a loan, those hamlet members not belonging to the *jikkō-kumiai* had to sign an explicit agreement with the hamlet and *jikkō-kumiai.*   But despite the fact that the financing was ultimately handled through the *jikkō-kumiai* and Agricultural Cooperative, all decisions were made by the hamlet council, and the collection of installments was handled as a function of hamlet membership.

(7) *Opportunity.*   Only the branch lines and feeders up to the meters were installed collectively.  It remained the responsibility of each household to install lines into their homes at their own expense.

(8) *Bifurcate Procedure.*   To the extent that any family in the hamlet could benefit, all families could.  Consequently, all families in the hamlet were required to, and ultimately did, participate in the provision of water lines into the hamlet. The criteria under which the hamlets, through the ward office, could apply for the modernization loan were all collective criteria: (1) local well water was susceptible to pollution from pesticides; (2) the area is drought prone; and (3) the ward is in the middle of the quasi-national park, and the danger of fire is great because of the dry pine forests in the surrounding hills and large numbers of hikers using the park trails.

The question of how to prevent "free riders," and hence guarantee participation of all hamlet members, was settled by agreement with the city water department.  All members paid equal shares in the first, collective, phase of the project.  In the second phase, only those members who paid in the first phase were able to participate in the second.  This participation, in the form of installation of lines directly into private houses, was considerably less than total:  by the fall of 1979, eleven families in Nohara hamlet had not yet installed water lines into their homes and continued to rely on their wells.

*(9) Overt Opposition.*   The available data does not indicate any overt opposition or advocacy.  The three cases in which the participation of ward families was in doubt are not based on opposition to the installation of water lines into the ward and hamlets on grounds other than inability to pay and take advantage of the opportunity.

## Case 5:  Fire Extinguishers, Gas Rings, and a Rice Cooker

*Narrative*

As a result of three separate decisions, two new fire extinguishers, a gas ring, and a rice cooker were purchased by the hamlet.  All three decisions were taken unanimously, or at least without overt objection, and all three purchases were made with funds already in the hamlet treasury.  In each case, the proposals to make the purchases were taken up first with the *gochōkai*, and on its recommendation in the form of motions by the hamlet head to the assembled hamlet membership, these recommendations were ratified by the hamlet membership meeting as the hamlet council.

When meals are taken in the hamlet hall by large numbers of people (more than about twenty), a delicious flavored rice dish (*gomokugohan*) is prepared and served in the hall.  Until June 1978 the rice was cooked in a large iron kettle over a wood fire in the kitchen.  The kitchen itself is a rather recent addition to the hamlet hall (December 1976), and before the kitchen was built, the rice was cooked outside.  After moving the kettle and fire indoors, however, it was quickly discovered that the kitchen was not well ventilated.  Both the kitchen and the hall would fill with smoke, and even with the windows and door open, tears and coughing were common.  This inconvenience was borne with bad jokes and something less than good humor for about eighteen months.

In general, opinion has it that rice cooked over a wood fire is more delicious than that cooked with either gas or electricity because it cools more slowly.  The convenience of smokeless cooking won out over good-tasting rice, and the demand for a new rice cooker took root.

The discussion in the meeting of the whole hamlet concerning the rice cooker was extremely brief.  Much of the meeting had already been devoted to an extended but inconclusive discussion of the feasibility of widening a hamlet path into a paved road.  The matter of the rice cooker was finally brought up by the hamlet head who, referring to his written agenda, stated that at the last meeting of the *gochōkai* it was recommended that the hamlet buy a rice cooker and that the decision be made as soon as possible.  He then circulated a manufacturer's brochure on which the model selected by the *gochōkai* had been circled.  He continued that the model circled was the one recommended by the *gochōkai*, that although its list price was ¥30,000, it could be purchased for ¥22,000 cash, and that it cooked rice for up to forty people at a time.  He then opened the matter for discussion.

What little discussion took place was primarily concerned with the advisability of purchasing additional gas bombs, which could be refilled, to insure that they would not run out of propane at a bad moment.  After about a five-minute discussion, several voices close to the hamlet head began to urge *"sansei, sansei"* (approval), and with that the hamlet head then said, "Well, what does everyone think?  Who is in favor of making this purchase?  Let me see the hands of those who are in favor."

During the discussion of the rice cooker most of the hamlet members had continued to talk among themselves in small knots around the room about the issue of the road, and few had paid any attention at all to the change of topics.  The hamlet head had difficulty in obtaining sufficient order in the room to get a response to his question on the rice cooker, and so Koichi, who had been sitting near the hamlet head and urging approval of the purchase, turned to the room and yelled, "Everybody be quiet for a moment.  We're trying to get a decision on the rice cooker."

Hearing this call for attention, Akira's mother, who had still been discussing the road issue with her back to the front of the room, turned and exclaimed, "Oh, the rice cooker, Is this the hands for or against?  If it's the hands for, then count me in, I'm definitely in favor of getting it."  And she began waving her hand around vigorously and laughing loudly.  But the room remained unsettled, and no count was taken of those who raised their hands in favor of the purchase.  Most continued to talk about the road, although in rather lower voices.  The hamlet head then said, "Well, then, is there anyone who is opposed to the purchase?  Let me see your hands."  No hands were raised at all, but this did get a brief moment's silence while everyone looked around the room to see if any hands were raised in opposition.

There was nothing unusual about this decision at all, except for the fact that the woman who wanted very much to be included in the vote in favor of the purchase had been only moments before speaking adamantly in opposition to the proposal to widen the road.  As women are most often in the kitchen while rice is being cooked, there is no doubt that she was wholeheartedly in favor of the purchase.  The new appliance was purchased two days later, and it was unanimously agreed at the next hamlet meal that while the taste of the old rice was missed, the smoke was not.

The new gas ring also runs on bottled propane. Three years earlier the hamlet had received a stove as a gift. It was not a commercial grade appliance and was a little small for the preparation of meals for large numbers of people. Each time the hamlet prepared a meal in the hall, there was talk in the kitchen about how welcome a larger set of burners would be, and the question became an item on the *gochōkai* agenda in July 1979.

Mrs. Tanaka, who was attending the meeting in place of her husband, had looked into the matter on behalf of the women of the hamlet and suggested to the *gochōkai* a particular model, a large set with two double gas rings of commercial quality. It could be purchased at the city Agricultural Cooperative store for ¥5000.

There was virtually no discussion of the need for such an item, and a few of the *gochō* commented that it was obviously a purchase the hamlet should make. Takeshi then suggested that the question would have to be put to the whole hamlet; it was beyond the powers of the *gochō* to authorize the purchase on their own. The hamlet head stated that since Mrs. Tanaka had been so kind as to investigate (*kenkyū*) the matter, the *gochōkai* would recommend its purchase at the next meeting of the whole hamlet. Mrs. Tanaka then repeated her description of the particular model she had admired at the cooperative and why that was just the model they needed. She was replaced at the meeting, some fifteen minutes later, by her husband.

The possible purchase of one or two fire extinguishers was also raised at this *gochōkai* meeting. The city had an annual program through which hamlets could purchase fire extinguishers to be placed in suitable spots around the hamlet. The city would subsidize one-third of the cost, and the list price of the model the city recommended was ¥12,000 per unit. This was a familiar program, and the hamlet had already bought one extinguisher, which hung in the entrance to the hamlet hall, three years earlier.

The notice from the city hall, along with its recommendation and an order blank, had arrived in the hamlet about a week before the meeting. (As with so many other programs subsidized by the city, the purchase was made directly from the retailer or manufacturer by the hamlet, and then the hamlet was reimbursed by the city upon presentation of the receipt and proper forms.) At this meeting the hamlet head brought up the question by saying, "Everyone is familiar with this program, so should we go ahead and get another one?" There was very little discussion about whether an extinguisher ought to be purchased. Rather, most comments were directed to possible locations for the new unit. Tanaka, who had replaced his wife by this time, suggested that the *gochōkai* should defer to the whole hamlet the decision to purchase, and Maeda suggested that the matter be brought up when the hamlet met a few days later, 15 July 1979, to clean the hamlet shrine. These two suggestions were agreeable to everyone present.

Before the members of the hamlet began cleaning the shrine, a brief meeting was held to organize the work itself and to take care of the issues of the fire extinguisher and gas ring. The hamlet head simply stated that the *gochō* recommended that two fire extinguishers be bought from money in the hamlet treasury and the decision on where to put them be deferred until the new extinguishers were received. Since application forms had to be returned before the end of the month, if it was satisfactory, he would go ahead and take care of the matter. There was no objection from any of the hamlet members present, but some discussion was raised concerning the locations of the new units. The hamlet head also asked the hamlet members to ratify the recommendation of the *gochōkai* concerning the purchase of the gas ring, and again there was no objection. A few voices suggested that it was about time that they got the new gas ring, and most of these voices were female. There was no further discussion of either of these issues.

*Discussion*

(1) *Decision Mode.* All three purchases were made with funds already in the hamlet treasury, and all three decisions were made unanimously.

(2) *Small Opposition.* This hypothesis is not relevant to unanimous decisions.

(3) *Consistent Orientation.* As the fundamental orientation of decision makers in this context is consensual, and there was no defection in these cases, the orientation did not change.

(4) *Incommensurability of Issues.* There was no evidence in any of the discussions or meetings concerning these purchases that anyone's support was gained other than through an appeal to the merits of the proposals alone.

(5) *Consent Criteria.* As these purchases were demonstrably "for the good of the hamlet" (*kumi no tame*) and required no assessments of private resources, there were no objections.

(6) *Exchange Commitment.* The assumption that any group other than the hamlet would or would not make these purchases was never put into question.

(7) *Opportunity.* The rice cooker and gas rings, of course, make preparing meals in the hamlet hall more convenient and the taking of the meals more pleasant. These values distribute to hamlet members only in so far as they participate in the affairs at which these facilities are used. The fire extinguishers have the same objective properties that the fire pump (Case 3) does insofar as opportunity and benefit are concerned.

(8) *Bifurcate Procedure.* Everyone in the hamlet hopes that the fire extinguishers are a total waste of money but believes that they will be better off with

them than without. Like the fire pump, fire extinguishers cannot provide benefit but merely lessen potential loss. But in order to benefit from the cooking facilities, it is necessary to participate at hamlet functions at which they are used. Benefits only accrue to individuals to the extent that they forego alternative opportunities and attend hamlet functions.

(9) *Overt Opposition.* There was no overt opposition to any of these proposals, and advocacy of the purchase of the rice cooker and fire extinguishers could not be identified with any hamlet member. There is some doubt as to whether Mrs. Tanaka's "research" into the gas ring should be considered advocacy, but in any event, it is clear that her advocacy was not in support of one course of action in competition with another: the question of the desirability of the purchase had long been discussed in the hamlet hall kitchen whenever meals were prepared. Her advocacy seems much more to have been for a specific model and based on her expertise—an expertise that the male *gochō* lacked. In this regard, her advocacy is of the same order as that of Jiro in the *seimaiki* case; it is based on the objective superiority of the unit purchased and not an overt expression of her (certain) desire to see the hamlet purchase a gas ring.

### Case 6: The English Class

*Narrative*

This and the following case concern decisions made within Nohara and Usoda hamlet, respectively, but both are substantively about relations between hamlets outside the context of ward membership. Although these two decisions were made by single hamlets, their results had repercussions for members of several other hamlets. Both cases demonstrate the extreme difficulty hamlets have in joining in concerted action at other than the ward level when decisions are not made by the whole ward council.

After I had been living in Nohara for about five or six months, several people from different hamlets in the ward asked me to teach them or their children, or even distant relatives, English. I still entertained hope at that time of being able to attend meetings in hamlets other than the one in which I was residing and thought that perhaps an English class would put me in contact with people from other hamlets in the ward with whom I might not easily become acquainted. I had earlier come to know Takayoshi, an elderly gentleman from a neighboring hamlet whose hobby was the study of English, and broached my plan to him, asking his advice.

He immediately thought it a good idea and suggested that we take the matter up with the ward council to see if we could get the use of the village hall for the class. He himself had served on the ward council as a hamlet head several times and had been the ward head twice and the ward treasurer more than a dozen times since the war. I certainly had no reason to doubt that the course of action he suggested was the correct one.

In February 1978, however, the ward council informed him that it would not be possible to use the ward hall. There was worry about fire, accidents, and responsibility for the youngsters in the hall. Three members were opposed to the plan, although any one member of the council may veto any course of action taken up by the council. Takayoshi then suggested that we wait and petition the new council, which would form at the end of the fiscal year in about one month. He approached the new ward head on 13 March 1978. On 4 April 1978 the new council also refused to let such a group use the hall, citing the reasons given by the former council and adding that "if the council had business on the same night that a class was scheduled, then the ward head would have to ask Mr. Marshall for permission to use the hall. That would turn the proper order of things upside down and could not be permitted." At this point it was necessary to look for an alternative location for the class or abandon the idea.

Takayoshi and I attended the *gochōkai* meeting in Nohara on 14 April 1978 and explained our plan, hoping for advice and suggestions. Yumei, that year's hamlet head, had already heard of the plan at the ward council meeting earlier. Following our presentation, discussion by the *gochō* was brief: he concluded that as long as the number of students was quite small, it might be possible to secure the use of the Nohara hamlet hall. I explained as carefully as I could that I had not had the intention of asking for the use of the hamlet hall but merely for suggestions for possible locations. Keiichi replied that, in any event, it was a matter that would have to be taken up by the whole hamlet, not just the *gochō* and the hamlet head. There was to be a hamlet meeting on the following Sunday, and the matter could be taken up then.

Takayoshi was not permitted to attend the hamlet meeting held on 16 April, but I was given several minutes to make my petition. I confined myself to stating my plan for a class for anyone in the ward who wished to learn English. It would be free because I was not running a *juku* (private school) for profit and only wanted to repay some of the kindness that had already been shown to me by ward members, and I hoped for suggestions for a suitable location for such a class. The hamlet head then repeated my proposal and recounted the ward council's position and the results of the *gochōkai* discussion of two days earlier. Again, there was not much discussion, and only the *gochō* spoke. The hamlet head recommended that the hamlet allow the use of the hall for such a purpose, and while there was no direct objection raised, the position taken was that Yumei and I work out the details of a plan for the class and the use of the hall to present to the hamlet members later.

Two evenings later I met with Yumei to work out such a plan. He told me that the previous evening he had called some of the *gochō* to discuss the plan and suggested the following: (1) there must be some fee charged to cover expenses, and ¥500 per student per month would probably be adequate; (2) the mothers of middle-school students must send one of their number to each session to maintain order; (3) if the number of students became too large, the hamlet hall could not be used; (4) Takayoshi would be treasurer and fees would be paid to him; (5) sessions would meet from 5:00 P.M. on Tuesday evenings, with the length depending on the number of students and their skills and interests; (6) I was to prepare a circular that would be sent to each hamlet to get an estimate of the number of students who might wish to participate; (7) the students could use the benches stored in the attic of the hamlet hall, but they would have to clean them first; and (8) the circular would contain at least the above items.

During the day of 19 April, I prepared the circular as I had been instructed and went the following evening with Takayoshi back to Yumei for his suggestions or approval. He thought it satisfactory, and we went with the circular to consult two other gochō, Keiichi and Hirahito, on its form and substance. They too thought it satisfactory, and I was told to begin circulating it in the village's six hamlets. The hamlet heads were to be asked to include the circular with the other materials included in the hamlets' respective circulating notice board (kairanban).

During the course of that evening's discussion, Yumei suggested that if the number of students who signed up was too large, then we would be in a good position to return to the ward council and have them change their opinion. This tactic, designed to secure the ward council's approval, had first been suggested by Keiichi at the gochōkai meeting on 14 April.

On 20 April I took the circulars to each hamlet head and explained the proposal to each one, asking if he would place the circular in the hamlet's kairanban. Each said he would do so. On 1 May Takayoshi and I returned to collect the circulars. Yumei had brought the Nohara copy of the circular to me earlier in the day. Twelve people from Nohara had signed up, including Yumei, his wife, and daughter, who was a high-school stuent, Takeshi, his wife, and daughters in middle school. The six circulars contained a total of forty-three names, but no one from Kitabora hamlet had signed up.

That same evening Takayoshi and I attended another Nohara gochōkai meeting. After seeing the list of names, Keiichi said that it would be best if only the Nohara people were taught in the hamlet hall and that twelve people would be a good size for a class. He continued that forty-three people was far too many for a class and could never fit into the hamlet hall. Further, no one knew how many more people would want to join once the class began. Yumei again suggested that it would be best if everyone were kept together in one place. He explained to Takayoshi and me that the hamlet hall certainly could not hold more than thirty people and suggested that we once again take the matter up with the ward council.

The first order of business taken up at the hamlet council meeting of 3 May was the English class. Yumei again outlined the steps taken up to that point, and the reasons the ward council refused to allow the ward hall to be used. He continued, "At present, forty-three people wish to study English. Does anyone have any suggestions on what should be done?" The circular I prepared as made available for inspection and passed around the room for everyone to see.

Tsuneo, the previous year's hamlet head who had been in favor of allowing the use of the village hall when he was a member of the ward council, made the point that it would be to the hamlet's shame if, after having said that the class could be held in the hamlet hall, it was later refused. It seemed to him, he said, that the hamlet was now responsible to do what it could to provide a place for the class. Yumei responded that it was clear in the circular that if the number of people enrolled was too great, then the hall could not be used, and that everyone understood that this was the case from the start. It was not as if the hamlet was going back on its promise or changing its opinion. Tsuneo then suggested that if the classes were to be held in the Nohara hamlet hall, the treasurer should be a member of Nohara hamlet and not Takayoshi, who belonged to another hamlet. This comment drew widespread agreement from those present.

Taiichi, who had been the hamlet head the year before Tsuneo (1976-77), then said that, in his opinion, the real problem was what the hamlet would do if there was still no suitable location for the class after we took the list of probable students to the ward council and it again refused. There was no specific reply to this question, but a number of voices appeared to agree with his phrasing of the problem. One or two other comments were raised concerning the conduct of children, but these were not addressed to the hamlet head "or anyone in particular and were not responded to directly." Yumei finally concluded the discussion with the suggestion that the ward council again be petitioned, and if the petition was unsuccessful, a new plan developed.

The next morning Takayoshi and I discussed the previous evening's meeting and began to develop a new plan. He had no confidence that the ward council would agree to allow the hall to be used. As most of the middle-school students were from Usoda hamlet, we thought of dividing the students in half, with the middle-school students meeting in Usoda and the high-school students and adults meeting in Nohara. That evening I discussed this plan with a member of Usoda hamlet, a man who had been among the first to ask about teaching English to his eighth-grade son. He thought that there was a good chance that the members of Usoda hamlet would go along with such a plan. He suggested that the middle-school students could possibly use the Usoda hamlet hall on Saturday afternoons, and if the hall could not be used, he and his wife were willing to have the middle-school students (only) in their home on Saturday afternoons.

I spoke with Takayoshi again on 8 May. Two days earlier he had spoken again with the ward head about the use of the ward hall. The ward head said that although he himself was in favor of the idea, there were others on the ward council who were opposed, and he would not try to force the issue in any way. He also said that he had not yet spoken with Yumei, but he would tell him the same thing when they next met. About two weeks later I had a chance to talk with the ward *doboku*, the officer in charge of public works in the ward and a ward council member, and he apologized for not being able to make the ward hall available. He said that he himself was in favor of the class and that his own daughter had signed up, as I knew. But he indicated that while education was very important to most people, some members of the ward council had voiced the opinion that an English class was not something from which everyone in the ward could benefit, and therefore, the ward should not sponsor or allow its facilities to be used. It was clear that only about 50 of the over 1000 people living in the ward had any interest in studying English.

I then told Takayoshi about my conversation with the father in Usoda and his comments. Takayoshi suggested that we take it up with Yumei and the *gochōkai* before going to the Usoda hamlet head with such a plan.

The following evening I talked with Yumei about the refusal of the ward head to review the matter before the ward council and told him about my conversation with the man in Usoda and his new plan. He thought it was a good plan and immediately phoned the hamlet head of Usoda, who was not as sympathetic to the idea as he might have been, according to Yumei. He then called Takayoshi. It had come to him that because the ward used a field belonging to Takayoshi for its annual summer dance, *bon odori*, the ward should be more willing to allow the use of the hall by the organization of which Takayoshi would be the head (*kaichō*). I left on Yumei's encouraging note that if we just waited a little longer, until Takayoshi had again talked with the ward head, everything would work out for the best.

I met with Takayoshi again on 13 May, and we discussed the course of events up to that time. He had, by coincidence, been contacted two days earlier by the ward head about the use of his field for the dance that year, to be held about the middle of August. He did not, however, bring up Yumei's suggestion during that conversation with the ward head. He also said that he had no intention of ever doing so and certainly would not forbid the ward to use his field whether or not the English class could use the ward hall. He continued at some length:

> The two things aren't related at all. It was Yumei's idea, but there
> probably won't be a field there this time next year anyway because we
> are going to build our own hamlet hall there next spring. But now I
> finally understand what has been going on, what the position of the
> *gochō* has been from the meeting we went to back in April [the

*gochōkai* meeting of 14 April]. They don't want other people [people from the other hamlets] in their hall. Yumei kept saying the problem was only "numbers," and so they never had a chance to come out and say what was on their minds. Now, there are "too many" students, and the result is the same.

But if the plan is changed and there are only twenty-three students here [if twenty middle-school students go to Usoda and twenty-three high-school students and adults go to Nohara], then there will have to be more discussion. Of course, if Yumei decides the hall can be used, then people will have to abide by it because it is the hamlet head's decision. But with everyone's feelings against it, it is not very likely that he can go against everyone. Then he will be in the position of having to say "no" to the use of the hall although he had already said that the only problem was "numbers." So the real decision is whether or not outsiders will be able to use the hall. And if the answer is no here [in Nohara], it's not very likely that any other hamlet will allow outsiders to use their hall either.

What happened at the *gochōkai* meeting on 14 April is that the *gochōs'* true opinion never really came out. The meeting ended with both the *gochō* and the hamlet head agreeing that if there were too many students, then the hall could not be used. But the *gochō* really didn't want anyone from outside to use the hall, while Yumei thought that it would be all right.

Now Yumei wants to carry the *gochō* over to his opinion that outsiders can use the hall if there are only a few of them. But the *gochō* opinion, that no outsiders can use the hall at all, is likely to be the one that gets support from the rest of the hamlet. I will go and talk to the ward head again, but I don't think that there is much chance of getting the ward hall. So the possibilities that remain are for the middle-school children to be taught in Usoda and the others in your home, or drop the project altogether. Still, maybe something will turn up.

Takayoshi and I agreed to meet at my house on 18 May.

I was surprised when Yumei and Takeshi arrived with him, shortly after Yumei had asked Takeshi to intervene in the ward council decision in his capacity as ward treasurer. Takeshi claimed that there was really nothing he could do to sway the opinions of those who were opposed to allowing the hall to be used for an English class. He was also certain that there was no possibility of getting the ward hall and that it would be futile to ask again. After that, there was no further discussion of the possible use of the ward hall, and the talk turned to using the Nohara hamlet hall.

Takayoshi at first suggested that the middle-school children be taught in Usoda if the approval of that hamlet for the use of its hall could be obtained, but Yumei shook his head discouragingly at this idea. Takayoshi continued that we might leave the adults and older students out for the time being, but I said that this was not what I had had in mind and that people of all ages had asked for instruction. I mentioned the offer of the man in Usoda to use his house for the younger children and that it was possible, although not convenient, to have the others in my house. Yumei thought that this was the best idea yet.

At this point, Takeshi finally realized that it was not my intention to run a profit-making private school (*juku*). He reentered the conversation saying that he thought it best if everyone met in the same place, that we should press for the use of the Nohara hall, and that the suggested fee of ¥500 per student per month could be reduced further.

I then suggested that perhaps the same plan Takayoshi and I had developed for the use of the ward hall could be applied to the hamlet hall, namely, that the group could be divided into approximate thirds and meet in successive groups of middle-school students, then high-school students, and finally the adults, all on the same evening. Takeshi said he thought this was a good plan and that the only remaining problem was the allocation of responsibility, the naming of a *sekininsha* (the person who is formally "in charge"). He suggested that Yumei, as hamlet head, be the official *sekininsha* and that he himself would check and close the building at night and be responsible for the key to the hamlet hall.

With this, the conversation ended abruptly. There were a few inconsequential remarks about teaching materials, a blackboard, and the reduction of the fee, but these were left unresolved. Yumei then thanked Takeshi profusely for his help and left. After that, Takayoshi explained to Takeshi (who had not been present at two of the hamlet meetings because of ward affairs on those nights) everything that had previously transpired. Takeshi said that he would present the matter before the hamlet members at the next hamlet meeting, which was scheduled for 20 May.

During the course of this conversation the mystery of why no one from Kitabora hamlet signed up was also solved. I mentioned this in passing, and Takeshi said that he had talked with the Kitabora hamlet head just a few days before. The hamlet head indicated that he had no word from the ward head about the circular. Thinking that he should not circulate in his own hamlet something that seemed to be a private matter (meaning something not officially sponsored by the ward council) from another hamlet, he simply had not sent it around with the *kairanban*. Thus, no one in Kitabora except the hamlet head had even seen the circular.

But when I said that I would then go back to Kitabora hamlet and try to get a few people to sign up, all three men discouraged me, saying that I need not

bother.  If anyone there should hear about the class and want to enter, that would
be alright, but there was no need to get more people involved than there were at
present.  I no longer felt able to state outright that I was anxious to have people
from all hamlets participate, and in fact no longer had much hope that the end I
sought through the English class would, in any event, result.  I let the matter drop.

The hamlet meeting of 20 May was originally called to discuss the issue of
widening the road, but the matter of the English class was taken up first.  Yumei
opened the meeting and immediately yielded the floor to Takeshi, who presented
the circumstances and events relevant to the English class.  His emphasis was primarily on the two facts that there was no possibility that the ward would permit
the use of the ward hall for the class and that the hamlet should not let the opportunity slip by simply because a few people from other hamlets might be involved.  According to his own count, forty-seven people had signed up so far, and
by hamlet, Nohara had sixteen, Yanigida thirteen, Nishioka seven, Usoda eight,
Beniya three, and Kitabora zero.  Although enrollment for other hamlets remained
the same as on the circular, four people had been added to the Nohara total.
Takeshi had, over the past two days, recruited four adults for the class--Keiichi
and Hirahito, both of whom were *gochō* that year, Masanori, the cofounder of the
Hakusan-kai (along with Takeshi), and Kazuhiko, a younger member of the
Hakusan-kai who was particularly friendly with Keiichi.

Takeshi's plan, as he presented it to the hamlet membership, consisted of
the following points:

1.  Everyone should meet in the same place and on the same day.
2.  There were more adults from Nohara than from any other hamlet.
3.  There would be three groups in succession, and therefore no
overcrowding.
4.  Part of the fee (¥100 per student per month) would go to Nohara
hamlet to cover expenses and wear on the hall.
5.  Masanori would serve as treasurer and collect the fees.
6.  Takeshi himself and Yumei, as hamlet head, would be joint
*sekininsha*.

He then asked if there were any questions.  There were several.

Taiichi:  "If the hamlet head was to be the *sekininsha*, would the next year's hamlet head become the *sekininsha* too, even though it might be someone who had not
entered the class?"

Takeshi:  "No, Yumei and I will remain *sekininsha* as long as the class is in
operation."

Tsuneo: "What about the insurance? There was an article in the paper the other day about a hamlet hall that burned down near Toyohashi City, and they lost everything because they didn't have the right kind of insurance. Will the present policy cover the use of the hall by the class, or will we have to get more insurance?"

Takeshi: "Yes, the present policy will cover such use of the hall. And of course, only adults, most of whom are Nohara people, will be allowed to smoke."

Keiichi: "What about the mothers who were originally supposed to come and keep the kids in line?"

Takeshi: "That was the plan before and there is no reason to change it. But they will not have keys to the hall and will not actually be in charge of the hall, just the children's behavior."

Jiro: "Well, who will have the keys then? Who will open and close the hall?"

Takeshi: "Takayoshi, who lives just across the street, will open the hall in the afternoon, and he will get the key from the hamlet head just before class. Either I or the hamlet head will make sure everything is alright and close up the hall afterwards."

There was a long moment of silence, and then Takayuki asked about the possibility of having the class rotate among the several hamlets, meeting each week in a different hamlet hall. This question was not answered, and then a number of people began saying that Takayuki's idea was not very practical. If they could not come to a decision about the use of their own hall, it was not very likely that any other hamlet would allow the use of its hall.

At this point Koichi, who had told me that he too wanted to sign up but had not yet had the chance, said that it seemed that the problem was simply whether or not they would allow the use of the hall. Masanori added that there seemed to be sufficient support for the proposal, and the hamlet should loan the hall one night a week for an English class.

But a few voices, among which Tsuneo's was conspicuous, said that it was not all that clear that the support was there and that there should be more discussion. Yumei then called for the hands of all those who were opposed to loaning the club one night a week. But before those hands could be raised and counted, both Keiichi and Toshihiro simultaneously asked that the hands of those in favor be counted first. This motion was seconded loudly throughout the room, and Yumei then asked for the hands of all those in favor. After counting the hands, Yumei said that it certainly looked like enough people were in favor, but Tsuneo indicated that he had doubts and that it would be only fair to call for the opposition's hands as well. Yumei duly asked for the hands of those opposed, and two were counted. Masanori said that by his count there were twenty-five in favor and two against, with two or three not voting or undecided.

Takeshi then resumed leadership of the discussion, stating that by his count there were twenty-seven for, two against, and one abstention. No one disputed this count. He then went on to present for discussion several points relevant to the use of the hall:

1. In the case of scheduling conflicts, the hamlet maintained priority.
2. Each week, two adults from Nohara hamlet would be in charge of the children and the hall on a rotating basis.
3. The money from the fees would, in part, be put toward the insurance premiums.
4. The treasurer would have the final say in allocating the fees collected from the students.

As these points were being presented, they were approved with shouts of "no objection" (*igi nashi*), "I approve" (*sansei*), and smatterings of applause. All had been touched on, at least briefly, in previous discussion, and no objection was raised to any of them. Nor was there any further discussion of these points. I was then given a moment to thank everyone for their support and cooperation, and the meeting moved on to the next item on the agenda. The entire discussion and vote lasted approximately forty-five minutes.

The two men who voted against the proposal were the two most recent hamlet heads. Both objected strongly enough to have their objections recorded in a vote even after it was clear that the majority easily had enough support to implement the proposal. These two men were also the only members of the hamlet, other than the hamlet head, *gochō*, or Takeshi, who took an active part in the discussion of the several conditions under which the hamlet hall could be used.

The fact that this issue, the use of the hamlet hall by members of other hamlets, was without precedent makes it somewhat unusual. But the general question of the use of the hall was resolved and a precedent established in writing at the next annual meeting. It is recorded in the minutes of that meeting in the hamlet head's notebook that:

1. Concerning the use of the hamlet hall: In the case of businessmen seeking a profit, requests will be decided on by the hamlet officers. A written guarantee must be received. (*Kurabu no shiyō ni tsuite: Rieki o ageru gyōsha no baai, yakunin to sōdan no ue. Issatsu kaite morau koto.*)

2. As for the Women's Association's lessons in wearing kimono, admission of members of other hamlets is forbidden. (*Fujinbu kimono kitsuke kyōshitsu ni tsuite wa tagumi no nyūkai wa kinzuru.*)

It is recorded in the hamlet head's notebook that the council's approval for the use of the hamlet hall for the English class was secured, but there is no mention of the vote that occurred.

*Discussion*

(1) *Decision Mode.* The prediction of the model fails in this case. Only corporate resources are involved, and thus, unanimity is predicted. But a vote occurred. While the hypothesis is not confirmed in this instance, it is possible to show why this is the case through an ad hoc explanation.

Neither man objected on the grounds that he himself could not afford to participate or that he did not have the opportunity to benefit from the proposal. In fact, to the best of my knowledge, both men supported the proposal until the issue was decided. Tsuneo had a daughter in the sixth grade, and he later told me that he hoped that I would not mind if his daughter joined the class if I was still in the hamlet when she entered the seventh grade. Taiichi, who taught Japanese language in the local high school all of his life, earlier in the course of negotiations told me that he fully supported the proposal and that he regretted that he was too old to begin the study of English in the class. He did, however, have a son who had done postgraduate work at an American university, and he appreciated what I was trying to do for the children in the ward.

Both men had always been extremely helpful and cooperative informants both before and after this decision, and both offered to show me their personal memoranda they had kept while hamlet heads. In fact, it was primarily due to Taiichi's early support that I was able to study in Kawasemigawa ward at all. It cannot be supposed that the source of objection for either man was opposition to me or my research, or to the English class itself.

The actual source of their objection was their interpretation that the agreed rate of exchange was being altered for the sake of expediency. Their objections took the form of a statement that two issues were being linked in an unacceptable way: a decision already taken earlier in the year was being annulled in order to make the administration of the English class more convenient.

At the annual hamlet meeting two months earlier, it had been decided without overt objection that the office of hamlet treasurer would be created, and a man was installed in the office. The reason that the office of hamlet treasurer was begun was to remove continuing responsibilities for hamlet projects from the person occupying the office after his term was completed. But the proposal at issue required the current hamlet head to continue to be responsible for the English class even after his term in office was concluded. Both men objected to this aspect of the proposal, and both had been involved in issues that required their attentions after they were no longer hamlet head.

Both of these former hamlet heads took the occasion of this decision as an opportunity to communicate a message to the hamlet. The message was that they disapproved of the way the matter of responsibility for the hamlet hall was being handled, not of the use of the hamlet hall for an English class to which members of other hamlets might attend. But because the discussion prior to the vote did not alter the proposal that the current hamlet head remain responsible after his term in office had ended, they could only use objection to the entire proposal as the medium to express their objections to one limited aspect of the proposal.

They expressed their objections in the least "costly" manner possible, and there can be no doubt that this fact was known to all the other hamlet members as well, and in particular, Takeshi and Yumei. That is, they knew beforehand that their objection would be insufficient to prevent the hamlet hall from actually being used, and it was only after it became clear that Yumei was not going to be able to separate his role as a member of the class from his role as hamlet head that they objected publicly. Neither man could expect to serve again as hamlet head because of the length of the rotation period. But because both had recently been hamlet heads and because issues that were taken up during their respective terms in office had prompted the creation of the office of hamlet treasurer, both felt that they had the duty to speak up in this matter affecting the "good of the hamlet." They were able to "make a point" without affecting the status of the proposal and, at the same time, to act in a way that showed they were only thinking of the good of the hamlet over the long run.

*(2) Small Opposition.* Although no opposition at all was expected in this decision, there was opposition and a formal division. The opposition, however, was small—two of the thirty-five members of the hamlet.

*(3) Consistent Orientation.* It is difficult to state unequivocally that defection was involved in this issue and its resultant decision by division. However, to the extent that Tsuneo and Taiichi supported the proposal to create an office of hamlet treasurer—and both did support the proposal strongly—there can be no doubt that they felt that their efforts at straightening out the lines of responsibility within the hamlet were about to come to nought. Having made their objections in public, however, both men seemed content with the ultimate result, and there is no evidence that either man reoriented his perspective on the hamlet decision-making process or that the stand taken by either of these men on this issue caused other hamlet members to regard either man differently in any regard.

*(4) Incommensurability of Issues.* In his attempt to resolve the issue at the ward level, Yumei did make a proposal that two issues, the English class and the

ward's *bon odori,* be linked. This proposal was not taken seriously by any of the other parties concerned.

The objections raised by Tsuneo and Taiichi were not an attempt to link two issues in their mutual resolutions but an attempt to prevent a decision taken earlier from being overturned for mere expediency in the present issue.

(5) *Consent Criteria.* It is precisely because the consent criteria given by the model are satisfied in this case that unanimity is predicted. That is, while this particular hypothesis is confirmed in this case, the decision mode did not follow as predicted. The conclusion is unavoidable that the proposal to allow the English class to use the hamlet hall would not involve any costs for either of these men, and neither would their objections. But had their objections involved any cost, especially if their objections had prevented the proposal from being implemented, then they would not have objected. As it resulted, both men were able to appear "public minded" without involving anyone in any costs not subsumed in the original proposal.

(6) *Exchange Commitment.* The source of objection during all stages of negotiation for the use of the hamlet hall was that members of other hamlets would be using the hall. That the proposal finally passed was due primarily to the fact that control of the administration of the class would be a function of the hamlet itself and not pass to members of other hamlets.

(7) *Opportunity.* My original proposal that the class be free was completely rejected on all sides. Ultimately, while corporate resources were used to create the opportunity, the money collected from the students ended up in the hamlet treasury.

(8) *Bifurcate Procedure.* See Hypothesis 7. The class was entirely voluntary, and anyone in the ward who wanted to attend and paid the fee could do so. The corporate resources of the hamlet were ultimately employed on a rental basis.

(9) *Overt Opposition.* Overt opposition occurred although it was not predicted. There also was overt opposition among the *gochō.* But Takayoshi, Yumei, and Takeshi were also overt advocates of the proposal. There is no doubt that if members of other hamlets had not been involved, there would have been no overt opposition, no difficulties with control over the administration of the class, and no overt advocacy.

## Case 7: The Usoda *bon odori*

*Narrative*

This case involves a decision taken in the Kawasemigawa hamlet of Usoda, and I did not hear of the decision until its effects were apparent. This case, as was the previous one, is primarily concerned with relations between hamlets and the relations of individuals to hamlets other than the one to which they belong.

Relations between hamlets are never smooth. In the main, they are confined to the ward level and dealt with in the ward council. Issues dealt with by the ward council generally involve all of the ward's hamlets. It is difficult to collect data on relations between only two or three of the ward's hamlets in interaction precisely because examples are extremely rare.

In 1976, Nohara and Yanagida hamlets jointly sponsored a *bon odori*, but because of mutual accusations of mishandling of funds, unfair divisions of labor, and general irresponsibility, they were unable to repeat the next year. In 1977 and 1978 the dancing and other festivities were sponsored by the ward council and the ward *kodomokai* (Children's Association) for all ward members. The presidents of the *kodomokai* acted as chief administrators in both years, but the ward was almost unable to have the dancing in 1979 because neither past president would release the previous year's accounts to her successor. Finally, however, the Wakaba, the Women's Softball Association, along with the support of the ward council, was prevailed upon to undertake the organization of the *bon odori*. The ward council does not organize the event but merely sanctions it and authorizes the temporary use of ward funds, which are later repaid through donations made to defray the cost of the dance.

Usoda, the largest of the ward's six hamlets, holds its own *bon odori* on the two successive nights following the ward dances. This hamlet's dance is sponsored by its *seisōnenbu*, the Young Householders' Association, men from thirty to forty-five years old. They have been holding their dance annually since 1976, and I was able to attend the dances of 1977, 1978, and 1979. No other hamlet holds a dance of its own.

These dances, both that of the ward and that of the hamlet, are said to be primarily for the children. Many of the women enjoy the dancing as well, but men rarely dance. The first year I attended the Usoda *bon odori*, I saw few men dancing, and those few only after they had had a few drinks. Of the many women dancing, however, I recognized only a few from other hamlets. I had only, however, been living in the village a few months, and I did not know many women by sight from hamlets other than the one in which I was living. I recognized several men from hamlets other than that sponsoring the dance, but none of them were dancing. The crowd, from 200 to 300 people, was only slightly smaller than that of the ward dance.

By the next year, however, the men of Usoda hamlet had formed a softball team within the *seisōnenbu* and wore their softball uniforms, each with "Usoda" written across the front. That year the men did dance in the innermost circle around the central drum tower (*yagura*), and the women and children danced in

two circles further from the center. Although many of these men also attended
the ward dance, they did not wear their uniforms to it nor did they dance there.
As I was told by one of the officers of Usoda's *seisōnenbu*, "Men don't usually
dance. They don't know the steps well and feel uncomfortable. We only dance at
our own hamlet's affair out of the spirit of 'social obligation' (*tsukiai*)."

But, of course, they do know the dances, many of them from childhood, and
in their own hamlet they perform them with considerable élan and even abandon.
By 1978 I was able to recognize most of the people, male and female, who were
present, although I remained unfamiliar with the children from the more distant
hamlets. By a rough estimate, about half of the women who were dancing were
from hamlets other than Usoda, and six were from Nohara hamlet. The women
who come and dance from other hamlets are women who enjoy dancing, although
most claim that they come "because we're neighbors and have relatives here, and
the children have such a good time." But the women who do not care for dancing,
even if they come to watch, do not dance. In 1978, as in 1977, the dancing both
nights lasted almost one hour beyond the time announced as the end of the dance,
10:00 P.M. It seemed to me, at least, that a good time was had by all.

The ward dances are held for two nights in mid–August, and then Usoda
holds its dance on the following two nights. In 1979 several women from Usoda
hamlet came to the ward dance wearing identical *yukata* (light, summer weight,
cotton kimono). That they had planned to do so seemed a well–kept secret since
none of the women from other hamlets whom I questioned about this phenomenon
had any idea that this would happen. The wearing of identical dress by members
of a group is not at all uncommon in Japan, but the fact that no one from other
hamlets knew of the plan was unusual. On the first night of the ward dance, about
ten women from Usoda came dressed identically and did not go unnoticed.

Several women wore these identically patterned *yukata* to both evenings of
the ward dance. They also wore them to the dances in their own hamlet. The men
of that hamlet also wore their softball uniforms, as they had done the year before. Unfortunately, the first night of dancing in the hamlet was cut short by rain
after less than one hour.

The second night the weather was excellent, and the dancing lasted until
almost 11:00 P.M. It began at 9:00 P.M. although the music began much earlier,
around 5:00 P.M. I did not see one man or woman from any other hamlet dance all
evening. A few children from other hamlets did dance some, and there were some
families from other hamlets who came briefly and watched from the perimeter.
Among these families were several women who had attended the ward dances and
the Usoda dance from previous years and who loved to dance. None danced that
evening, however.

As a result, the inner circle was composed of the hamlet's younger men
dressed in their softball uniforms; the second circle contained about twenty-five

women of Usoda hamlet all dressed in identical *yukata*; and in the outermost circle danced the children, relatives of Usoda members who had returned to the ward for the holidays, and the few young women of the hamlet who were unmarried (such as students), living with their parents, and ineligible to join the hamlet Women's Association. Of those few members of other hamlets who did attend, none danced. Although the previous year perhaps half of the women dancers were from other hamlets, in 1979 none were. And everyone from other hamlets had returned home by 9:00 P.M., with most returning home shortly after appearing and paying their respects to their relatives and neighbors who were Usoda hamlet members and present at the dance.

As soon as I realized what was happening, I asked some of the women from other hamlets who I knew liked to dance why they were not dancing. Their responses varied: "Oh, I just don't feel like it tonight. I must be getting old," or "I'm a little tired tonight after all that dancing at the village *bon odori*." One response was a little more specific: "They all have those identical *yukata* on, and it makes it hard to join in" (*minna wa yukatta ga sorotte'ru kara, odorinikui wa*). And yet I saw several of these same women at other dances held elsewhere in the following days, and they danced then.

The effect of the identical *yukata* is clear: they prevented members of all other hamlets from dancing at the Usoda dance. We may ask whether this effect was intended and, if not, was it foreseen; or if not intended or foreseen, was it regretted. I was unable to obtain definite answers to the first two questions. None of the women or men from Usoda hamlet would admit that the effect of barring "outsiders" from dancing was intended, and likewise no one admitted to me that they had thought beforehand that such an effect would be likely. On the other hand, everyone in Usoda thought that the 1979 dance had been a smashing success, largely due to the beauty of the identical *yukata*, and that they would wear them every year whether or not anyone from other hamlets came. I could detect no regret that their *yukata* had inhibited the other women from dancing.

The *yukata* cost approximately ¥6000 each and were made by two women in the hamlet who had the necessary skill. Only those members of the hamlet Women's Association who thought they would dance participated, as I was told, but as a practical matter, all the women members under about forty-five had *yukata* made. They each saved ¥1000 a month from "household expense money" (*hesokuri*) for six months after settling on the plan in January 1979. The primary effect was to have been aesthetic: "Wouldn't everyone look nice dancing together in identical *yukata*." (The dance steps are performed individually, with each dancer performing the same movements simultaneously in a circle revolving around a central drum tower.)

The men and women of Usoda hamlet told me that the idea of making the *yukata* had originated with the women. Outside the hamlet, however, there were suspicions that the women had been put up to it by the men, who wanted a further demonstration of hamlet solidarity (*danketsu*) with which to confront the other hamlets of the ward.  The hamlets themselves are ranked or have reputations based on their solidarity.  Usoda is acknowledged as the hamlet with the most solidarity, and the other hamlets are only now beginning to come out of a period of unstable leadership.  It was even insinuated in more than one other hamlet that the plan must have come from the men because the women in leadership posts or positions of influence in the hamlet are "far too hairbrained to have ever come up with such a plan themselves and would never have been able to carry it out without the urging of their husbands and fathers-in-law."

A few days after the festivities, I asked the woman who was the ringleader of the younger set in that hamlet if she had noticed that no women from other hamlets had danced, although many had the year before and the year before that. Her answer and a subsequent discussion took place:

"Yes, of course we noticed.  But we don't invite people from other hamlets to come.  We don't send out invitations like the village does.  Sure, we want people to come and look, but we really hold the dance for the children and old folks.  The money we get in contributions goes for the children's *undōkai* (field day) in this hamlet.  Every single family in this hamlet made a contribution, but you were the only person outside the hamlet to bring one.  *Danketsu* in this hamlet is very strong, and we're the only hamlet able to have a *bon odori* and a field day for our children."

"But didn't you notice that people from the other hamlets not only did not dance but also didn't stay long and didn't watch either?"

"Oh, some did, but we don't send invitations, after all.  People from other hamlets can come or not come just as they like."  She also mentioned that they would continue wearing the *yukata* every year, and so I asked if she thought anyone at all from other hamlets would come the next year.

"Oh certainly, people will come so the children can have a good time.  Everyone enjoys seeing these kinds of dances, and more people always watch than dance anyway."

But the women from other hamlets were not so sure that they would attend in future.  One woman, who enjoys dancing very much, responded, "Well, our children are getting older now and don't really need me to take them just across the road.  It's not really much fun to just go and watch when you can't dance."  Replies from other women in other hamlets were much the same, and none was certain that she would attend the next time.

*Discussion*

The only hypothesis that this case addresses directly is Exchange Commitment. Attempts to arrange productive exchange transactions between hamlets in contexts other than the ward council seem generally to end in failure, as the arrangements and later accusations involved in the Nohara-Yanagida joint sponsorship of a *bon odori* demonstrate.

But the fundamental issues here are (1) the nature of the ties between families in contexts other than that of the hamlet as hamlet members and (2) the central position of the hamlet itself as the local nexus for productive exchange transactions.

As long as women from other hamlets could remain inconspicuous among the dancers, individuals among other individuals, they could dance freely and rely on individual ties of kinship or neighborhood to justify their presence. They need not be recognized as members of "other hamlets." From the perspective of the hamlet holding the dance, however, while any individual woman from another hamlet could justify her presence, the collectivity could not. All of these individual women, together, amounted to "too many" women from other hamlets. These women did not bring contributions because they were not "really there." That is, they were merely individuals in a crowd, and the ties that justified their presence at all were not to the hamlet sponsoring the dance but to friends, neighbors, and relatives. The relationship of these women to the dance did not continue on to the hamlet but stopped with the individuals to whom they were tied and who were also at the dance.

The *yukata* were not the result of an impulsive gesture, an aesthetic fling, as it were, but a well-planned and carefully guarded symbolic statement through concerted action. They effectively identified those participants who were "really there," who had ties to the hamlet itself and could not dance for free. The women without matching *yukata*, those who were not "really there" and who belonged to other hamlets, could no longer sustain the illusion of absence, of anonymity, of mere faces in the crowd. The overriding importance of the direct hamlet tie was brought to consciousness again.

The effect was achieved by mapping hamlet membership onto the dress of the dancers, by indicating an identity between dancer and hamlet member. This was done by raising everyone's investment in the hamlet, which was, after all, the nexus through which the dance was organized and actualized. Women from other hamlets simply had no basis in previous investment in that hamlet upon which to construct effects due to "further investment." The women from other hamlets were without the opportunity to invest in *yukata* of the same kind, although it is certain that, even if they had known that such a plan was afoot, they would not have purchased *yukata* like those made in Usoda but, if any, different patterns for matching *yukata* in their own hamlets.  The secrecy was intended entirely to prevent women from the other hamlets from making their own identical *yukata*. Without knowledge that such a plan was in the offing, it was extremely unlikely that any other hamlet would have had identical *yukata* made since no other hamlet had its own dance.

While it is sometimes, though only very rarely, possible for someone to get "a free lunch" in a hamlet not his own, participation in hamlet affairs by outsiders is never possible on a regular basis.  The ties between individuals in different hamlets always remain individual or aspects of temporary statuses, such as hamlet or village offices.  Ties between members of different hamlets, except as aspects of hamlet relations, never become collective because the resources of hamlet members are already committed to their own hamlets.  Unable to match the new level of investment required (the contributions which they had, until then, been able to avoid making, plus the cost of the *yukata*), the women from the other hamlets were obliged to withdraw and refrain from participation as dancers (in their own eyes) and as freeloaders (in the eyes of the members of Usoda hamlet to whom they had no individual ties).  They chose not to absorb the cost of seeing their own hamlets humiliated, which they would have done if they remained as mere spectators.  This seems to have been a uniformly unacceptable choice for the women from all of the other hamlets, and they all retired from the field early.

This is the essential problem of relations between hamlets, and it is a necessary correlate of high mutual investment within hamlets.  The ties between individuals who belong to different hamlets can never become the basis for collective action among two or more hamlets, and in fact, such ties are always suspect in the eyes of fellow hamlet members precisely because they require resources that all hamlet members know must be available to claims within the hamlet first.  All hamlet members have ties outside their own hamlets, but no one is willing to recognize that his neighbor's extrahamlet ties have a legitimate priority over claims originating in his own hamlet.  Because the ties between individuals in different hamlets are individual, it is never possible to raise the level of investment between hamlets to levels within any hamlet; the resource base achieved by a hamlet cannot be duplicated by an ego-centered network, in which all members are already members of hamlets and hamletlike groups, without initial investments beyond the reach of individuals or without raising the likelihood of defection to unacceptably high levels.  Consequently, there remains a residue of suspicion of defection that is debilitating in the extreme between individual hamlets, and hamlet members remain unwilling to invest in interhamlet projects when they cannot rely on their own ties directly to individuals in other hamlets.  But again, this multiplicity of individual ties cannot serve as a basis for collective action because the lack of direct ties between members of the two hamlets is greater. And where there is no tie of mutual investment to avoid defection in exchange, exchange becomes both more costly and more risky.  Insofar as Usoda's *bon odori* was a function exchange in that hamlet, we must consider the participation of women from other hamlets as a form of deception. Not one of those women was able to continue her behavior without the cloak of invisibility.

Resources are limited, and so hamlet solidarity can only be achieved at the expense of limiting opportunities elsewhere. Because the mechanism of mutual investment requires claims on all of a member's resources, opportunities outside the group must be limited completely, at least in theory. They are not, however, because of differences in individually controlled resources, with the lowest common denominator determining the level of activity possible in such a group, and because there is a time lag between the proposals within the group for action and the implementation of such proposals.

In this particular ward, each hamlet has the formal power to veto any proposal made in the ward council. I was often told that if the hamlets and not the ward were the units officially recognized by the city as administrative units, the ward council and the ward organization would become moribund. Before the war the ward council was primarily the organ of the landlords, who maintained ties with landlords in other hamlets and villages. Now, because it is a ward in the city, the village organization is almost entirely supported from above, by the city. Despite the fact that ward members believe that "it is necessary to organize and use large numbers of people when dealing with the city," the ward organization continues to serve primarily as a conduit for information passed from the city to the hamlets. If there were no ward and no ward council, however, each hamlet would continue as a viable nexus for productive exchange among its members. Relations between hamlets, however, even at the ward level, are tenuous at best, and between or among individual hamlets, virtually nonexistent. This fact is less due to the internal strength of the hamlets than to the mechanism through which hamlet members are able to lessen the likelihood of defection in exchange within the hamlet.

# CHAPTER 5:
## DECISIONS: DIVISION AND SOLIDARITY IN HAMLET SOCIETY

Where the previous chapter specifically analyzed each decision in relation to each relevant hypothesis derived theoretically in chapter 2, it is the task of the present chapter to trace out the more general effects of this way of making decisions on the overall tenor of hamlet society. In particular, this chapter examines the problems of participation, opposition, and membership in relation to the public pursuit of private interest.

The process of group decision making brings together, focuses, articulates, influences, and even creates private preferences. But while the way in which the decision-making process generally influences the social milieu in which decisions are made is a question of particular interest to students of decision making, decision makers themselves can only be interested in such matters to the extent they affect the distribution of influence over outcomes of concrete decisions. Where the two—pursuit of private interest in public settings and the effects of decision-making procedures on social relations—come together, we shall expect to discover an already developed native theory concerning their relation. Such theorizing can only be an interested theorizing, however; it may or may not diverge from disinterested theorizing, or at least theory embedded in a different social matrix, but its aim must always be the production of strategy and tactics for use in a specific decision-making procedure. This is not to say that, within the scope of this study, rural Japanese are more or less calculating as decision makers or decision theorists, more or less compassionate than other human beings, or even more or less able decision makers than members of other cultures and social situations, but only that the task of disinterested theory is not to provide an alternative to native theory but to demonstrate the sociological basis within which it operates and has developed. In the case of rural Japan, this basis is the hamlet productive exchange relation governed by mutual investment. Consequently, we must leave open the possibility that interested theory developed on this specific premise, however unconsciously perceived, incompletely articulated, differently expressed, or conceptually refined, will have generated many strategies and tactical maneuvers that have no place in other theories, such as those based on simple exchange governed by contract.

145

The findings of this study suggest that while the culture at large may or may not include specific instructions on how collective decisions ought to be made, unless this information is acquired by induction and presented as a rule of thumb for the practical pursuit of private interest in a specific exchange context, it remains irrelevant to the determination of the mode in which any particular group decision is taken. "Voting" may or may not be regarded by many of the participants in decision-making processes in Nohara or Japan generally as an element in the strategic repertoire entailing negative evaluations, or even as an importation and imposition. The tendency toward division in hamlet collective decisions, however, is a direct result of the dramatic increase in postwar years of privately, compared with corporately, held resources in the hamlet, together with the commitment to productive exchange within the hamlet that is implied by hamlet membership.

It remains a fact, however, that whatever is *said* about collective decision making in hamlets of rural Japan by native participants, native theorists, or scholarly observers, hamlet members must still make public choices. Thus, the relation of decision mode to resource control (or any of the other hypotheses offered here) as a generalization from the consequences of practice and the model of exchange that explains this relationship is fundamentally irrelevant to decision makers. They cannot "trust" these generalizations in actual practice any more than they can "trust" their own or their neighbors' theories concerning how they themselves collectively make decisions. What are always at issue are applications of the rate of exchange and, hence, the distribution of resources within the hamlet. As Bourdieu (1977: 19) points out:

> The informant's discourse, in which he strives to give himself the appearance of symbolic mastery of his practice, tends to draw attention to the most remarkable "moves," i.e. those most esteemed or reprehended, in the different social games, . . . rather than to the principle from which these moves and all equally possible moves can be generated and which, belonging to the universe of the undisputed, most often remain in their implicit state. But the subtlest pitfall doubtless lies in the fact that such descriptions freely draw on the highly ambiguous vocabulary of *rules*, the language of grammar, morality, and law, to express a social practice that in fact obeys quite different principles. The explanation agents may provide of their own practice, thanks to a quasi-theoretical reflection on their practice, conceals, even from their own eyes, the true nature of their practical mastery, i.e. that it is a *learned ignorance* (*docta ignorantia*), a mode of practical knowledge not comprising knowledge of its own principles. It follows that this learned ignorance can only give rise to misleading discourse of a speaker himself misled, ignorant both of the

objective truth about his practical mastery (which is that it is igno-
rant of its own truth) and of the true principle of the knowledge his
practical mastery contains.

It follows that the hypotheses presented in chapter 2 do not necessarily
embody forms that replicate the discourse of informants on their own behavior.
The hypotheses concerning consent criteria are specifically not the conscious
products of the participants in the decision-making process I have observed.
These criteria are as follows:

1. There must be a demonstrable potential to benefit for each member of the group.
2. Where there is no such potential, participation cannot be induced
and no liability assigned.
3. No benefits can flow differentially to any member as a direct
function of initial private expenditure or the expenditure of corporate
resources.
4. All opportunities for benefit must provide the possibility for
individual members to benefit by further expenditure of production
costs that are not coerced in any way or, where that good to be supplied does not exceed demand, by a share in those benefits equal that
of other members who share equal liability.

The "back translation" of this set of criteria, which are established from
the point of view of the collective process, is simply expressed as a judgment of
each participant on the likely outcome of each alternative, namely, "Can I do
better than this, or am I being misled?" If the issue has been thoroughly re-
searched, and if none of the above criteria have been violated with regard to any
member of the group, then no member will feel that he is being deceived or that
he can do better within the framework of the alternatives offered by the issue at
hand. Ultimately, each member must ask himself, "Well, if this is all the better I
can do in this group, can I do better elsewhere?" Historically, in this hamlet, the
answer to this question has been overwhelmingly in the negative. But insofar as it
is a question answered within the privacy of the individual household, the range of
the values defining the answer's parameters falls outside the scope of this study
and inquiry into collective, rather than individual, decision-making practice.

The primary implication of this set of criteria is that group membership
will not become, in and of itself, a liability to any member. It insures that group
members cannot be stripped of the means of production and resources necessary
for production and consumption by other members acting in concert as a coalition. The importance of this element in the collective decision-making process
cannot be overemphasized because it defines the maximally effective distribution

of resources within the hamlet with regard to the collective creation of opportunities for production and productive exchange.  The hamlet in which this study was conducted is not a collectivity in which the membership is so specialized and interdependent that the removal of any one member implies the immediate extinction of the entire group or even another member.  Japanese hamlets have never been like that and are not now becoming collectivities of that sort.  Rather, they are becoming less mutually dependent, even as the total amount of resources available for collective undertakings grows.  No member is indispensible.

As a consequence, all members must at some time face the decision whether or not they would be better off as nonmembers.  And conversely, the coalition in favor of a course of action must decide whether such a member (faced with that decision) ought no longer be a member of the group.  The satisfaction of the above criteria within each decision reduces the number of such side-decisions to the absolute minimum and, thus, assures the stability of the group to the greatest possible extent.  It also provides for the widest possible participation in the implementation of each decision.

Unanimity in the form of a lack of overt objection in itself does not guarantee willing participation, especially if the expression of opposition is blocked rather than encouraged.  It is clear that no goods of any kind will be produced unless the distribution of those goods can be limited to those who combined to provide them, or the cost of nonparticipation can be raised above the cost of participation.  Unless costly applications of force are introduced into the equation, these criteria provide maximum benefit at least cost to all members without requiring any member to directly or indirectly subsidize any other member.

That each member must be satisfied with regard to these criteria for each issue reveals the major structural effect of the operation of mutual investment. Implementation of collective decisions will not redistribute resources around the hamlet *differentially* and, thus, not provide only some members with the resources necessary to move up to higher levels of investment, production, or consumption than can be maintained within the group.  And not all proposals will be implemented in any event.  But the commitment of resources to the relationship requires that resources be made available to productive exchange within the relationship and not outside it for the same set of opportunities.  Consequently, group members may choose among proposals available outside their own group only if their own group cannot provide the same opportunities internally (e.g., wage labor and marriage markets).  But a member cannot, in good faith, enter into an external opportunity simply because his own group has decided not to exploit that particular opportunity.

This constraint on the ability to exploit opportunities for exchange implies that interaction will be maximal within the group and minimal between groups or members of different groups over the same range of opportunities.  Those opportunities that will be exploited by members outside the group, when the group has decided not to undertake them itself, must always contain the promise of a much higher return or lower initial investment to be at all attractive. Unless a group member is prepared to risk discovery of his defection from the relation, the opportunity must provide a steady source of further alternative opportunities for exchange and not merely a casual alternative to the ongoing exchange relation in which he finds himself embedded. To the extent that such an opportunity appears attractive, the risk of defection by these potential new partners also increases. This fact is well known to the members of Nohara hamlet from both practical experience and anecdote.

At issue is not merely the sentiment of hamlet members and their idiosyncratic attachment to the collective representations of a shared identity, but the limited resources that can be collectively applied to the exploitation of an opportunity at any one time. The resulting structure of groups and relations among and between groups is similar to that described by Nakane (1970): there will be a sharp tendency toward hierarchy and replication of functions within groups and extreme difficulty in raising the level of exchange by merging groups of the same structural order, which provide the same range of exchange opportunities to their members. Although returns may be lower within a group for any particular transaction when compared to those offered by alternative partners external to the group, the risk of defection is also lower within the group. To the extent that the entire field of opportunity is organized by mutual investment, awareness of the likelihood of defection becomes the primary orientation toward exchanges among members of different groups.

It is through consideration of the criteria of consent, stemming from the impossibility of reconciling the subsidization of some hamlet members by others with participation in everyday hamlet affairs, that we must conclude that there is no actual privileged position corresponding to "the good of the hamlet as a whole" from which the hamlet productive exchange relation itself can be observed. While the group may be involved in simultaneous consideration of several different issues, the tensions involved in each issue do not result in a summation of all tension and do not present themselves as a single obstacle that immobilizes the decision-making capacity of the group, unless defection is discovered. Not only are decisions settled independently of one another, but they are never settled by regarding any or all issues at hand as one issue with multiple solutions. This is precisely because each issue is strictly confined to those circumstances in which it presents itself; each member must satisfy himself that the rate of exchange determined within the relationship is accurately (or adequately) applied to each issue as it arises.

Contrary to the statements of participants, who easily express their belief that it is always the same individuals who are in the opposition and that this tendency is a function of the personality of the individual or his household, a review of the data shows that the support and opposition on each issue is formed independently on the basis of objective interests in the alternatives presented by that issue. Group members found themselves allied with different members on every issue, and coalitions only formed around single issues, not personalities. This state of affairs neither tempts members to resolve issues en masse nor prevents them from resolving "easier" issues while more "difficult" issues remain unsettled. Neither convenience nor expedience overrides the demand of all members that each (for his own part) be satisfied with regard to the above criteria of consent on each and every issue.

It is only by refusing to merge issues into single, over-arching settlements that each member is able to "keep his books straight"—to assess the impact of each issue on his continued ability to remain a hamlet member and avoid subsidizing other members of the hamlet. It is the rate of exchange itself that, if applied to each member's satisfaction in each issue, makes such "bookkeeping" automatic. What is of concern, within the application of the rate of exchange and the collective interpretation of the distribution of potential to benefit among the membership as a social process, is that "bookkeeping" as such not become part of the exchange process in any immediate way. Underlying this concern, and the reason for it, is the major mechanism that makes such decision making, and such groups, possible, namely, that an indefinitely numerous series of transactions with the same partner(s) is one way to reduce defection in exchange. And this series must also be well regulated to avoid involuntary consumption of resources in the form of subsidies to other members. By avoiding "bookkeeping" altogether, no one can "juggle the books." Over time, such subsidies as would enter through constantly negotiating a new rate of exchange would not lead to a "balance of results" among members but the breakdown of the relationship. Within the decision-making process, the accumulation of subsidies is uni-directional when the resource pool is finite.

In the following section, these general findings are related to the specific features of the cases previously presented.

### Decision Mode and Participant Orientation

The idioms in which consensual and adversarial discussions and negotiation are conducted in Japan are extremely clear in most instances and appear to be deliberate exaggerations to Western eyes. A brilliant photo essay on the Minamata pollution case by W. Eugene and Aileen Smith contains several accounts of adversarial negotiation and decision making (Smith and Smith 1975). Robert Smith (1978) also provides something of the flavor of the atmosphere in which such deliberations are conducted, with armbands, posters, placards, and angry threatening voices.

None of the discussions that I was able to record in this fieldwork, with one possible exception, was conducted in this idiom or with this orientation. This one exception occurred in the late summer of 1977, at which a presentation by city engineers of plans to expand the municipal trash-burning facilities was disrupted by local farmers. The farmers yelled at the engineers, and the engineers ignored the farmers. Finally, one of the farmers tore the elaborate diagram of the planned facility from the wall on which it was hung, rolled it into a ball, and hurled it at the chief engineer. That brought the meeting to a close.

Later, however, the man who had done this told me that it was all for show and that "if you don't take a tough stand with city hall, they simply will not listen at all." Whether or not his anger, and that of the other farmers, was as intense as they wished it to appear, I do not know. But what is clear is that there is local understanding of the idiom of adversarial discussion and orientation to decision making. It is an idiom and orientation that I did not once see inside the hamlet or its subgroups.

The adversarial orientation requires direct confrontation and the close identification by adversaries with competing alternative courses of action. The case of the softball equipment purchase reveals an idiom of discussion in which the participants are closely identified with alternative courses of action and yet remain within the consensual orientation. This alternative is found in the use of "politeness language" (keigo). Such language allows each participant to defer to the other and show respect for him without showing agreement with his position. It allows the individuals to demonstrate that they do not identify the other with the position he presents and to avoid unambiguous insult when criticizing a partic- ular course of action. It was in this idiom that much of the discussion between Koichi and Hirao was conducted, and they resorted to this idiom as soon as they realized that they were both committed to opposed positions on the issue.

The above shows that there are two distinct idioms of discussion when two parties find themselves opposed. One leads to confrontation and an open break, and the other to a separation of the speaker from his opinion. In the consensual orientation, there are also two distinct idioms. The first is that which is ex- pected: discussion is carried out in more or less friendly language and with a disinterested air. This is the idiom that I most often encountered. Another is when putative antagonists work to achieve a mutually satisfactory agreement. This idiom, the use of the garb of public protest in which there is the appearance of an open break, seems to occur most often in labor negotiations in Japan and serves to symbolize the distance between labor and management even though both parties are sincerely concerned with the welfare of the company (Hanami 1979: 42-45). In this idiom, within the consensual orientation, we see the railroads' annual one- and two-hour strikes at contract negotiation time, for example. Perhaps it was an example of this juxtaposition of idiom and orientation I witnessed when the diagram was removed from the wall and thrown at the city's representative.

These various combinations of idiom and orientation of discussion do not, however, correlate with the mode, division or unanimity, in which the decision is made.  Of the eight cases presented here for which a definite conclusion was reached and known, four—softball, fire pump, English class and rice polisher— appear to have been settled even though there was division. The others were settled unanimously—fire extinguisher, rice cooker, gas ring, and city water. I do not insist on this particular partitioning of case by mode, however. It might be possible to consider the English class as a unanimous decision, and city water, division.  But in any case, both modes have representative cases, and there are no empty classes of decision mode.

It is useful here to discuss exactly what a vote is and can do and the overall importance of the ability of a group to raise the costs of members who do not consider the decision of the group binding.  There is, first, no sense in which a vote may be thought binding on a member opposed to it unless the costs of disregarding the decision are higher than those involved in the decision. Obviously, where this is not possible, only unanimous decisions are possible. Conversely, where an individual finds that his only alternative to abiding by a decision is death, his active participation can hardly be said to be necessary to the implementation of the decision, except in hypothetical cases.  Such cases are not likely to arise in the setting in which this research, at any rate, was conducted because production and consumption remain fundamentally independent among members of hamlets.

Second, a vote may carry either one or two messages. When it is not clear to participants where support for any alternative lies, a vote may make this clear.  This function is extremely useful in decisions made by large groups. At the same time, the result of the vote conveys the message to each participant that he must then make a decision himself on whether or not he will regard the decision as binding.  This individual decision must make reference to the costs that the group can, and is likely to, assess for noncompliance.  But when the first message is redundant and the likely result known beforehand, only the second message is conveyed by a vote; those in opposition to the result must either appeal the vote or be prepared to decide whether they will consider it binding or absorb the costs the group will impose.

The one parameter that will affect this decision is whether or not the course of action can be implemented without the participation of those who chose to absorb the costs for noncompliance the group will impose. The decisions taken in this hamlet make this point extremely clear:  when the resources necessary for successful implementation must be contributed directly by the membership, no decision is worth implementing that will require more than one or two members to think carefully about the alternatives to noncompliance.

But this is also true for those members who wish to see a certain course of action implemented; they must always consider whether or not they wish to implement any course of action that is likely to remove members from the group. Such a course of action is rarely seen as desirable because they will have to absorb the costs that would have been paid by those who do not comply on that decision and, if these people are removed from the group, on every future decision as well.

It is for this reason that a small majority will not decide any issue, but only a majority that leaves, in this case, only one or two members in the minority. This point is apparent in the decisions on the purchase of the rice polisher and fire pump. In the issue of the rice polisher, it was clear who was opposed to the purchase and who was in favor, even without a vote. What had to be established was not so much the distribution of opinion but the grounds for assessing penalties for noncompliance. These grounds—objective potential to benefit—were found at the point that insured a minimal opposition, even at the expense of a dislocation between what was said in public and what was actually done. This solution was also adopted for the softball equipment.

When resources needed for the implementation of a course of action are already corporate property, and implementation is possible without the active support of each member, no member will find it worthwhile to leave the group merely to voice opposition to that course of action that he cannot, by noncompliance, prevent being adopted and implemented. Whatever the result of the decision, an individual member can only lose access to resources that he could not, in any event, allocate at his own discretion. Hence, if there is agreement by a majority, there will be unanimous agreement in such cases.

A vote, as pointed out, is not merely a mechanical device for dividing participants in a decision by opinion. It may also serve as a medium of communication for messages other than the expression of opinion. In the case of the fire pump, it was used simply to pressure the opposition, which was small. The issue of the installation of city water does not seem to have come to a vote precisely because legitimate grounds for objection—poverty and lack of potential to benefit—were of primary concern to each member, or to the group as a whole, from the beginning. It may in fact be that this issue *did* come to a vote at some time. But if it did, then the fact, and the results, have been expunged from the records, and this information, as is usually the case, is not now recoverable. But whether objections were raised in a vote or not, conditions were ultimately provided so that no objection could be sustained by any member unless that member was willing to leave the group to avoid compliance.

The example of the decision on the English class shows how the simple mechanical procedure of voting, however, can serve as a means of communicating messages other than the two mentioned above. There is no doubt that this issue could have been settled unanimously and that, ultimately, there was not even opposition to allow the use of the hamlet hall. Opposition was expressed through the vote to an issue that was not being considered at the time and that was thought to have been settled. This represents the one occasion in which two separate issues were linked by participants. In this case, it was not a matter of trading off interests in issues but in expressing opposition to one course of action through the decision being made on another. Both of the men expressing that opposition, however, would only have done so if they knew that their opposition would not prevent the adoption of the course of action being decided at the time. They did not, in fact, want that course of action prevented.

In all of the cases analyzed here, no issue was raised that might have caused any member to seriously consider leaving the group rather than comply with a collective decision. In all of these cases, an argument was made so that the criteria for participation were satisfied for each participant and the cost of compliance was lower than the cost of noncompliance.

It is in this connection we return to what seems the prevailing "last straw" theory of division in hamlet affairs. Smith (1978) provides an account of this theory of hamlet conflict as well as an extended example in the Clover Affair. It is argued that the harmony and solidarity of hamlets is provided at the expense of suppression of points of irritation and conflict within the hamlet. When conflict does erupt in hamlets, it does so with an extreme bitterness that only the "pressure cooker" environment of close face-to-face relations makes possible. While Smith does not subscribe wholeheartedly to this theory, neither does he offer an explanation for the Clover Affair beyond the cogent observation that the trend toward economic independence of members has "undermined the power of the hamlet to defend itself against outside incursions" (1978: 241).

The model developed here favors a unified approach, which might be best thought of as a "quantum jump" model, in which both harmony and solidarity are real and do not suffer pressures where *any* issue might convert into direct hostility. On the contrary, the appearance of conflict is not directly related to the results of past decisions and repressed hostilities but can emerge at any moment if an issue arises in which the returns to some members are great enough that they will never recover the value of the opportunity lost through future interaction within the group. The model might also be thought of as a "main chance" model, or a "once-in-a-lifetime opportunity" model. As Smith (1978: 246) points out, "People are sufficiently aware of the practical benefits of these relationships to be persuaded that, unless they are prepared to make the final break and move away, it is well worth nurturing them carefully and restoring those that have been ruptured." This sentence implies a variant of the model advocated here, the "take the money and run" model.

There are two crucial points with regard to the circumstances under which the Clover Affair developed and that determined the direction of its development. First, the Clover company, to implement its own decision to locate in Kurusu, only needed to purchase one small piece of land in the area owned by a Kurusu family. Second, the resources that the company needed, in effect an environment that could absorb the effluvia and other pollution its plant would generate, could be obtained without the individual consent of each hamlet member. These two features made possible the rapid implementation of the company's decision. Any hamlet member who did not intend to take a job in the factory could never regain what would be lost through hamlet interaction of the traditional sort. There was no means by which the families opposed to the plan could raise the cost of participation for those who favored the plan beyond the dissolution of the hamlet as a nexus for productive exchange. Thus, we see that it was not the group in the hamlet in favor of the plant that gave way, but the Clover company itself, whose original proposal seems to have contained no small element of deception as well.

It is clearly a matter of the stakes involved and a comparison of the payoffs expected from investment outside the hamlet to those within. For such hostility to break out, it is necessary that some members believe that they will never get such an opportunity again, that the opportunity can never be matched within the hamlet, and that they can implement the decision without the participation of any members who disagree. This does not involve a majority and a minority, and a minority can undertake such a project as well as a majority. There is no reason to think that "old wrongs" or old alliances are involved. When such an opportunity arises, we must always expect it to be taken, and those who take it will be prepared to accept the conversion of past investments into losses. This case represents the limits to which the strategy of mutual investment is efficient. Such opportunities often require a strategy of unilateral action, if not outright deception: the true cost-benefit ratio is not made apparent. When defection is not required, such opportunities cannot be abandoned or lost. They must be taken or they will amount to nothing more than subsidies of one's partners. The interests of all members are never completely identical.

## Minimal Criteria for Consent

The Clover Affair demonstrates what can happen when an attempt is made to implement a decision before all participants are satisfied that the criteria given here have been satisfied. In retrospect, it is possible to imagine that these criteria could have been satisfied for all members within the decision-making process in its normal state, but it is not now possible to know with certainty. What is certain is that the members in favor of the plant did not care whether everyone in the hamlet was satisfied or not, and they were not willing to risk the plant to find out if it would even have been possible to satisfy everyone. This can only be the case when some members believe that the hamlet must be sacrificed to such an opportunity or that those who are not satisfied can be co-opted into participation after the fact.

It must always remain a matter for the interpretation of participants whether or not they have the potential to benefit from any issue in which they are involved because of hamlet membership. The issues of the softball equipment and the rice polisher both turned upon this point. Of course, such an interpretation must be possible if there is to be consideration of a motion at all. Consequently, much of the political activity in the hamlet consists precisely of the struggle of opposing interpretations concerning the distribution of the potential to benefit in any issue. The kinds of resources that are employed in this struggle can be seen in the issues of the fire pump and the rice polisher. Group members, after all, must participate where they can benefit; they cannot remain group members if they do not participate where they can benefit.

It is the potential to benefit that forms the basis for consideration of any proposal for action. Where such a basis is lacking, to the extent it is lacking, support and participation will diminish. When a psychologically oriented student of Japan, such as Lebra (1976: 158), writes that Japanese "comply with the will of the group against their own will," we must interpret such statements against the background of a system of relationships within groups where participation is not expected at all if there is no potential to benefit but is expected where there is such potential, even though that potential is not easily activated or realized. That is to say, "free will" is only "free" from the point of view that each person can and must assess the costs and benefits of any action open to him. It does not mean that any segment of the universe is responsible for the gratification of any individual's wants. In many groups in Japan it is clear that, while the alternatives within the group are not all that they might always be, they are better than those available to its members outside the group, and certainly freer of defection. Within the group, individuals have at least two grounds for legitimate opposition to any proposal, but that opposition must be legitimate, or the relationship cannot be sustained. Individuals do not yield their legitimate interests to the will of the group, but they do find, over the long run, that they must participate in the group if they are to benefit from it.

The presence of these criteria allows judgments to be made about the wisdom of participation at all and not about ideal cost-benefit ratios in risk-free situations. Again we must return to the fundamental point: the mechanism of a series of indefinitely numerous transactions with the same partner(s) is only effective if the resources of those partners are committed to that series of transactions. But this by no means implies a totality of interest among partners; what identity of interest is present must be renegotiated with each transaction and within the circumstances in which each transaction is embedded. The danger of using such a mechanism unconsciously lies precisely in the opportunity for defection that an extensive common interest presents: the good of the group may be offered by the unscrupulous as an alternative to the good of each member. Unless care is taken, the caution implied by the necessity of having each of these criteria satisfied on each occasion, one member might be deceived by another into mistaking an extensive range of common interest for a totality of common interest.

The issues of the rice cooker, the fire extinguisher, and the gas ring were "simple" precisely because the common interest was so obvious, and the issues of the softball equipment and the rice polisher, because it was not. In the case of the fire pump, it was obvious that the common interest was being served, and the question was merely if it was worth the cost. But it is the interpretation of "common interest," not at all obvious in every issue, that is important.

## Hidden Costs and Structural Implications

Whether the presence of the mechanism of mutual investment for the regulation of transactions fosters trust among partners or reduces defection is probably a moot point. This mechanism, with all other mechanisms of similar function, is incapable of generating a total identity of interests among members. It consequently is unable to preclude the possibility that the advantage gained by one partner will not be made from the loss of another. It can, however, make opportunities in which such transactions are possible less attractive than transactions in which gain is a function of different utilities, as in simple exchange, or in which gain results from the concerted action of two or more partners for some benefit that is not available to any acting separately, as in productive exchange. Such a result in itself is no small achievement and can provide the basis for long-term stability in exchange relations.

Nevertheless, there are costs involved in the employment of this mechanism. The feature of mutual investment that makes it a viable alternative to contract is that its costs are not diverted but remain available to production as long as exchange remains free of defection. To operate effectively, however, the resources of the members of the exchange relation must be thoroughly committed to exchange within the relation. When they are, they will not be available to investment in opportunities external to the relation. And these external opportunities, if not exploited, can never be known to be worse than those exploited within the group. This difference in apparent potential must also be considered an investment in the relation.

The other cost involved is apparent in the different utilities members have for consuming or investing their resources. Members of such exchange relations must participate in the creation of collective opportunities when objective consent criteria are satisfied. The possibilities remain, however, that a member will prefer to consume his share of capital costs or that those costs will leave him unable to both subsist and still meet production costs. In this case, capital costs can only be considered absolute losses when there is no likelihood of future rectification: depending on the potential of the opportunity, interest on a loan may be a justifiable expense. Of issues resolved in Nohara, the installation of city water lines makes this point most clearly. Several households have ¥210,000 tied up in water lines that, until they install lines into their own homes, provide them with no return whatsoever.

One possible cost that can never be avoided and that is never referred to in public is that some participants may be able to fortuitously benefit relative to others despite an equitable distribution of initial liability. For example, a fire pump must be housed somewhere, and wherever it is housed, it will be closer to a water supply and to the houses of some members than others. There is little that can be done about this. It is the sort of differential advantage that participants must assume will "even out" in the long run. In any event, such benefits do not come at the expense of other members.

Another potential source of costs inherent in mutual investment is, perhaps, not as important as those previously mentioned but is one that, nevertheless, remains unavoidable. This is the cost of limiting access to "public goods." The simplest method to limit access is by requiring further investment in the form of a "toll" or use tax. This strategy is clearly seen in the matter of the *bon odori* in Usoda hamlet. To the extent that there was any desire to prevent the dance from being enjoyed by those people who did not contribute toward making it possible, it was found more expedient to resort to further investment in *yukata* than try to forbid people from other hamlets from attending and risk the result of overt confrontation. This further investment is functionally equivalent to the requirement of individual provision of production costs.

The issue of the installation of city water raises the question of the potential cost of not being able, even collectively, to free resources easily for investment with other groups. While the water-line project was ostensibly organized at the village level, all important transactions were conducted at the hamlet level. One hamlet did not even participate.

In this particular case, all financing was handled by each hamlet separately, and each hamlet that participated did so as an independent unit. It was only when it was obvious that installation of lines to hamlet members by their own hamlets would be prohibitively expensive that they agreed to install lines by neighborhoods instead. Still, the groups that undertook the financing of these lines were not the neighborhood groups, which would ultimately use water from the lines they shared, but the hamlets. This resulted in the odd situation of several households throughout the ward paying for lines they do not use and using lines for which they did not pay. Such an arrangement was possible only because all of the members of the participating hamlet bonded themselves for ¥50,000 each, thus insuring members of their own, and other hamlets, that they would pay for the water lines in that hamlet.

Within Nohara hamlet, there was some question of whether or not those hamlet members who did not belong to the *jikkō-kumiai*, through which organization the financing was in part made available, should be allowed to enjoy the benefits provided to members. Alternative sources of financing were investigated, and when it was finally discovered that there were none, all hamlet members not belonging to the *jikkō-kumiai* were asked to make their commitment in writing.

The attempt by Nohara and Yanagida to sponsor a joint *bon odori* shows how difficult it is for two or more hamlets to engage in concerted action. One amusing anecdote illustrating the difficulty of mixing hamlets comes from the ward softball league. Tiny Nishioka was unable to field a complete team at a league tournament. Rather than use men from teams with surplus members, they used women, both from their own hamlet and from other hamlets, all members of the women's softball team.

Another episode involving the men's softball league was rather more serious. One of the member hamlets nominated a candidate for league office who was clearly unqualified. The hamlet was asked by the current officers to nominate an adequate person, and it refused to do so. At a general meeting of the league, it was suggested that the team either be removed from the league, barred from using the village field, or fined. All of these suggestions were shown to be impractical or undesirable, and it was finally decided that the team would be suspended for one year, the following year, if it was not able to offer a reasonable candidate one year later. For the moment, the previous year's officers would serve another year. This was decided as expected: after lengthy discussion, the league president reviewed the alternatives discussed and the objections raised to each. Finally, he stated the only alternative left, that of doing nothing, in effect, until the next year. This was phrased in such a way that the noncompliant team could consider themselves on a one-year probation. The difficult decision about what to do if the recalcitrant team did not mend its ways after a year was left undecided. The league president asked if there were any further suggestions or if anyone was opposed to that course of action. No one was, and he undertook to inform the team, which sent no members to that meeting, of the decision. Interestingly enough, it was the team from the same hamlet that did not have city water installed. Because this hamlet's nonparticipation in the city water did not endanger anyone else's chances of having the mains installed, no conflict arose. But the clearly blatant attempt by one team to enjoy the benefits of league membership without absorbing any of the cost cannot long remain unanswered without the dissolution of the league sooner or later.

I do not know whether the failure of that team to supply a league officer as agreed earlier was the result of a collective decision by the team to avoid sending a candidate or the refusal of all of its members to accept the position. From the point of view of the members of the league, however, this information is not relevant. Whatever the reason, no team can be allowed a privileged position within the league.

What is important is that it is exactly this unwillingness to transfer resources from the hamlet to structurally equivalent groups that is at the root of the failure of hamlets, and individuals in different hamlets, to engage in potentially beneficial transactions. This is a problem implied by the hamlet relationship itself. "Hamlet solidarity" is based on the commitment of unspecified levels of resources by all hamlet members. This relationship requires hamlet members to participate in all hamlet activities from which they can benefit. This requirement in turn implies an unspecified claim on the resources of each hamlet member. After dividing resources into those claimed by the hamlet and those earmarked for consumption, there are few left for transactions in which the risk of defection is high.

## Incommensurability of Issues

Bailey (1965: 11), in his seminal paper on collective decision making, suggests that unanimity, true consensus, cannot be achieved in groups numbering more than about twenty members. The reason he gives is that the mechanism employed in reaching consensus is the linking of several issues in which the participants have different interests and control, and that this mechanism is too cumbersome and complicated to be manipulated successfully by large numbers of participants over a large enough number of issues. He calls this mechanism "squaring," or "horse trading." It is the same as "log rolling," however, if difficulties arise in matching issues and decision makers. El-Hakim (1978: 68) essentially agrees that this is the mechanism employed in Sudanese decision making and that it requires participants to exchange control "of what interest them little in return for greater control over what interest them more."

Such a mechanism would indeed be unwieldy in situations where several participants are involved in a wide range of issues over long periods of time, but there is no evidence that "squaring" is employed in Nohara (although it may have a place in other contexts in Japan). The mechanism employed in Nohara produces both unanimity and voting, and it does not require either the linking of issues by participants with different interests in them or the trading off of these interests. On the contrary, such "horse trading" requires an implicit terminal transaction, a limited set of issues over which interests can be correlated. This is not the case in Nohara. "Squaring" is, in fact, anathema to mutual investment, which requires that there be no terminal transaction to the exchange series.

What does occur is the apparent paradox that participants reduce expectations for issues that interest them greatly in return for greater control over issues
that interest them less. In other words, issues in which the gain of one party is
the loss of another, "zero-sum" issues, are simply not decided upon positively. On
the rare occasion in which such results cannot be avoided or resolved, the exchange relation itself, the hamlet, is dissolved, as in the Clover Affair. This was
the case with the hamlet head's suggestion to Takayoshi in the English class issue,
that he trade off the use of his field for the village *bon odori* in exchange for the
use of the village hall. This notion was not taken seriously by anyone except
himself, however. Although there is none but negative evidence, I suggest not
only that issues cannot be linked in this manner when the mechanism of mutual
investment is employed but also that differential payoffs—"side payments"—
cannot be used to induce participation. That would merely be a weakened form of
"squaring."

What we see in each case is not an exploration of possible "deals" among
participants but an examination of the circumstances in which the issue is embedded for assurance that no member will be victimized by participation and that the
minimal criteria for acceptance of a course of action are satisfied for each participant. Consequently, each issue becomes an opportunity to benefit only if each
member who must suffer any liability also has the potential to benefit. The result
is a series of low-return, low-risk transactions. The major implication of this
mechanism is that it encourages production and productivity in a way that neither
"horse trading" nor zero-sum transactions ever can. Production is both demanded,
because participants must have resources to invest in collective action if a terminal transaction is to be avoided, and encouraged, because it is virtually certain
that there will be returns, however relatively low in relation to investment. It is a
mechanism that is suited to stable social relations over the long run and guarantees a low risk of defection in exchange transactions while providing for unusually
high rates of production and the collective encouragement of productivity. These
are, in fact, predominant features in Japanese society and have been for perhaps
the past few hundred years. Much of what Japan is today is due in no small part
to the employment of the mechanism of mutual investment to insure the integrity
of productive exchange transactions.

# CHAPTER 6:
## CONCLUSIONS

A central conclusion of this study is that the mode in which a collective decision is taken is an emergent property of the decision-making process itself and not the result of participants' preferences, culturally or otherwise determined, for particular decision modes. Mueller (1979: 270) concludes his extensive review of the voluntary-exchange-oriented public-choice literature with the observation that both modes—unanimity and division—involve dilemmas:

> The basic challenge facing a community is achieving a consensus, or the dilemma of decision-making in its absence. Public choice has shed light on these issues, but much remains to be done. The positive literature is riddled with demonstrations of the instability, inefficiency or irrationality of various voting outcomes, the normative literature by impossibility proofs.

I suggest that these problems are at least in part due to the fact that collective decision-making events are an expression of the underlying exchange relations of the participants and that the act of exchange itself is never without risk of loss due to the ever-present possibility of defection from an agreement. Precisely because parties can come to an agreement, reach a consensus, the rates of expected utility implied by the agreed-on rate of exchange can never be realized.

It is consequently fundamental to the explanation offered here for the emergence of unanimity or division in decisions that the mode in which a decision is taken is the result of the interaction between the requirements of the particular defection-reduction mechanism governing the underlying exchange relation and the interests of the participants in the resources at issue in the decision. Overall frequency distributions of decision modes in any social arena can thus be understood as the results of participants' relations to the resources at issue and the exchange relation obtaining (or failing to obtain) among participants rather than as expressions of externally determined preferences for particular decision modes. In turn, such preferences, or the disguising of preferences, must be seen as elements of tactical maneuvering in overall strategies for securing desired results through public-choice episodes rather than ever-present components in the preference schedules of participants. The three decisions requiring only hamlet treasury funds—rice cooker, fire extinguisher, gas ring—all resulted in unanimous agreement of the hamlet acting as council. The decision on the English class provides additional confirmation of Hypothesis 1 insofar as opposition was raised to the apparent negation of a previous decision and not to the use of hamlet resources *per se*. Three decisions requiring individually held resources—softball equipment, rice polisher, fire pump—resulted in division. The mode of the water-lines decision remains ambiguous, but accommodations were made for members with insufficient resources to allow participation. It is possible for decisions to be recorded ambiguously because the goal of a proposal's supporters is to generate participation, not opposition. Division of opinion in this case was reconciled by the same method used in the decision to construct a hamlet hall in Nishioka, the redefinition of the conditions for participation to align them more closely with the objective circumstances of members in opposition. In no case was the opposition in a division ever more than two or three members.

The theory of productive exchange governed by mutual investment presented here also provides a number of additional hypotheses related to public-choice events beyond expectations for the emergence of specific decision modes.

(1) The consensual orientation of participants remains unchanged across the entire series of decisions. The orientation that participants bring to the decision-making process is not created by the decision-making process but derives from the underlying exchange relationship and the defection-reducing mechanism in operation. Even the presence of a demonstrable "common goal" (i.e., a mutually agreeable rate of exchange) will not produce a consummated exchange without a reliable defection-reducing mechanism. Consequently, the orientation of the participants, whether consensual or adversarial, will not change unless the defection-reducing mechanism itself is changed.

(2) Issues are not treated as commensurate. The attempt to link issues is merely the attempt to reach a rate of exchange. In productive exchange relations governed by mutual investment, however, each issue is already maximally linked to each other issue. In other words, decisions in this context are not attempts to find a satisfactory rate of exchange but to apply a predetermined rate of exchange to the specific features of each issue as it arises. The question to be settled is not what is a mutually agreeable rate of exchange for this issue but whether or not this issue can be fitted to the prevailing rate of exchange.

(3) Consent depends on the absence of grounds for objection. If a proposal is productive, incentive for agreement is already present. In practice, objectively sound proposals will be assumed satisfactory in the absence of objections, which in turn must also be based on objective grounds. Such grounds can arise from only two sources, namely, that the proposal "victimizes" a participant by requiring him to contribute without possibility of future benefit or that, even having potential

for future benefit, capital costs will leave him with too few resources to exploit the new opportunity.

(4) Individual participation in productive exchange transactions is a function of membership rather than opportunity among structurally similar productive exchange relations. Within such groups, the tendency is always toward self-sufficiency. The mechanism of mutual investment demands continuity of the group and commitment of the members to the group's future. Thus, what members look for are opportunities for productive exchange with the partners they already have, not new partners. Whether this arrangement is inefficient cannot be determined because relative efficiency must be measured over the entire series of exchanges within the group, which itself is indefinitely long. Consequently, the tendency will be to attempt to introduce new opportunities within one's own group where the risk of defection is low rather than to join in opportunities external to the group.

(5) Productive exchange transactions within the corporate group create opportunities for production but do not directly distribute benefits to members. This is not to say that the results of production are not ever consumed, but rather that the tendency is to increase opportunities for production rather than consumption. For a proposal to be successful, it must allow for divergent levels of demand for the specific good to be produced, and this can only occur if members are permitted to meet their individual levels of demand independently. Barring this incentive, only those proposals for which utilities of both capital costs and returns on investment were equal for all participants, an obviously impossible requirement, could succeed. The famous distribution rule, "From each according to his ability, to each according to his need," fails in the long run precisely because it does not provide this incentive across transactions but encourages participants to under-report their abilities.

(6) Productive exchange transactions governed by mutual investment always follow the same bifurcate procedure. Capital costs are met as a function of relative resource control, and production costs are met individually. This hypothesis is a restatement of the underlying idea that the rate of exchange is fixed across the entire series of transactions and not determined anew with each transaction. But this restatement is important insofar as it emphasizes the continuity and interdependence of the exchange relationship. Decisions are never made solely on the basis of the attractiveness of the issue at hand. The effect of the decision on the relationship itself must be considered. But this effect is not so much consciously considered in itself as the issue is made to conform to this fundamental procedure. By conscientiously applying the prevailing rate of exchange to each transaction, the feedback component of the distribution rule assures the continuity of the relationship.

(7) Overt advocacy of a particular course of action by individual members is much less likely than overt opposition. Objectively sound proposals are assumed support even in the absence of advocacy; objections to such proposals will only be raised on specific, limited grounds. The distinction to be made here between simply offering a proposal for consideration and advocating a course of action is a pragmatic one: in the decision-making process, advocates become identified with specific courses of action while those who suggest appealing proposals do not. The productive exchange relation implies a willingness, even eagerness, on the part of all members to make suggestions for possible transactions. Thus, from a strategic point of view, an advocate runs a needless risk that a member with a legitimate objection is already prepared to take, the accusation that his action will lead to defection from the prevailing rate of exchange. Given that all members of the group are predisposed to participate in novel productive exchange relations at acceptable resource levels, any advocacy beyond an objective, disinterested presentation of the features of a course of action can only result in suspicion directed toward the advocate.

Taken all together, these hypotheses yield a decision-making practice in which a great deal of attention is paid to the information-gathering process, consultation of interested parties is wide (and often prolonged), issues are treated as amenable to "objectively best" solutions, maximal participation by all participants is encouraged, rhetorical usage is characterized by the appearance of objectivity, and personalities are treated as irrelevant. Pains are taken by participants to dissociate themselves from specific courses of action, and comments are largely confined to concrete aspects of the issue at hand. Participants do not refer to their individual interests in the issue at hand; this information is assumed to be based on widely shared knowledge of participants' circumstances in relation to the issue under discussion. It is the task of the chairman or moderator to draw these recommendations, objections, comments, and tacitly shared understandings into a coherent proposal.

This process is, as are all decision-making processes, open to manipulation. Because legitimate grounds for objection are not fundamentally subjective and because issues are not resolved through compromises that link issues, the most sensitive point in the procedure is not the chairman's attempt to reach a "sense of the meeting," a consensus solution, but the distribution of information regarding the objective circumstances surrounding the issue in relation to participants' interests. The notion of an "objectively best" solution implies an identity of interest among participants to the extent specified in the distribution rule, i.e., that all members have the potential to benefit by the transaction and that capital costs are not so high that members have no resources left to exploit the opportunity created through the transaction. To apply this distribution rule, however, all participants must have access to the same information. For the decision-making process to remain above suspicion, the information-gathering process must be as public as possible. The well-publicized phenomenon of preconsultation in Japan, *nemawashi*, or *shita sōdan*, is not so much an aspect of the search for information that will help in the discovery of an objectively correct solution as an attempt to clarify that which is not overt and public, but tacit, assumed, and ultimately private, the specific interests of the participants in the issue in relation to their objective circumstances. In groups where accurate information of this order is widely shared, little of this kind of consultation is necessary, but the public aspects of the information search process remain imperative under all circumstances. And, of course, the possibility always remains that, despite the objection of a small minority, other members will see a particular course of action as so desirable that they are willing to pursue its implementation without the consent of all members. Here again, we would expect capitulation or resignation rather than compromise and, in resolving such apparent impasses, emphasis on "misunderstanding" and "apologies." This process is based, as much as possible, on shared information and objectivity and not whim; dissolution of the relationship can only result from complete resignation or defection from the prevailing rate of exchange.

This decision-making process is found in hamlet society in rural Japan because the foundation of hamlet society is the productive exchange relation governed by mutual investment that includes all hamlet members. As a result of this exchange relation in combination with this defection-reducing mechanism, minimal constraints are placed on production within the hamlet, while the flow of resources to alternative exchange opportunities is greatly reduced. The general result, in hamlet society, is an extremely competitive and conservative social fabric receptive to a very high degree to innovation in production. Through productive exchange and mutual investment the hamlet converts its social exclusivity and internal competition into high levels of cooperation. The resultant solidarity and high rates of consummated exchange transactions produce a corporate identity that depends neither upon kinship criteria to define potential exchange partners nor upon a costly system of external guarantees to assure the integrity of transactions.

These characteristics are not common to hamlet society alone. A well-known element of Japanese folk sociology holds that family life and hamlet social organization are both replicated in even the largest commercial enterprises; Atsumi (1975: 5) cites no fewer than five authorities on this point, and no doubt more could easily be found. The common thread that binds these different kinds of social entities together, gives them a similar appearance despite their many differences, is their common foundation of production, in general, and productive exchange relations governed by mutual investment, in particular. It is the capacity of this mechanism to consistently condition and coordinate virtually all productive exchange relations within a circumscribed social field that encourages the habit of viewing even large firms as if they were *ie* or *buraku*. Beyond decision-making practices, there are many features of Japanese society that encourage further investigation in terms of the theory of productive exchange governed by mutual investment presented here. Another possibility lies in the general absence in Japan of conflict-resolution patterns based on advocacy and direct confrontation, as well as the small number of professional advocates (Holden 1980: 752) and infrequent recourse to the formal legal system (Haley 1982). In general, however, it is apparent that Japanese society is oriented toward "the long run" to an extraordinary degree, exhibits an equally high degree of social integration, encourages participation, and expects commitment from its members. All of these features are expected in groups organized for productive exchange and governed by mutual investment.

NOTES TO CHAPTERS

*Chapter 1*

[1]Discussions of *buraku* decision making can be found prominently in Akimoto (1973), Dore (1959, 1978), Dull (1954), Scalapino and Masami (1962), Steiner (1956, 1968), Sutton (1953), Ward (1951a, 1951b, 1953), and Beardsley, Hall, and Ward (1959). Brown (1974), Kerlinger (1951), Lebra (1976), and Nakane (1970) offer generalized accounts of decision making throughout Japanese society. Decision making in historical settings is discussed in Befu (1966), Hackett (1968), Hall (1968), Ike (1964), Scalapino (1968), and Yoshida (1964, 1975). For accounts of contemporary decision making in government and business, see Abegglen (1958), Clark (1979), Dore (1973), Silberman (1967, 1973), Tsuji (1968), and the several contributions to Vogel (1975).

*Chapter 2*

[1]It is worth noting here that even simple association courts the dangers entailed by advocacy. The messenger is sometimes blamed for the message he brings: "Although the post of headman is an honor and a mark of general confidence, it is generally assumed with real reluctance. It takes time which many farmers can ill afford to give, and it obliges its occupant to initiate action or make public recommendations that are certain to incur the ill will of at least some members of the buraku" (Beardsley, Hall, and Ward 1959: 356).

*Chapter 4*

[1]This was the only occasion where I heard hamlet men use such language among themselves. This unusual occurrence is emphasized by the region's national reputation for blunt, informal, and even impolite speech.

[2]The "fifteen *kankeisha*" referred to here are the thirteen or fourteen regular users of the *seimaiki* noted in figure 2.

[3]Loans from the hamlet treasury could only be considered at this time because the ¥500,000 received from the railroad had not yet been spent.

# BIBLIOGRAPHY

Abegglan, James
    1958    *The Japanese Factory: Aspects of Social Organization.* Glencoe,
             Il: The Free Press.

Akimoto, Ritsuo
    1973    Leadership and Power Structure in Local Politics. Pp. 167–80 in
             *Japanese Politics: an Inside View*, Hiroshi Itoh, ed. Ithaca: Cornell
             University Press.

Atsumi, Reiko
    1975    Personal Relationships of Japanese White-collar Company
             Employees. Ph.D. dissertation, University of Pittsburgh.

Axelrod, Robert
    1981    The Emergence of Cooperation among Egoists. *American Political
             Science Review* 75.2: 306–18.

Axelrod, Robert, and Hamilton, William D.
    1981    The Evolution of Cooperation. *Science* 211: 1390–96.

Bailey, Fredrick
    1965    Decisions in Councils and Committees. Pp. 1–20 in *Political Systems
             and the Distribution of Power*, Michael Banton, ed. London:
             Tavistock.

Barth, Fredrick
    1966    *Models of Social Organization.* Royal Anthropological Institute
             Paper 23. London: Royal Anthropological Institute.

Beardsley, Robert, Hall, John, and Ward, Robert
    1959    *Village Japan.* Chicago: University of Chicago Press.

Befu, Harumi
    1966    Duty, Reward, Sanction, and Power. Pp. 25–50 in *Modern Japanese Leadership*, Bernard Silberman and H. D. Harootunian, eds. Tuscon: University of Arizona Press.

    1971    *Japan: an Introduction*. New York: Chandler.

    1974    Power in Exchange: Strategy of Control and Compliance in Japan. *Asian Profile* 2.6: 601–22.

Ben Dasan, Isaiah
    1970    *Nihonjin to yudayajin* [Japanese and Jews]. Tokyo: Yamamoto Shoten.

Blau, Peter
    1964    *Exchange and Power in Social Life*. New York: John Wiley and Sons.

Bloch, Maurice
    1971    Decision-making in Councils among the Merinda of Madagascar. Pp. 29–62 in *Councils in Action*. Audrey Richards and Adam Kuper, eds. Cambridge: Cambridge University Press.

Brown, William
    1974    Japanese Management: the Cultural Background. Pp. 174–91 in *Japanese Culture and Behavior*. T. S. Lebra and William Lebra, eds. Honolulu: University of Hawaii Press.

Clark, Rodney
    1979    *The Japanese Company*. New Haven: Yale University Press.

Cole, Robert
    1976    Review of *Modern Japanese Organization and Decision-making*, edited by Ezra Vogel. *Journal of Asian Studies* 35.2: 503–6.

    1979    *Work, Mobility and Participation: a Comparative Study of American and Japanese Industry*. Berkeley: University of California Press.

Coleman, James
    1964    Collective Decisions. *Sociological Inquiry* 4: 166–81.

Dore, Ronald
    1959    *Land Reform in Japan*. Oxford: Oxford University Press.

1973    *British Factory-Japanese Factory.*     Berkeley:     University of
        California Press.

1978    *Shinohata: a Portrait of a Japanese Village.* New York: Pantheon.

Dull, Paul
1954    The Political Structure of a Japanese Village. *Far Eastern Quarterly*
        13: 175-90.

El-Hakim, Sherif
1978    The Structure and Dynamics of Consensus Decision-making. *Man*
        (NS) 13.3: 55-71.

Emerson, Richard
1976    Social Exchange Theory. *Annual Review of Sociology*: 335-62.

Fjellman, Stephan
1976    Natural and Unnatural Decision-making:     a Critique of Decision
        Theory. *Ethos* 4.1: 73-94.

Fukutake, Tadashi
1972    *Japanese Rural Society.* Ithaca: Cornell University Press.

Gaenslen, Fritz
1980    Democracy vs. Efficiency: Some Arguments from the Small Group.
        *Political Psychology* 2.1: 15-29.

Hackett, Roger
1968    Political Modernization and the Meiji *genrō.*  Pp. 65-97 in *Political
        Development in Modern Japan,* Robert Ward, ed.     Princeton:
        Princeton University Press.

Haley, John
1982    Sheathing the Sword of Justice in Japan: an Essay on Law without
        Sanctions. *Journal of Japanese Studies* 8: 256-82.

Hall, Jay, and Watson, W. H.
1970    The Effects of a Normative Intervention on Group Decision-making
        Performance. *Human Relations* 23.4: 299-317.

Hall, John
1968    A Monarch for Modern Japan. Pp. 11-64 in *Political Development in
        Modern Japan,* Robert Ward, ed.  Princeton:  Princeton University
        Press.

Hanami, Tadashi
    1979    *Labor Relations in Japan Today.*   Tokyo:   Kodansha International,
            Ltd.

Hare, A. Paul
    1982    *Creativity in Small Groups.*   Beverly Hills, CA:   Sage Publications.

Heath, Anthony
    1976a   *Rational Choice and Social Exchange.*   Cambridge:   University of
            Cambridge Press.

    1976b   Decision-making and Transactional Theory.   Pp. 25–40 in *Meaning
            and Transaction,* Bruce Kapferer, ed.   Philadelphia:   Institute for the
            Study of Human Issues, Inc.

Hobbes, Thomas
    1651    *Leviathan.*   Reprinted 1955.   Oxford:   Blackwell.

Holden, Constance
    1980    Innovation: Japan Races Ahead as US Falters.   *Science* 210: 751–54.

Ike, Nobutaka
    1964    Political Leadership and Political Parties.   Pp. 389–410 in *Political
            Modernization in Japan and Turkey,* Robert Ward and Dankwart
            Rostow, eds.   Princeton:   Princeton University Press.

Kerlinger, Fred
    1951    Decision-making in Japan.   *Social Forces* 30: 36–41.

Klein, Benjamin
    1980    Transaction   Cost   Determinants   of   "Unfair"   Contractual
            Arrangements.   *American Economic Association Papers and
            Proceedings* 70: 356–62.

Klein, Benjamin, and Leffler, Keith B.
    1981    The Role of Market Forces in Assuring Contractual Performance.
            *Journal of Political Economy* 89.4: 615–41.

Kuper, Adam
    1971    Council Structure and Decision-making.   Pp. 13-28 in *Councils in
            Action,* Aubrey Richards and Adam Kuper, eds.   Cambridge:
            Cambridge University Press.

Lebra, Takie
    1976    *Japanese Patterns of Behavior.*    Honolulu:    University of Hawaii
            Press.

Marshall, Robert
    n.d.    Giving a Gift to the Hamlet:    Rank, Solidarity and Productive
            Exchange in Rural Japan.    Unpublished manuscript.

Mueller, Denis
    1979    *Public Choice.*    Cambridge:    Cambridge University Press.

Nakane, Chie
    1967    *Kinship and Economic Organization in Rural Japan.*    London School
            of Economics Monographs on Social Anthropology 32.    London:
            Athlone.

    1970    *Japanese Society.*    Berkeley:    University of California Press.

Oishi, Shinzaburo
    1956    Edo-jidai ni okeru nōmin no ie to sono sōzoku-keitai ni tsuite [On *ie*
            and inheritance patterns of peasants and landowners in the
            Tokugawa period].    *Kazoku-Seido no Kenkyū* [The study of family
            systems] 1: 97-121.

Olson, Mancur
    1956    *The Logic of Collective Action:    Public Goods and the Theory of
            Groups.*    Cambridge:    Harvard University Press.

Popkin, Samuel
    1979    *The Rational Peasant.*    Berkeley:    University of California Press.

Ramseyer, Robert
    1969    Takachiho, 1868-1968:    Evolving Patterns of Community Decision-
            making in a Developing Nation-state.    Ph.D. dissertation, University
            of Michigan.

Richards, Aubrey, and Kuper, Adam, eds.
    1971    *Councils in Action.*    Cambridge:    Cambridge University Press.

Scalapino, Robert
    1968    Elections and Political Development in Pre-war Japan.    Pp. 249-91
            in *Political Development in Modern Japan*, Robert Ward, ed.
            Princeton:    Princeton University Press.

Scalapino, Robert, and Masami, Junnosuke
    1962    *Parties and Politics in Contemporary Japan.* Berkeley: University of California Press.

Schelling, Thomas
    1978    *Micromotives and Macrobehavior.* New York: W. W. Norton Co.

Silberman, Bernard
    1967    Bureaucratic Development and the Structure of Decision-making in the Meiji Period: the Case of the *genrō*. *Journal of Asian Studies* 27: 81-94.

    1973    *Ringisei*—Traditional Values or Organizational Imperatives in the Japanese Upper Civil Service: 1869-1945. *Journal of Asian Studies* 32: 251-64.

Smith, Robert
    1961    The Japanese Rural Community: Norms, Sanctions, and Ostracism. *American Anthropologist* 63: 522-33.

    1978    *Kurusu: The Price of Progress in a Japanese Village 1951-1975.* Stanford: Stanford University Press.

Smith, Thomas
    1959    *The Agrarian Origins of Modern Japan.* Stanford: Stanford University Press.

    1977    *Nakahara: Family Farming and Population in a Japanese Village, 1717-1830.* Stanford: Stanford University Press.

Smith, W. Eugene, and Smith, Aileen
    1975    *Minamata.* New York: Holt, Rinehart and Winston.

Steiner, Kurt
    1956    The Japanese Village and Its Government. *Far Eastern Quarterly* 15: 185-99.

    1968    Popular Political Participation and Political Development in Modern Japan: the Rural Level. Pp. 213-48 in *Political Development in Modern Japan*, Robert Ward, ed. Princeton: Princeton University Press.

Sutton, Joseph
    1953    *Rural Politics in Japan.* Center for Japanese Studies Occasional Papers 4. Ann Arbor: Center for Japanese Studies, The University of Michigan.

Telser, L. G.
    1980    A Theory of Self-enforcing Agreements. *Journal of Business* 53.1: 27-44.

Tsuji, Kiyoaki
    1968    Decision-making in the Japanese Government: a Study of *ringisei.* Pp. 457-76 in *Political Development in Modern Japan,* Robert Ward, ed. Princeton: Princeton University Press.

Vogel, Ezra
    1979    *Japan as Number One.* Cambridge: Harvard University Press.

Vogel, Ezra, ed.
    1975    *Modern Japanese Organization and Decision-making.* Berkeley: University of California Press.

Ward, Robert
    1951a    *Patterns of Stability and Change in Rural Japanese Politics.* Center for Japanese Studies Occasional Papers 1. Ann Arbor: Center for Japanese Studies, The University of Michigan.

    1951b    The Socio-political Role of the *buraku* (hamlet) in Japan. *American Political Science Review* 45: 1025-40.

    1953    Some Observations on Local Autonomy at the Village Level in Present-day Japan. *Far Eastern Quarterly* 12.2: 183-202.

    1956    Village Government in Eastern and Southern Asia. *Far Eastern Quarterly* 15: 175-83.

Williamson, Oliver E.
    1979    Transaction-cost Economics and the Governance of Contractual Relations. *Journal of Law and Economics* 22: 233-61.

Wittevogel, Karl
    1957    *Oriental Despotism: a Comparative Study of Total Power.* New Haven: Yale University Press.

Yoshida, Teigo
    1964    Social Conflict and Cohesion in a Japanese Rural Community. *Ethnology* 3: 219-31.

    1975    Technical and Social Change in a Japanese Fishing Village. *Journal of Asian and African Studies* 9: 1-16.